AUTOBIOGRAPHY
BOOK 3

DRUMS UNDER THE WINDOWS

Each volume in the evocative and richly entertaining autobiography of Sean O'Casey is essential reading for a proper appreciation of this major Irish dramatist whose plays were among the most exciting developments in modern drama.

Born in the back streets of Dublin, suffering from weak and diseased eyes, he lived in poverty and physical hardship for many ye___ ___ his late teens he became a manual labo___ ___r working on the roads or in th___ ___in the morning to six at ni___ ___ings helping the ca___ ___inn Fein. He h___ ___zen Army and a___ ___ Labour Party. Althou___ ___k was in 1907, not until the su___ ___he Paycock in 1925 did he give up m___ ___ and become a full-time writer.

Here are a nationalist's views of his country and countrymen from 1906 to that 'rare time of death in Ireland' – Easter, 1916. From his stay in hospital came people and incidents for *The Silver Tassie*, and out of his personal experiences of Dublin during the Rising arose *The Plough and the Stars*.

The photograph 'Arran Quay' by Evelyn Hofer, reproduced on the cover is from Dublin: A Portrait *by V. S. Pritchett and Evelyn Hofer, published by The Bodley Head.*

By the same author in Pan Books

AUTOBIOGRAPHY (BOOK 1):
I KNOCK AT THE DOOR

AUTOBIOGRAPHY (BOOK 2):
PICTURES IN THE HALLWAY

AUTOBIOGRAPHY (BOOK 4):
INISHFALLEN, FARE THEE WELL

AUTOBIOGRAPHY (BOOK 5):
ROSE AND CROWN

AUTOBIOGRAPHY (BOOK 6):
SUNSET AND EVENING STAR

AUTOBIOGRAPHY
BOOK 3

DRUMS UNDER THE WINDOWS

SEAN O'CASEY

UNABRIDGED

PAN BOOKS LTD : LONDON

First published 1945
by Macmillan and Company Ltd.
This edition published 1972 by Pan Books Ltd,
33 Tothill Street, London, SW1.

ISBN 0 330 02933 9

2nd Printing 1973

Printed in Great Britain by
Richard Clay (The Chaucer Press), Ltd, Bungay, Suffolk

CONTENTS

DRUMS UNDER THE WINDOWS

Study that house.
I think about its jokes and stories.

To Dr Michael O'Hickey

A Gael of Gaels, one-time Professor of Irish in Maynooth College. In a fight for Irish, he collided with arrogant Irish bishops, and was summarily dismissed without a chance of defending himself; taking the case to Rome, he was defeated there by the subtlety of the bishops, helped by a sly Roman Rota, ending his last proud years in poverty and loneliness.

Forgotten, unhonoured, unsung in Eire, here's a Gael left who continues to say Honour and Peace to your brave and honest soul, Michael O'Hickey, till a braver Ireland comes to lay a garland on your lonely grave.

AT THE SIGN OF THE PICK AND SHOVEL

PUG-FACED, pleasant-hearted Georgie Middleton had pulled him to the job, hearing he was idle; big gang at work on a railway siding, more wanted; make a man of you. He brought Sean straight to the foreman, had whispered into his ear, One of ourselves, and the foreman, a modified true-blue, had decided to give him a start. A big man was the foreman, over six feet and broad-shouldered. A handsome face, spoiled by a big crooked clumsy chin, falling away from a large mouth, well shaped; deep clefts from each corner of a handsome nose furrowed the cheeks to the frame of the chin, looking like taut ropes keeping the heavy chin from falling away altogether; but he'd taken him on, and that was a decent thing to do.

The ganger, Christy Mahon, looked doubtfully at Sean when he came to the job with a navvy shovel on his shoulder. Mahon was another big and powerful man of fifty or so, wide-shouldered and deep-chested; lazy as sin, and as ignorant as a kish of brogues. Doesn't know the name of his own religion, couldn't recognize the number on his own hall door, and hardly make out a bee from a bull's balls, one of the workmen whispered to Sean, a few days later. He had a rugged, rather distinguished face, a heavy grizzled moustache, a bush of the same sort of hair, tousled as if it had never come within sight of a comb, and his chin, hardy and strong, was covered with a week's growth of hair. There was one remarkable thing about him – he had a very small arse for such a big man, and the part of his trousers there looked like the drooping mainsail of a ship in a fitful wind when he walked. Too much beer, whispered another workman to Sean, a few days later. This ganger mostly remained torpid, but was under the habit of sudden fits of passion for an hour's occasional work to show the others how it was done; and would seize a shovel or a pick to work like a nigger for a spell, the effort gradually declining till the tool dropped from his hand, and he sank into torpidity again. He spoke through his nose in a querulous way, and got good-humoured only when he was half-seas-over by drinking the bullage from empty whiskey barrels, made by steeping the damper ones with boiling water till the whiskey still in the wood had soaked its way into the water. He lived in Yellow Walls, near Malahide, the stronghold of the Talbots, where he had a white-washed cottage with clay floors, a wife, two children, less than an acre of ground, and an animal that he said was a cow. He was the richest man in the hamlet. All life centred round the cow. Up every night he had to be when she was calving, squatting on the bare earthen floor of the byre, a huge, shaking, shadowy figure in a dim pool of light from a storm-lantern, watching every twist and turn of the cow, sensing her condition in every moaning bellow she gave, echoing each moan in his own aching, wondering heart; with his wife at home in bed on her back, ears cocked to hear a possible yell from her husband to come and give her fellow a hand with the suffering animal; while the few houses round hers sank into the night's silence, for they had not on them the care of a cow calving. There he sat in the darkness and dirt, cooped in with the cow, the heat from her body and the steam from her nostrils enfolding them both and making them one, a thick needle threaded with a thick cord nearby, ready to stitch her belly up if it got torn during the delivery. His life, literature, art, and leisure were all embedded in the cow calving.

Every morning at four o'clock, this ganger forced himself from bed to catch the four-fifteen coming from the black north, nodding in the cold carriage with three comrades till it was five to six, and time to climb from the carriage resting in a Dublin siding, when they heard the bell calling them all to begin a day's work. He got home again, with his comrades, at eight o'clock, so doing sixteen hours a day at his everyday job with a few hours added to till his patch of ground and care for the cow; yet withal, he had plenty of leisure to go to Mass on all the Sundays.

This shaggy, lumbering, dim-minded man looked at Sean doubtfully, shrugged his shoulders, and grumbled to his gang, God in heaven! What kind of a scrawl am I gettin'? For Sean stood mute before him, a blink of fear in his eyes as if he expected to be set to move a mountain. Didja never ever have ne'er a shovel in your hand before in your life? he asked.

—Ay, said Sean; but not this sort of a one.

—An' which would you liefer start with – pick or shovel?

—Don't mind, said Sean carelessly; it's all the same to me.

—Ay, it's all th' same because you don't know how to use nather.

—Give him a shovel, said a stocky, red-bearded man anxiously, for he'll be penethratin' one of us if he thries to use a pick.

Sean thrust the shovel feverishly into the earth already hacked out of the little hill that was to make way for the new siding. It was a hard push to the broad-bladed shovel, with a short handle, and a crook like a crutch on the end of it, a push given by all the strength in his forearm only, unaided by the thrust of the knee the navvy gives whenever he forces the shovel home. He emptied what was on the shovel into a waiting cart, and thrust the blade into the hacked-out heap again. By the time a crawling half-hour had passed his hands were smarting; the veins in his forearm seemed to be knotting themselves together; salt sweat was trickling down his forehead and cheeks, oozing into his eyes, making them burn and veiling their vision with a salt smart. Now his chest was getting so tight that he could breathe only in short intermittent gasps. The first quarter of this work would do him in; he could never come back to this ordeal by sweat, pain, and breathlessness. He was flabby, soft, inalert, and useless. Through a reddish mist he saw the rest of the gang working away easily as if they were made of well-oiled steel. He sensed that they were enjoying themselves watching him, grimly glad to see his staring eyes, groggy legs, and hear his gasping breath.

—Not worth a damn to me, he heard the ganger mutter as he turned away to miss the new man's agony; lifts up as much on his shovel as a new-hatched hen 'ud lift up in her bake.

A low lot, thought Sean, a low lot to have to work with, and all rejoicing at the poor show I'm making. The less I'm able, the more hilarious and comfortable they'll feel. Oh, if Georgie was only here, but he's a tradesman, and above this crowd.

A tall, dark, raven-haired man edged closer to him, saying softly out of the corner of his mouth, Go easy, take your time, draw it mild; watch me. You'll kill yourself the way you're goin'. Lower the shovel, bend quietly, don't jerk; now, the knee against the crutch of the handle – shove! Lift gently, don't jerk, and fling with a slight swing of both arms – see? Don't be afraid to straighten your back when you feel a sthrain, so's to keep yourself from gettin' too stiff. It'll all come to you in a few weeks, and you'll be as good as the best.

Try as he would, it only grew worse in spite of Bob Harvey's attempt at tutoring, and through the mist Sean saw the ganger shaking his head with annoyance, though he had kept his back turned on Sean's agony. His arms had grown into things torturing his body, and his gasping breath seemed to cling to where it was in his lungs, stifling him, rather than to tear a way through his gaping mouth. Sweat was hiding the blue sky above him; the sky itself was damp with sweat, the whole earth was tired and aching, all save only those dim figures working by his side, laughing silently at him for thinking he could become a navvy; but it was for food, for security, for freedom from want, and stick it he must. Now things at a distance seemed to be swinging about, as if they had suddenly gone tipsy, and the earth shook like a thing infirm. Every shovelful now pulled a bigger strain out of his taut, rebelling muscles; put a sharper ache into his creaking back. He was going slower; he could barely get the heavy shovel from the ground. He got reckless, gave a mighty lift and a jerking throw, sending a shovelful of earth and stones clattering against the neck and over the head of the startled ganger, knocking a pipe from his big mouth so that it fell to the ground and smashed itself into many pieces.

—What th' hell! he roared. What d'ye think y're throwin' — thunderclaps, or wha'? Is it buryin' poor men alive yeh want to be? He looked down at the shattered pipe. A year's hard work seasonin' her gone for nothin'! Here, get a hold of a pick instead, th' way we won't have to be diggin' people outa what you've buried them in!

But the pick in Sean's lacerated hands was worse than the shovel, for he didn't know how to swing it neatly back over his shoulder within a small space, but swung it clumsily and widely so that those who worked next to him hurried away to give him room, and stood bunched together, watching in wonder the wild swing of the pick, effective in his hands as it would be in the hands of a child of twelve.

—Oh, Lord, what am I goin' to do with the boyo at all! burst out of Christy Mahon; keepin' three men from work to let him do a little. You're only ticklin' it, man. You'll kill somebody, so you will; that waypon's deadly in your dangerous hands; you'll drive it deep into the broad of somebody's back before you're done. You'll never do on this job. It's not fair to me. *Christy Mahon, is this all you've done for the day?* the foreman'll say when he sthruts up; an' he after sendin' me a man that's burnin' to hamsthring half th' men workin' with him; an' afterwards their mothers or widows comin' in black blamin' me for permittin' murdher to be done in all innocence be a fella fortified be not knowin' what he was thryin' to do! Go on, an' get into it! he

roared to the others, for it's a risk yous have to take, dependin'
for safety on a smart lep outa th' way when yous see the point of
the pick comin'.

So it was, too, carrying sleepers, slippy, hot, and pungent with
the soak of creosote, he at one end, and a man at the other. They
fought shy of joining him for fear he'd let his end go before the
right moment, jabbing their end into their bodies, or nipping a
finger by failing to give the heavy baulk of timber a tuneful swing
before casting it from the permanent-way wagon. Bob Harvey,
the tall, raven-haired ex-Guardsman, was the only one ready to
man the end opposite to him, giving him slow sage counsel,
showing him how to keep a proper poise forward or backward,
counting the swings quietly, one, two – go! and in a little more
than no-time Sean swung sleepers out of a wagon, or on the
ground and on to the ordered piles, in perfect tune with his
partner's help. Carrying the twenty-five-foot rails, six or eight
men at one end, and the same number at the other, he was always
opposite the ex-Guardsman, and his and Sean's shoulders and
hands were always interlocked; and though he went home, night
after night, a clumsy-moving mass of aching stiffness, seeing
when he got home an anxious look in his mother's eyes, and heard
her murmur, when she saw the raw red on the palms of his hands,
Maybe the job's too much for your strength, he stood up to it,
silent, with no shadow of a song near his lips, and no sigh either,
grim and grand; mouth-clenched resolution his armour, and the
determination to become as good as the next his shield and
buckler. His first fortnight's pay opened the heart of the dirty
little grocer, purveyor of the workers' district, so that for the
first time for a year and more he and his mother fed well. He
went on wringing power and confidence from the passing hours,
till the aches gradually left him, and the stiffness was gone. His
body now became flexible, his arms strong, his legs firm in tackling
shovel, pick, crowbar, rope, scaffolding-pole, wheelbarrow, hod,
or sledge with the best of them, beating the ex-Guardsman who
got pale and whimpered when asked to mount higher than the
sixth rung of a ladder; and, at last, found himself the one man in
the gang who could mount a ladder with a hod carrying near
eight stone in it, balancing it with equal ease on right shoulder or
on left.

God, he felt proud all right. Felt as proud as he did when he
first fell into step with Shakespeare. His body now was in fine

alignment with his mind. *Mens sana in corpore sano*, that's how it
went, he thought; and, if the words were curious, the sense was
sane. He often inflated his chest now, forty-four inches round
normally; often felt the sturdy muscles in arm and thigh; and as
he swung pick or sledgehammer, thrust in shovel, hung on a rope,
or swarmed up a ladder with a hod on his shoulder, song once
more bubbled brightly from his lips. And to him, most of the
songs were new; songs of an Ireland astir, awake, and eager; an
Ireland forging fresh thought out of bygone history and present
hopes to create a glowing, passionate, and permanent chapter
from which a great nation would be born. Oh, silver trumpets be
ye lifted up, and call to the great race that is to come! cried Yeats,
and Sean cried the call with him too. The sword was being
polished, the rifle cleaned, and a new banner of green, white, and
orange was being attached to the old staff, and was nearly ready
to be broken out to fly in the four winds of Eirinn. Dr Douglas de
Hyde was rushing round, shouting in at the Dublin Castle gates,
It's a Gael I am without shame to meself or danger to you; in at
the windows of Trinity College, A country without a language is
a country without a tongue; on every hill in the country, Waken
up your courage, O Ireland; and in at the doorway of Maynooth
College, in rather a quiet way, Irish in the New University – or
else! . . .

Gaelic Leaguers were pulling reluctant and timorous native
speakers from the darkness of their little grey homes in the west,
hardly waiting, when they laid hands on one, for him to get his
coat on, shoving him where he didn't want to go, amid the
clapping of white hands; mixing his tatters with the elegant array
of tweed suits, high white collars, and poplin ties of civil servants,
doctors, chemists, revenue officers, and teachers, hauling the
frightened fellow into the midst of garrulous emotion, declaring
that the native speaker was all in all to Ireland, was Ireland, all
Ireland, the whole Ireland, and nothing else but Ireland, so help us
God; the long-hidden Ireland, chidden Ireland, forbidden Ireland
by the Ascendancy gang that ruled the land. The native Irish
speaker was forced to walk upright through a fierce white light
beating on him everywhere, and he seeking often in his heart a
kindlier darkness so that he could slink into the friendliness of
gloom again; but they placed him to the forefront of every
meeting, applauded every word that came out of his mouth, assuring him that the day of shame for the native speaker had gone

for ever; for now whenever two or three were gathered together in the name of Ireland, there was the native speaker in the midst of them.

And while all these respectable, white-collared, trim-suited Gaelic Leaguers, snug in their selected branches, living rosily in Whitehall, Drumcondra, Rathgar, Donnybrook, and all the other nicer habitations of the city, nuzzled round the bewildered native speaker, away went, without money, with often an empty belly, on rusty bicycles, under scorching suns or pelting rain, eyes gleaming, backs bent, hands blenched by the tight grip on the handlebars, unmindful of the hawthorn in June, changing the hedges into never-ending miles of nuns' veiling, or the sparkle of frost on the twisting roads, or of mountains towering up around them to threaten or protect, or of the gentle lap-lap of the waves on a summer sea, or of their battering on to the beach when the winds of winter blew, went the travelling teacher; backs bent, eyes gleaming, hands asweat or frozen on the handlebars, their feet going round endlessly on a glorious treadmill, went the travelling teacher, rushing here, dashing there, to teach a class, to help found a new branch, spreading the Irish as a tree sends forth its pollen, seeking neither to gain a reward nor to pay a penance, but for thee, only for thee, dear land, and for thy language that it may come back to us, be brought back to us by persuasion or by force; snatching time reluctantly to take a meal, spending a few restless hours in jaded sleep, exposed to sun and rain and wind and frost and snow and black sleet, hot and cold by turns, many of them sliding with a wan sigh into a grave by the wayside where they went, worn and worried, into a quiet end from the warm fight and the hope that flickered wanly in most hearts save their own fiery ones; others seizing their bicycles ere they had flattened in their fall, to bend their backs, evoke a gleam in their eyes, to grip the handlebars till the knuckles whitened, and dash off, too, through shower and shine and storm, wet with summer's dew, or soaked in wintry sleet; on, on endlessly, endlessly, reckless and frenzied, endlessly cycling on through country road, through village street, by hilly paths, lifting the heads of grazing mountain-sheep to glance and wonder, skirting mountains alive with their loneliness, a goat, browsing rapidly, lifting a bearded chin to cast a sudden look at the stir that marred his solitude, unawake to the need of the fevered man's hurry to keep a step ahead of time; to bring their lovely language back to the Gael, he hastened on, endlessly, hastening on, the muinteor taisdal, the travelling teacher; Cathleen ni Houlihan busy in the woods nearby searching for leaves to weave a garland, but finding naught but bramble and coarse gorse, thistledown and thorns, jagging her bare feet, but searching still, and silence everywhere.

Here and there, in one or another hole or corner, Tim Healy was mocking Dillon, while down South William O'Brien was trying to fight everyone in his All For Ireland League, unaware, the fools, that when they killed Parnell they killed themselves too; while their followers sauntered in and out of the House draping their souls with all the moods and manners of their masters, carrying in occasionally a stuffed wolf-dog to give a mechanical bark to show that Ireland still lived through joy and through tears, while Johnny Redmond smilingly waved a bright-green flag smelling sweetly of the fragrant English rose.

Far away from it all, a tiny group of men followed Jim Connolly through the streets to the cul-de-sac curving round the circular side of the Royal Bank of Ireland, a large slouch hat covering Connolly's head, a large round head, fronted by a rather commonplace face, its heaviness lightened by fine, soft, luminous eyes; the heavy jaws were jewelled with a thick-lipped sensuous mouth, mobile, and a little sarcastic, bannered peacefully by a thick and neatly-trimmed moustache. His ears were well set to the head, the nose was a little too thick, and gave an obstinate cast to the bright eyes, and a firm fleshy neck bulged out over a perfectly white hard collar. The head and neck rested solidly on a broad sturdy trunk of a body, and all were carried forward on two short pillar-like legs, slightly bowed, causing him to waddle a little in his walk, as if his legs were, in the way of a joke, trying faintly and fearfully to throw him off his balance. Silent, he walked on, looking grim and a little surly, followed by the tiny dribble of followers, one of them carrying a box so that, when Connolly spoke, he he might be lifted up before the people as he preached the gospel of discontent smoking faintly in the hearts of most men. Up on the box, the soft slouch hat came off, and the hard, sparsely-covered head turned this way and that, the mobile mouth flickered with words, red with the woe of the common people, words that circled noisily over the heads of the forty or fifty persons hunched clumsily together to oppose the chill of the wind that whipped around the corner of the curving, graceful, classical hip of the Bank, murmuring in the mellowed, matronly, plump loveliness of its lines and curves, *Here in my ample and elegant belly lies safe the golden life of Ireland, fructifying warmly there, fulfilling the Jehovahian command to multiply and replenish the earth.*

A step aside, within the counter-spoiled building, lay the dead ashes of the last fire lit in the Assembly Room of the Irish House of Lords; a fire that had warmed the backsides of the lords in their crimson-plush coats and black-satin breeches, or black-satin coats and crimson-plush trousers; or of them that strutted in a bright-blue Volunteer military coat, gleaming yellow trousers, all bedecked with crimson braid and the richest of gold embroidery, that voted for the Act of Union with England, side by side with the Maynooth Catholic bishops; or against the Act, side by side with the Orange Lodges of Dublin and Belfast.

Here was Up Griffith's seed of life for Ireland, needing but her King, Lords, and Commons to form a coloured trinity that would forge a terrifying power in Ireland of the Wise Welcomes, darken the seven seas with Irish shipping, deaden the song of birds with the bum and whirr of machinery, and flood the quays, the streets, the homes of the two gigantic Atlantic ports of Galway and Sligo and the one-way street town of Blacksod Bay with corn and wine and wool, oil and amber, mahogany, teak, and rosewood to build houses for the Irish to live in; juniper gin and jars of spices; Indian muslin, cashmere shawls of crimson and white, or green and turquoise for every Irish snowy-breasted pearl, each colleen dyas, for every girl milking her cow, each dark rosaleen, every dark woman of the glen, and every red-haired man's wife; tobacco the rarest the sun could season, peculiar birds for all the parks, bales of shimmering silks from China, and snowy ivory, too, for beads; luscious figs and pomegranates in curious coloured wickerwork baskets, lying in down of the Tibetan ducks, all gums and perfumes of Arabia; and dainty leather for ladies' shoes, all tooled for style in a Persian garden; sherbet rich in crystal vases for a ploughman's drink through the pull of the harvest. Jasus Christ, the vision was lovely!

It was all written in the book of *Resurgamise Upsadaiseum Hungarius*, a huge tome five feet long, three feet wide, and two feet deep, containing in itself all the lore that is or ever was, all laws, licences, customs, pardons, punishments, perquisites, genealogies, constitutions, magna chartas, social contracts, books of rights, das kapitals, origins of species, tallboy talmuds, speeches from the dock, carried about everywhere on the back of Up

Griffith Up Davis, as a pedlar carries his pack, compiled from the
original sources by the sage himself, deep in a corner under a
secret rowan tree, in the dim cloisters of the old Abbey of St
Fownes, the Soggart Aroon acting as secretary, assisted by Kelly
and Burke and Shea all in their jackets green, with the Bard of
Armagh stringing the harp to *He's the Man You Don't See Every
Day* to give their minds a lift.

Here Sean was now, free for the moment from the pick and
shovel, for it was Sunday, of a January, on his way home after
playing centrefield in a hurling match, and having had tea with a
comrade hurler, stopping for a few seconds to listen to this man,
Connolly, who was trying to destroy the fine work being done by
Up Griffith, and make a medley of his cut-and-dried Hungarian
Gospel. A thin, haggard, lugubrious young fellow, wearing a red
tie, moved aimlessly through the little crowd, droning out the
titles of a bunch of colour-covered pamphlets that he carried in
his hand, a drone that was half a whisper and half a threat,
Socialism Made Easy, a penny a copy, only a penny the copy;
tuppence each, *Can a Catholic Be a Socialist?* only tuppence each;
the truth for tuppence; Hubert Bland's great work, *Can a
Catholic Be a Socialist?* The gaunt young man, whose name was
Tom Egan, was the most cheerless sight ever seen by Sean.
Everything about him had a downward drag; his jaws sagged
down to the edge of his chin; his long nose seemed to be bent on
pulling itself out of his face; his eyes were mirrors of energetic
despondency; his lips were twisted into lines of deeply-cut
complaints; but in the midst of all this misery his red tie blazed
in his shallow bosom.

—Who's th' big-bodied man gettin' up to speak? asked a man
of him as he passed displaying the pamphlets.

—That's James Connolly, our Secretary, an' if you knew all
you should know, you'd know without askin'.

—Secretary of what? asked Sean.

—Aw, God, th' ignorance here's devastatin'! said Egan, giving
a wryer twist to his melancholy mouth; Secretary of the Irish
Socialist Republican Party, an' if you knew all you should know,
you wouldn't have t' ask. Penny each, *Socialism Made Easy*, be
the renowned Socialist leadher, James Connolly.

—It doesn't look to be a mighty force of a Party, murmured Sean.

—Aw, you count be numbers, d'ye? and he looked with pitiful
tolerance at Sean.

—There's certainly something in them, said Sean; God fights on the side of the big battalions, you know – or so Napoleon said.

—We aren't concerned with Napoleon, an' God has nothin' to say in this meetin'.

—Jasus, don't we know it! burst from the man who had asked the first question.

—An' if you were with us, comrade, said the gaunt one, laying a hand on Sean's shoulder, and ignoring the ignorant remark of the ignorant man, you'd make one more.

—I thought you said you didn't put any pass on numbers?

—With a hurley stick under your arm, a gay blue-and-green jersey on your chest, and, I suppose, a cushy job, you can well afford to mock the woe of th' world!

—I am a labourer, and that's not quite a cushy job; I have no desire to mock anything, and there's more things than woe in the world.

—What more is there, comrade?

—There's joy and a song or two: the people sang as they went their way to tear the Bastille down.

—You're too oul'-fashioned for me, mate, said the gaunt one. Look! there's your proper leadher there, and he gestured to the fringe of the crowd, a little way from where they stood; Arthur Griffith, who's stooped to have a little quiet silent laugh. Well, he'll wake one day before he knows the night is gone to find himself and his gang swept away by what he's scornin' now.

Right enough, there was Up Griffith Up Thomas a Davis, hunched close inside his thick dark Irish coat, a dark-green velour hat on his head, a thick slice of leather nailed to his heels to lift him a little nearer the stars, for he was somewhat sensitive about the lowness of his stature. His great protruding jaws were thrust forward like a bull's stretched-out muzzle; jaws that all his admirers spoke of, or wrote about, laying it down as an obvious law that in those magnificent jaws sat the God-given sign of a great man. And Arthur Up Griffith, to give him his due, did all he could to give the fiction substance and fact. As plain as a shut mouth could say, he said he was Erin's strong, silent man.

What was he thinking of as he stood there, grim and scornful? Tormenting himself with the fading vision of a most lovely lady whose golden hair was hanging down her back, so full of fire that a tress of it would give light to a group threshing corn in a black barn on a dark night. Maybe stroking the right hand, oh! worthy

right hand, that had laid a whip on the back of a little tittle-tattle
Dublin editor of a gossip journal when he whispered *spy* about
the Helen of Eireann who had the loveliness to launch a battle
and go through it with the walk of a queen. He hid his hatred of a
rival in the wrapping of Erin's noble emblem, boys, the green
flag, around him; he composed gnarled remarks in his weekly
paper against him who embroidered lovely cloths to put beneath
the feet of the fair one, to shelter their grace and whiteness from
the dust of the street; and sang songs that made a flame of her
fair ear and sent a swell into her bosom with the pride of what a
singer can say out of a purple-and-white love. Art Up Griffith Up
Thomas a Davis' cold eyes saw the black-maned head of Yeats
in the clouds, saw it on the earth beneath, looking at him from the
Book of Kells, and staring down from the ceiling of the simple
room wherein he slept. So he began to mock at the phantoms,
saying that the fashioner of the play *Cathleen ni Houlihan* had
become a king's pensioner; that he had walked away from her
four beautiful green fields into an English paved court; Ochone,
widda Malone, d'ye hear me talkin? And widda Malone said
she'd heard right enough, and th' name that was once a jewel in
Erin's girdle had dwindled into a dull stone; and Willie Reilly and
his dear colleen bawn said, He was never much; he is nothin' now;
and the Rose of Tralee said that he was just a lonely gateway now,
where no one enthered; and Mary sitting on the stile murmured
it was all very shocking; the minstrel boy went about saying that
Yeats now was no more than the seams on the grass showing
where a house once stood; while Nora Creena closed her eyes,
nodded her pretty head sagely, and murmured the less said
about it all the better. A pensioner of an English king – pooh!
bah!

Instinctively Sean stood by Yeats, in spite of the little he could
guess then, and the less he knew. We have too few, too few such
men to spare a one like Yeats the poet, and the Gaelic Leaguers
who heard him grew silent. Devil a much you fellows do to keep
a few shillings jingling in the poet's pocket. What about the
Israelites who took gold, silver, and jewels from the Egyptians
before they left them? If England pays the man's rent, then let it
be counted unto righteousness for her. None of you know a single
poem by Yeats. Not even *The Ballad of Father Gilligan*. And the
poor oul' gaum, Cardinal Logue, condemning *Countess Cathleen*
though he hadn't read a line of it. We were paying a deep price

for that sort of thing since Parnell went away from us. He himself had read the ballad only.

There the little squat figure of Griffith stood, no tremor stirring the spectacles on his nose. Probably thinking more of Yeats than of Connolly, thought Sean. It wasn't Connolly's face Griffith saw, but Yeats', and the evening was full of the poet's verses. Well, the golden tresses would gleam no more for Yeats, at any rate. The small white feet would seek another pathway, one of thorns rather than of broidered cloths or dreams. Oh, Cathleen ni Houlihan, your way's a thorny way! And Ireland's rock of ages, Griffith, stiffened with elation, firm in his Irish woven tweed, armoured with the stamp of Deunta in Eirinn on its collar and on the seat of the pants. And wasn't Up Griffith a poet himself? You bet he was. What about the one written to give Major McBride a lift in the Mayo election?

> God bless you, John McBride, aroon,
> God bless your Irish corps!
> With courage of the Keltic race you've gone to help
>   the Boers.
> True friends by Bann and Liffey banks,
> By Suir and Shannon side,
> Send you their hearts' best sympathy –
> God bless you, John McBride!

Let Yeats arise now and go to Inisfree, and stay and hide himself well there in his strict cabin of clay and wattles made – though, if y'asked me, thought Griffith, he wouldn't know what wattles were – and let him sow and hoe and crow over his nine bean rows, and live on them, with honey from the hive of the honey bees, and his evening full of the linnet's wings, regardless of the fact that no one in Eirinn wants an evening full of a linnet's wings. Far more profitable for them to go to hear me lecture on how Hungary hitch-hiked herself into independence; or to listen enthralled to the gallant deeds done by the wild swans of Coole – whatthehell-amisaying – by the wild geese in far foreign fields from Dunkirk to Belgrade, the O'Haras, Maguires, Reillys, McGauleys, O'Briens and O'Bradys, with hosts of other leaders, and men of many clans, fighting for anyone that would furnish them with a sword, a good word to go on, and a glass of malt at the end of a battle.

Sean edged nearer to where the great man, Griffith, stood

surrounded by the gaunt one, now behind, now to his left, to his right a moment later, and then circling in front of him, murmuring balefully in Griffith's direction, *Socialism Made Easy*, by the renowned James Connolly, only a penny each. But the great man with the brain of ice, in the greatcoat, underneath the green velour, never moved. The widely-lensed spectacles and the thick moustache and the thrust-out chin listened in cold silence to Connolly's words; and Sean remembered how, at meetings in the rooms of the Sinn Fein Central Branch, Up Griffith had often called on Sean to speak, and he had spoken eloquently in Irish and English, amused that Connolly, Pike, Ling, and a few other Irish Republican Socialists had to listen silent and respectful to the flow of the Gaedhilge, understanding not a word of what was being said; with Up Griffith sitting bolt upright and grim in the chair, huge jaws forced forward, ears cocked, though he understood no more than he'd understand the sad songs sung by the Children of Lir tossed about on the foam of the Swanee river. So he edged nearer till his elbow gently touched the stiff frame standing in the greatcoat.

—It's cold it is the night that's in it, he said in Irish.

The widely-lensed spectacles, velour hat, and intrusive moustache turned towards him, the rocky road to Dublin jaws thrust themselves farther out over the turned-up collar of the greatcoat, but the clenched mouth remained shut; then all turned, and, without a word, went their way.

—Little bourgious bastard! growled the gaunt one, glaring after the little conceited figure. Not enough banks in the counthry but he must start another – him and his Sinn Fein Bank! The dumb yahoo! Curse o' God on the bit he is above an ordinary little bourgious bastard!

Thinking, most likely, of what Connolly has been saying, thought Sean as he followed the great man slowly. *Cheek of those fellows stating the English were brothers. Connolly should know better. But my icy brain can never be deceived.* A capitalist government would never destroy capitalist property. *Bah! As if an' English government cared a damn about Irish property.* Dog won't eat dog, says Connolly. *Nonsense! Besides the Irish aren't dogs, even if the English are.*

Griffith doesn't understand Ireland, thought Sean; no, in no way. He is simply delighted to dream as he walks through Ireland's junk-shop of all the tawdry paraphernalia of 1882. He hasn't the slimmest connexion with a Gaedhilge proverb or a Gaedhilge song. He has no inkling of what burns in the breast of him who looks back on, and lives with, the

> Outlawed man in a land forlorn,
> He scorned to turn and fly;
> But he kept the cause of freedom safe
> On the mountains of Pomeroy.

He never even walks with the shade of Swift, for if I brought him tomorrow to be with them who work with me; among Christy Mahon, Bob Harvey, Bob Jones who'd sell the King of Ireland's son for a pint, Ned Smith who'd steal a cross off an ass' back, and all the rest, he'd be lost. His highest vision is no higher than the counter in his Sinn Fein Bank. He strikes a match, and thinks it the torch of freedom. A lighter of little gas-lamps to show the Irish where to walk. The Sword of Light would turn him to ashes if ever he tried to hold it. Ah! he's thinking of Trinity College; for he saw the green velour turning to look at the austere façade of the memorable building, sighing, probably, that the young men inside didn't hear ear to ear with him. More inclined to Yeats' poetic bombast than to me. One of England's strongest bastions. Here was a group of them coming along now, singing *Daisy, Daisy, Give Me Your Answer, Do*, shouting it out with vengeance and vim. Oh! the vulgarity of the anglicized Irish mind! To think that Thomas a Davis had once gone in and out of those gates. Hardly believable. They surged uncivilly around him, jostling him out into the gutter. Oh, Cathleen ni Houlihan, your way's a thorny way!

—God, it's Arthur Griffith! shouted one of them.

—*Alumna licentiae, quam stulti libertatem vocabunt*, bawled another, waving his cap over his head, shouldering Up Griffith with a sly sliding movement, making the man nearly lose his balance; but he recovered, walked slantwise back to the sidewalk, bypassing the students, and marched on without either a word or a gesture.

Sean felt angry, for Griffith was something of a leader, deserving jail from the point of view of the conquerors, but deserving respect as well. Strange, he thought, swinging his hurley into a poise that could swiftly jab the ribs of anyone likely to try to jostle him from the pathway. Strange and curious, he thought,

that one able to speak Latin, who got a golden education denied
to Griffith or himself, having a fine home in the country or in
Rathmines, son, maybe, of a clergyman, a doctor, or a judge,
strange he didn't know what decent manners were. He could
calmly understand them hotly cracking skulls in the emotional
medley of a royal visit, when the Dubliners were out with the
battle-cries and their green flags; but in the cold of a quiet wintry
night when citizens moved about intent on business, recreation,
or love, indifferent to their national submission for the moment,
to spout abuse on a citizen without warrant even of English law,
or the gallant provocation of opposing tirades, was, to Sean, a
thing that couldn't be understood of common sense or tangible
decency. Let them look to it if they pushed him a hair's breadth
away from where he was walking. But they didn't; they passed
by and took not the slightest notice of him as he followed Arthur
marching on sturdily ahead as if nothing had happened.

The next day of a dark cold morning, Sean in the forge blowing
the bellows to make the fire roar so that the smith might repoint
his pick blunted by the work of the day before, for the soil of the
deep trench navvies dig, to sow great iron pipes to carry a main
supply of water, is hard and stony, and the point of a pick is soon
deprived of its eagerness to bite: here in the yellow-and-red gleam
of the flame of the fire, watching the smith Dick Bagnal's lanky
form waiting for the pick to redden, one sooty hand on the butt
of the pick, its point in the heart of the fire, Sean saw again the
meeting of the night before, the squat, swaying form of Connolly
speaking from his box, and the cold staring lens-covered eyes of
Griffith watching, the big mouth beneath the great moustache
grim and clenched and silent. Both of them out for Ireland, all for
Ireland, yet neither of them could understand her. Both were a
wide way from the real Ireland, and it was not in either of them
to come closer. One man alone, of that time, had in him all that
prophesied of the Ireland yet to come; the Ireland that would
blossom into herself many, many years from now. This man alone
had the hand to hold the Sword of Light. He held it now, and its
rays were sparkling all over the valley of the Boyne. There were
visions of handicrafts, of furniture, of woven garments, new, yet
full of the scent of the days gone by; of pottery decked with the
coloured glory of Keltic spirals and intricate, waving, twisting
patterns, new too, but touched with the grandeur of the Book of
Kells and the gaiety of the Book of MacDurnan; here, where of

old time Protestant men for King William wrestled to the death with Catholic men for King James, falling with the arms of hatred round each other by the borders of the Boyne, was seen again the sway of the scarlet, green, grey, or saffron kilt; here was heard the musical scream of the war-pipes; here were heard the countless stories of Eireann, long in thrall, with the scent of freedom clinging round them still; and song burst out, and filled the valley with hope; and the plough and the cross shone on the biggest of banners; and *The Irish Peasant*, one of the finest papers Ireland ever had, told all about them; while among all this gay-coloured energy and excitement walked the dark-eyed, black-haired W. P. O'Ryan, shy, sensitive, one with the peasant, the worker, and the scholar. All aglow he was, and firm set to make the Pope's green island a busy place and beautiful. Half a step behind came a Man, a bacon-curer, the surety of the paper, and a helper with money for the things they thought of doing, whose heart was warm with the coloured resolution all around him. All was fine till the clergy came to murmur against it, and Cardinal Log lashed out to yell that it was a shame to undermine the holy faith! And the Man's wife said to her husband, You've got to hearken to what these holy men witness against them and thee. Have nothing thou to do with this bad bold man, O'Ryan, but cast him off, and come thou into the house, lest an evil thing befall us here, and lest worse befall us when we pass away to Purgatory. And he hearkened unto his wife, and shut himself up in his own house, condemning certain things written by O'Ryan, already condemned by the Cardinal, though never read by him; for the Cardinal had the power to see a hole through an iron pot; and so O'Ryan was left alone to fight a host of snarling clergy who silenced song and story, drove away the marching, kilted men, hunted O'Ryan from the Boyne to the Liffey, then to the Dublin Quay, and finally from the last spot where his clinging feet still stood, away, away with you, from Ireland altogether, away from her for ever and a day! And Sean wondered that Hyde said nothing, that the Gaelic League made no moan, and Griffith, indifferent to a greater man, shook no angry fist, but let him go, and so he went for ever. And Sean was sad, for it was O'Ryan who first gave his written words a value, and spaced his thoughts over a fine column of *The Irish Nation*; words, under the name of *Sound the Loud Trumpets*, that struck at the educational system Augustus Birrell was hanging around Ireland's neck. Over the grave of this brave man, this cultured man, a silent hurrah; a big, broad, and scornful spit on the grave of the Cardinal.

Down in the deep trench, shored up with planks and cross-pieces, a long way from Ireland's four beautiful green fields, side by side with the huge glossy black cylinders, Sean watched the broad backs of the navvies bending, rising, and bending again, as they worked on, making way for another length of the monster black pipe, looking like a prehistoric ebony worm that men were uncovering now after a rest of a million years; while far above their heads a dim damp dawn crept slowly over the sky. Not one of these brawny boys had ever even heard of Griffith or of Yeats. They lived their hard and boisterous life without a wish to hear their names. A good many of them had done seven years' service in the British Army, and now served on the Reserve, for sixpence a day wasn't to be sneezed at. What to them were the three Gaelic candles that light up every darkness: truth, nature, and knowledge? Three pints of porter, one after the other, would light up the world for them. If he preached the Gaelic League to any one of them, the reply would probably be, Aw, Irish Ireland me arse, Jack, not makin' you an ill answer, oul' son. What would the nicely-suited, white-collared respectable members of the refined Gaelic League branches of Dublin do if they found themselves in the company of these men? Toiling, drinking, whoring, they lived everywhere and anywhere they could find a ready-made lodging or room. They didn't remember the glories of Brian the Brave. Beyond knowing him as an oul' king of Ireland in God's time, they knew nothing and cared less. Their upper life was a hurried farewell to the *News of the World* on Sunday morning, and a dash to what was called short twelve Mass in the Pro-Cathedral, the shortest Mass said in the land; and then a slow parade to the various pubs, and a wearisome wait till the pubs unveiled themselves by sliding the shutters down, and let the mass of men crowd in for refreshment. And yet Sean felt in his heart that these men were all-important in anything to be done for Ireland. Well, there was no sound of a linnet's wings here; nothing but the thud of the pick, the tearing sound of the shovel thrust into the gravel, the loud steady pulse of the pump sucking away the surface water, and the cries of the men handling the derrick from which the huge pipes swung, and the irritating squelch of the men's boots as they sunk into, and were pulled out of, the thick and sticky yellow clay. While he swung the sledgehammer down on the hardy head of the bright steel wedge imprisoned in a gad held by a comrade, to break through a harder crust the pick couldn't penetrate, he cursed himself that he couldn't afford to spend a month, a fortnight, or even a week in a summer school at peace in an Irish-speaking district. Three or four visits, and he would be as fluent a speaker of the Gaelic as any in Ireland. Even now, with all their chances, all their means providing them with the best of books, there were few of them could speak as well and as rapidly as he; and none of them with such a fire of eloquence. Few of them hadn't heard him speak at one time or another, yet never a one of them had even asked why he didn't go to Rinn or Tourmakeady when the summer sun shone, and share with them the joy of living with their very own. If he went up to a meeting of the Coiste Gnotha, the Head Executive of the Gaelic League, and, leaning over the table they sat around keeping time in their talk to the snores of Edward Martyn, asleep in an easy-chair, said, Look here, boys, I love the Irish; I've learned a lot; I want to spend a holiday in an Irish district, Connemara for preference, but I've no money; couldn't you people fork out enough to fix me there for a week or two, so that my Irish may be as the rain falling on the earth, or the lightning splitting the black clouds, what would happen? The tidy-minded, uninspirable Secretary, Paddy O'Daly, would come over, grip his arm, lead him to the door, and say, Now, now, we're engaged in very important business. The like of them would hurry by Whitman spitting out of him as he leaned by a corner of the Bowery. And doing so, they'll die, for whoever walks a furlong without sympathy walks to his own funeral dressed in his shroud. Ah, to hell with them!

—Eh, there; look out, Jack! warned his mate: the sledge near missed the wedge that time!

POOR TOM'S ACOLD

SEAN STOOD silently in the room looking long at the fearful figure of his brother, Tom, crouched in the comfortable armchair before a sunnily-blazing fire, for the night was cold, and a white frost was calmly settling down on the paths and street outside.

He felt a choking in his throat, and tears trickled down his cheeks, but Tom couldn't see them, for his eye-strings had broken, and he was blind.

Tom had done well and done ill since he had come home from the Boer War, jaunty in his khaki uniform, helmet and puggaree, the Queen's coloured box of chocolate in his kitbag still full of the sweetmeat, for what soldier could eat chocolate given by a queen? And he had kept it just as it had been given to him during a parade on the brown veldt, in the shadow of high kopjes when many bugles had blown the cease-fire, and the ragged De Wet, with many a curse, had stabled his horse, and had flung his rifle and whip into a corner, easing his sweating body on a sofa till another chance came to strike again, galloping over the veldt or crouching behind a kopje.

War's wager won, Tom had gone back to his job as a postman, was shortly after promoted to his old job of a sorter, finally becoming head sorter in the morning mail running from Dublin to Belfast, this job bringing another and much higher one almost within his reach: he was getting on well and worthily. Then he married: married an ignorant Catholic girl who in some way had influenced him towards a newer home, and a companionable bed. Agatha Cooley was a yellow-skinned, stout woman, badly built in body, and mind-sly in a lot of ways, as so many toweringly ignorant persons are; her best knowledge lay in guessing what a newspaper was trying to say. She could struggle through a short letter with pain and anxiety, her finest phrase always being that of hoping all were in the best of health as that left her at present. A lid that drooped halfway down over one eye gave one side of her face the appearance of falling into a jocular sleep, and, watch as he would, Sean had never seen it lift or fall; it stood still like a fading yellow blind whose worn-out spring refused to send it more than halfway up on a dark and dusty oval window. She dressed in a very dowdy, slovenly way, and spoke in a voice from which a rough life had mobbed even the dimmest tinkle of music. She was a cook-general when Tom met her, and how or where they met, or how the rather fastidious Tom had been gathered into her bosom, none of the family ever knew. Before they were married, Tom had brought her once or twice to see his mother; but do all we did to make things merry and offhand, the core of every effort was uneasiness, for poor Agatha could do nothing but sit straight on her chair, prim and fat, sipping her glass of beer, making herself look as unrefined as possible; giving a flat yes or a flatter no to every question, till one grew tired of asking, turning away to other thoughts, leaving her there to sit and sip her beer in peace. She had got Tom, and there she sat, thick and stout, like a queen cactus on a kitchen chair of state.

Mrs Casside had an anxious time of it, for she had an old Protestant dread of a mixed marriage, and all her time now was a silent prayer that, in some way or another, the marriage would drift into a happy unfulfilment. She told her trouble to but one outside the family – the Rev Mr Griffin, who agreed with her in a scholarly way, though Tom had only once ever put his foot inside his church, feeling very uncomfortable till he got out again. The Rector prayed in the little room, with Mrs Casside, that God in His goodness would see the dear woman's son safe, and lead him from the tangible danger of marrying one alien in religion, and different in manner and outlook in life, his words mingling with the laughing shouts of children swinging from a rope tied to the lamp-post just outside the window. Sean wasn't bothering about her alienism in religion, even for Tom's sake, for he knew that Tom had slid away from all of them. The smell of a pub was incense to Tom, and its portals had the beauty of a Persian garden, with an everlasting fountain of sweet waters in the midst of it. The hold of the faith had weakened well on Sean himself. Though he hadn't said farewell, the anchor was getting weighed, and his ship of life was almost about to leave the harbour. He no longer thought that God's right hand, or His left one either, had handed the Bible out of Heaven, all made up with chapter and verse and bound in a golden calfskin. Darwin's flame of thought had burned away a lot of the sacred straw and stubble, and following men had cleanly shown how incredible much of the Bible was, contradicting itself so often and so early that no one could argue with it, rearing up an imposition of fancy, myth, and miracle coloured by neither fact nor figure; depending on a crowd who, as Coleridge said, didn't believe, but only believed that they believed, ready to strike at, and drive away, any sincere and sorrowful heart daring to murmur, I can believe no longer.

No, it wasn't Agatha's religion that troubled Sean, for she had none save to eat and drink and sleep and be afeared of fancies; it was her slovenliness that tortured him, her drowsy ignorance and deep-set superstition that seared his imagination; for Tom was the one brother whom he liked, and, in his heart, he knew

that this marriage would be the end of Tom, and that he would
be separated even from the bawdy exhilaration of the pub.

God was no good, and the marriage took place, how, or where,
no one seemed to know. Tom just came to the home one day and,
in a silent silence, took his box away. For some years after, he
was rarely seen, and it was gossip that told us where he was living.
Occasionally at the railway station, Sean, with his dinner in a
handkerchief fixed to a billycan tied to his belt, hurrying to his
train for a country job at the screek of dawn, met Tom who
murmured a hurried hello, and Sean gave him the railwaymen's
signal of greeting of a raised index finger as he passed by to his
train. All the same, three fine kids came out of the mating, Sam,
Sylvester, and Sally; the little girl, a real handsome kid, the
younger boy, handsome and sturdy, and the older one strong too,
his boyish face an annoying blend of his father's good nature and
his mother's tireless querulousness. They rented a small house
with three steps up to the door, a shining brass knocker, and a
bow-window. This residence, with a few others, stood out grandly
in the narrow terrace, for the rest on the opposite side had only
iron knockers, no bow-windows, and no steps up to the doors.
Here with a selection of fair furniture, especially what was in the
room with the bow-window, fine lace curtains on the window,
with dark-yellow blinds at night, and a plant on a round mahogany
table, Tom made quite a splash, and for a time all went well as a
marriage bell. Once in a blue moon Tom would pay a flying call
to see the mother, send out for a jug of porter, and, with bread
and butter, drink it with her, chatting rapidly about what had
happened at work, but never a word about what had happened
at home; and Sean gave a guess that these lunar visits were spell-
snatched out of acrimony and thorny-worded leisure time. Once
Sean caught a glimpse of what was happening. It was Tom's day
off, and Sean had taken the day to help in a local election, and
when he came to Tom's terrace he came on the bould boy polish-
ing the brass knocker. Tom brought him in for a cup of tea, pointing a thumb warningly upwards, and murmuring, She's up in bed,
not feeling too well. In the kitchen, Sean noticed a pile of Delft
draining on a shelf, the things of yesterday mixed with the things
of today, and he knew that Tom had washed them.

—What's wrong with her? asked Sean, with a pointed gesture
of a thumb upwards.

—Not feeling too well; just not feeling too well, he murmured.

Down the road, in one of the houses on the opposite side of the terrace, Sean was told that this was a common thing on Tom's day off; and that it was he who kept the children's hair combed, bathed them often, and tried to see that the boys got their meals in time to allow them to attend, without blame, the local Christian Brothers' schools.

The time came when Tom himself wasn't feeling too well, and came oftener to see his mother – not to complain, but, maybe, to look at the old, hardy, encouraging face that had weathered so much of the stormy world. At first Tom took his inability to work with pretended joy – a holiday on full pay, he called it. The Post Office doctor attended him, gave him remedies, but Tom got weaker and weaker, and nothing stayed on his stomach. One day, out with the pipers' band, Sean hurried home to get a letter about a festival they were to attend, found Tom there, sitting heavily on a chair, his breath coming in gasps, and when asked what was wrong, I came upstairs too quick – all right in a minute, came staggering out of his mouth. When he came to himself a little, he sent for a pint of porter, but this time his mother drank it alone. His face, once so ruddy and confident, had waned into the pallor of a half-dead man.

—What's wrong with you, old man? asked Sean.

—Dunno right; something; I'll be all right again soon.

—But what does the doctor say 'tis?

—Didn't say, Jack; can't be anything serious, or he'd say, wouldn't he?

—You'd think so, said Sean doubtedly.

—Well, I'll be getting back home to rest a while, and a flash of meek panic at the journey before him flickered over the pale face; getting back now, I'd betther. He stood up slowly, and a shaking hand put a hat on his head. Well, so long, Jack; so long, old woman; and his shaky legs carried him out of the room.

—I don't like the look of him, said Mrs Casside; I don't like the look of him at all. A man of his age, only, should be fortified with all but the full strength of one of twenty. Whisht! He's callin', Jack – run!

He ran down the stairs to find Tom sitting breathless and near fainting on the last step of the flight, a kid with a squint staring at his panting breast and gaping mouth. He stood for a moment beside Tom, a hand resting on his shoulder, afraid that he would have to help Tom home, and he in full piper's dress, and sorry for himself that he had come home, and so plunged into all this annoyance.

—What's wrong with you, man? he asked, a little harshly; but Tom went on panting his breath out through an open mouth, motioning with a death-nacred finger for Sean to keep silent. So silent he stayed till the fit passed, and the breath of his brother came more softly again.

—Ran down the stairs too quick, he said at last. Could you manage, Jack, to see me home a bit of the way? and a tense look of appeal shot into the gentle grey eyes of the sick man.

—I've got to join the band again, Tom, we're advertising a coming concert, and the work has to be done.

—Right, old man, I know, murmured Tom. Never mind; I'll manage; but he bent his head to hide his frightened disappointment, for he dreaded to be weak in the presence of strangers.

—I'll see you a little of the way, said Sean, softening. Cheer up, old sweat – you'll be all right yet.

—All right yet, echoed Tom; yes, all right yet; but Sean didn't like to look at the glassy film creeping over the eyes of his brother.

He helped him to his feet, putting an arm around his body, while Tom put one over his shoulder, and so they went down Church Road, slowly, slowly, gradually getting nearer to Tom's halfway home, the sick man frequently stopping to get his breath, the passers-by stopping to stare back at a death-faced man whose legs were like loose bending wires trying to keep straight, kept going with the help of another in a green kilt, shining brooches in breast and at knee, jaunty balmoral cap, and flowing crimson shawl.

—Don't talk, don't even try to talk, advised Sean; just do your best to move, and lean well on me, for he was anxious to get his brother home, and flee to sunnier company, to march stiffly proud by the side of the pipers. Suddenly he heard the roll of the drums, and buried in the roll the opening and unruly skirl of the pipes being filled with air before the pipers got into the start of the tune at the end of the second roll.

—There they go now, he thought; at a distance, thank God, for he didn't want the band to come swinging past, and he carrying a half-dead man home. He felt the sweat running down his belly and along his legs, for the kilt was warm and heavy, seven yards of material swinging from a man's hips; and his arms were aching. Worse than a hard day's work, this!

On the two of them struggled up the quiet terrace; quiet no

longer, for all the doors were opening to let the people see where
the music was coming from, and what band was playing it. On
and on, past all the little doors, little windows, little front gardens
with little gates, each with different-shaped beds, but with the
same flowers growing in them all: tansy with its hotly fragrant
smell, its deeply-fronded leaves, and its humble yellow button of
a blossom; mignonette sending out its dainty, delicate perfume,
a little disdainful of the vulgar scent of the tansy; purple rockets
whose seed-pods turned to wonderful discs of nacred silver, fit to
make tiny wings for tiny angels; blood-red dahlias, portly and
pompous-looking, like eighteenth-century gentlemen ripened into
a stout dignity with rich wine; orange marigolds with their ragged
and crooky stems and dishevelled leaves looking like harridans of
the Coombe wearing patched disordered skirts round their bodies
and gorgeously gay orange bonnets on their heads. Variegated
clumps of sweet-william prim and apart in their own private
corners; brown, yellow, white, and blue-purpled pansies living
for themselves, and taking notice of nothing; hurrying, gaudy-
coloured nasturtiums, trying to climb everywhere, like upstarts at
a sedate garden party; and bushes of violet and delicately-mauve
michaelmas daisies, their dark, sober green leaves and tall stems
gathering together for company, silently sneering at the richer
display of the other blossoms.

—Do you think you could go a little quicker, old son, asked
Sean, before the band brings the crowd surging round us?

—Must try, must try, Jack, Tom panted back; and with a gal-
vanic power of will he stiffened his poor wavering legs, and
hastened on past the rest of the gardens, till they passed through
his own little plot, asway with neglected blooms, Sean knocking
impatiently at the door, while Tom lay almost lifeless against it,
his waistcoat coming out and sinking in like a blown and pricked
ballon, with the dint of palpitation, his glazing eyes bulging, and
his mouth again agape in an effort to pacify the turbulent commotion of his frightened heart.

Sean's mind held only thoughts of the concert that was to raise
funds to help Dr O'Hickey with his fight in Rome against the
bishops who were opposing Essential Irish in the New University
Ireland had wrenched from the hand of her enemy. Irish in the
New University, or else! That was the one way to talk, to fling a
challenge right into the teeth of the snarling Birrell and his hoary
henchmen, the bishops! Dr O'Hickey go brath! A lion's roar, a

wolf-dog's bay beside the pigeon-cautious coo of Dr Douglas Hyde, and the scholarly and elegantly brushed phrases of Eoin Mac Neill, an Aaron's rod that rarely bore a bud. Hyde would venture a boo to an English goose, but ne'er a boo to an Irish bishop. That would be asking too much. Oh, O'Hickey, me jewel of Ireland – there's one man left in Ireland yet! No priest, bishop, archbishop, cardinal, or pope is going to be let impede the onward march of Ireland. Such a scandal has never been seen here since the dastard who, having sold his country, successfully sought the votes of the citizens of Athlone, leaning on the arms of two bishops. Sadleir and Keogh, be God, and the Pope's brass band! But *ne plus ultra* O'Hickey – a Parnell with a Roman white choker round his neck, fighting the battle of Banba's language. I hear you speaking: If the New University is to be a West Briton one, it will be made so by an act of treachery to Ireland on the part of the University Senate, five of whom are distinguished clerics, two of whom are bishops. These lords and gentlemen of the Senate must be told that, wily as they are, they will not be suffered to cozen and delude the Irish people. Michael O'Hickey, you are my soul within me; our love and our strength in the day of strife, our rosc catha, a piercing eye of battle leading us on to a new and freer life!

Here they come, now, chests out, eyes proud, aswinging grandly round the corner, drummers and pipers in full play, mantling the narrow terrace with martial music; the rolling of the drums echoing through the little houses giving them a proud passion to find a sword somewhere; the shrill of the war-pipes sending a thrill through every ear that had been already half stuffed with the dust of death – like poor Tom's; the green kilts, crimson shawls, and gay ribbons draped on the drones fluttering winsomely whenever a breeze blew, fanning a new resolution and a strict courage into all who followed; here they come, here they come, the pipes and drums of war, to scatter away the quiet resignation of timorous people, their big crimson banner before them, the silver lion asparkle on its bloody field, roaring out, forward, forward! Forward for Ireland, like the Scots Wha Hae at Bannockburn; march on, march on, to liberty or death, like the French with bloodied fingers tearing down the stones of the Bastille; march like the marching of the Men of Harlech, for of battle we'll not cheat them; on like the whirlwind riders on the desert sands of Abdel Kader, son of a slave, first of the brave,

swift-riding Abdel Kader; farther, farther on, for the rifle brown
and sabre bright can freely speak and nobly write, and prophets
preached that truth right well, like Hofer, Brian, Bruce, and Tell
– Christ, will the pendulous-lidded, yellow-faced bitch never open
the door!

The door opened, and Tom's yellow-skinned wife glared at
them sleepily from the half-lidded eye, and balefully from the
wide-open one, like a lassie direct in descent from the one-eyed
coon – no, like a woman Balor of the Blows. Sean caught up Tom
in his arms and carried him into the little bow-windowed room,
laying him down as gently as his hurry could, in the easy armchair
by the empty fire-grate. Mercy on us! his bones were like flints
against his breast, and pressed sharply into Sean's arms. Then he
patted the sandy-haired head and turned to go.

—A nice state to bring the poor man back in! said Agatha
bitterly. Dhrinkin' with his oul' wan I suppose he was, forgettin'
all about his wife an' childher. Well, it looks as if he was bein'
punished for it. Thryin' to get all she can outa th' poor man,
that's what it is, so it is. I'll put a stop to it, so I will. I will, see
now. Now run off in your gay get-up an' leave me here with all
th' trouble.

A rich surge of rolling drums and valiant skirl of a defiant
march came sweeping into the lonely room as the band swung by
outside the window, and Sean caught a glimpse of crimson shawl,
crimson banner, and the jaunty feathers rising out of the pipers'
balmorals, set a little rakishly on their boyish heads.

—A nice noisy commotion to bring to th' ears of a poor sick
man, she said. God forgive you! – that's all I can say.

Sean noticed that Tom's lips were moving. He bent down close
so as to hear the pale words from the thronging sound of rolling
drums and skirling pipes that filled the room with martial animation.

—Cold, Jack, he heard Tom whispering; feeling bad and cold,
very cold.

—You'd better light a bit of a fire for him here, said Sean to
Agatha – he says he's very cold.

—I'd betther, had I? I'm to take insthructions from you, am I?
Your money'll pay for it, I suppose, will it? An' what has him
cold, I'd like to know? If he'd ha' stayed in his own home, he
wouldn't be cold now. His lawful wife's th' proper person to
know whether he's cold or no, if y'ask me. Sorra mend him, if he

is cold, aself, for his flighty way o' goin' on. Is it any wondher he's cold, an' has no luck th' way he regards his poor patient wife? Oh, ay, slink away now when th' harm's done, do. Guttherbred highlandher, guttherbred highlandher! she said loudly, following him to the door.

Through the harp blows the cold wind. Ah, Tom, if it had only been a comely face, a rustling petticoat, and a slender leg that had betrayed your poor life to a woman, enhanced by a shimmer of a little silk. But no! It was pendulous breasts, a ponderous belly, a clumsy foot, and a vacant yellow face that brought you close to this! A drab, hard cushion on which to stretch your life. But a small spark left now, all the rest on's body cold.

He was again amid the roll of the drums and the skirl of the pipes, forgetting Tom, and thinking only of Ireland. The drums of Ireland, of Inis Fail, the Isle of Destiny, beaten by tempestuous hands, were tossing the patriotic air into wildness, shaking every window in every city, town, and hamlet, and tapping a tocsin at every door, giving a quiver to the tidy walls and corbelled ceiling of the Viceregal Lodge, sending the cloth-covered butlers and plush-covered footmen to whisper in corners where they couldn't be seen, hurrying out to the wind-swept plains of Kildare to circle slowly round the lonely grave of Wolfe Tone to liven his dust-filled ears with the sound of the drums at the head of an Ireland marching!

Busy in the circle of drumming, Sean had a visit from Tom's eldest son, who said his Da felt bad, very bad, and wanted Sean to come to him. Catching up the latest issue of *Sinn Fein* to leave with his brother, he hurried along, warning the young boy that he hadn't time to stay long. He found Tom crouched in the armchair beside the fire, his tawny head sunk on his shrunken breast, his white handsome hands resting on the arms of the chair.

—Well, old man, how goes it?

He sat there silent for a long time, never stirring, making Sean feel uneasy, for he had no time to think of these things. Then he lifted the finely-formed head a little to murmur, I'm beginning to think, Jack, I'm on the edge of the end.

—Aw, nonsense, man, you're only a little downcast. Not a condition of thought for an old Dublin Fusilier. I've brought a copy of *Sinn Fein* for you to lift your mind away from depression. And he laid the paper on his brother's knee, putting a gentle and encouraging hand on his shoulder.

—No use, now, Jack; I'm afraid I'll never read again: my eyes have gone; something burst – the strings, I think.

Jesus have mercy on us! Tom was going from them. Like their father before them, he was trying to die on his feet. Well, Sean could do nothing. He wasn't a Hercules to wrassle with Death and throw him down with a half-nelson.

—Where's Agatha? he asked.

—Don't know. Shopping, I think. Kids outside playing. It's a hard thing to keep alive, Jack; hardly worth the effort. Then he fell silent again, his bony hands resting motionless on the arms of the chair. I think I'll give in, and go, he said suddenly; help me up and into bed, Jack, me oul' son.

—Ah, thought Sean, he's about to leave the view from the little bow-window for ever. He took off his coat so that it wouldn't come in his way, helped Tom up out of the chair, and saw that he couldn't even try to walk. He edged him gently over to the wall, leant him against it, and then turned his back to his brother.

—Now, me son o' gold, fall forward on to my back, put your arms around my neck, hold tight as you can, and I'll carry you up the way an Indian woman carries her papoose.

Tom fell gently forward, and clasped his thin arms around Sean's neck. With a gentle hoist he had Tom up; up the ten stairs he bore him as he'd often carried a sixteen-stone bag of cement, into the little bedroom. There he laid him down against the wall, squirming round with a hold still on him, lest he'd fall; lifted him up in his arms, and carried him like an infant to the bed. Here he stripped him to his shirt, got him in, and covered him up warm, standing still to look down on the pallor-stricken mask of what was so short a while ago a lively, laughing, proud, and buoyant face; a handsome one too, with its straight nose, bold forehead, the blue-grey eyes full of the animation of taking things as they came – now unsightly cavities of decaying jelly – the fierce-looking tawny moustache veiling the kind mouth, and the poor neck, thin now as a pipe-shank, that had once bulged out the stiff stern collar of his soldier's crimson coat.

—Tom, oul' son, he asked in a gentle whisper, do you really feel very bad?

—Only for the three chiselurs, I'd be all right; I'm doing me best to live.

—He's game to the end, thought Sean. He's deliberately fighting it alone; no murmur against the dark dullness of the grave. He isn't asking me to stay; he doesn't seek a wife's sympathy, or a mother's comfort. Happier are the dead that are already dead, more than the living that are yet alive. Not a mother's son of a gun of us knows whence we came or whither we go. Some shout that they do, and carry banners of belief in their hands; but the banners, too, will soon be dust sprinkled on the dust of the bearers. Kindly Tom, poor kindly Tom. He rushed into the brightness of the pub, the one brightness within his reach. Well, God is as likely to be there as in the Viceroy's satin-walled residence, or the Guinness' mansion of high style and tabinet. Not a son of a gun of us knew who he'd meet, or what he'd see, or a ha'p'orth when the time came to go. A bird's flight from the ground to the roof-top, and then the same bird's flight from the roof-top to the ground, and life was over. He bent down towards the bed till his mouth was close to Tom's waxy ear. You know Mr Griffin, don't you? A grand man. Would you like me to bring him to you for a minute's talk?

—Anything you like, Jack; only for the three chiselurs, I wouldn't care a lot.

—I'll go get him then; I just heard Agatha coming in, so you won't be by yourself. So long, oul' soldier!

He hurried out to where Agatha was taking off her hat in the hall, and touching her on the arm, said, I'm off to bring Mr Griffin to him. Keep an eye on him, and stay with him, for he may slip off any minute now.

—Yous would all like him to go, wouldn't yous? Oh, I know well, but he'll stay in spite of yous all. An' don't throw any ordhers at me, if you please; I know quite well what a wife's duties to her husband is.

Sean left the house, and ran, and hurried, when running lost him his breath. What was he hurrying for? To bring the Rector to say a word in season to a fellow hurrying off in an opposite direction. What word? The word that was in the beginning? Possibly. The word that was with God; the Word that was God. He was hurrying to bring God to the dying Tom who was on his way to meet Him, as it were, halfway home. But Tom had never bothered his head about what the word might be. His holy grail was a pint tankard filled to the brim. Yet Sean could proclaim to all the angels of Heaven, to all the gilded prelates of the Church militant here on earth, that Tom was a decent fellow. He had done foolish things early and late and often, but who the hell hadn't? The pint tumbler in the midst of a pub's glow, or the half-gallon can at home were Tom's own true guiding star. But what about the boyos who made what filled them? The fellow who rebuilt St Patrick's Cathedral out of some of the profits made out of the stuff that thousands of poor Toms swallowed? The National Church of Ireland balanced now and for evermore on barrels of beer and whiskey. The church where Ormond Butler's men and Kildarian Geraldine's men sliced each other to death right before the altar, like alto-relievos come to life there, making the Pope himself to force the Lords Mayor of Dublin City to bereave themselves of their flaunting red gowns and lengthy golden chain of office every single Corpus Christi Day, and go walking barefoot, weeping away, a yellow tip of flame on a lighted candle the one ornament in a sad token of humiliation for a sin cleverly and enthusiastically committed by others; the church where the Irish were told straight off and straight out that Henry the Eighth was their lawful, legitimate, legible, rightful king; and only an hour or two later the city was deluged with banners of orange and blue, and Dutch troopers wearing big-plumed, high-rimmed, three-cornered hats, and thigh boots, with spurs with rowels on them as big as circular saws, came clattering through the streets, led by King Billy with his long sword on one side of him, and a Bible broad hanging by a silver chain from the other side of his saddle-girths, who led them into the church to get rid of their thanks to God for the vast victory of the Boyne, burying the Duke of Schomberg in a copper coffin under the tiled floor with his martial cloak around him; and here, too, Edward the Seventh, when he was but a prince, was made a knight of the illustrious blue-ribboned, quiz seberrabbit Order of St Patrick, sitting near the chained shot that whipped off the head of General St Ruth and he leading the French cavalry at the battle of Aughrim; and it was here, too, that poor Swift constantly kept tormenting God to stir up the Irish into burning everything English except her coals.

It was this history-chequered church, so wittily and winsomely built in the form of a Latin cross by placing a lot of absolutely equilateral triangles together, showing the choir, nave and transepts to be a perfect Latin cross according to its kind, and the aisles, nave, choir, and transepts, surrounding this one, in the same accurate system of trinified triangulation, presented another perfectly proportioned Latin cross that must be seen to be believed:

it was for this church that Benjamin McGuinness forked out a quarter of a million of the best to keep the walls from falling asunder, amid cheers and beers, thanksgivings, blessings, songs of praise and appreciation, brandishing of croziers, waving of embroidered copes, throwing-up of ornamented mitres, swinging of bells; the archbishops, bishops, deans and deacons leading the vast multitude in the singing of He's a jolly good fellow that nobody dare deny, while peers of the Order of the Goose that laid the Golden Eggs and knights of the Coined Cross of St Croker Crispin led McGuinness up the long aisle by the hands, a scene unequalled anywhere at any time on this terrestrial ball, though, singular to remark, no mention at all was made of the thousands and thousands of Toms who lowered millions and millions of pints of porter fundamentally providing the where-withal to allow this church to stay standing for the certain shelter of God and His greater glory.

But he mustn't forget Tom lying alone and dying alone and facing a never-ending future alone. He must argue it out with himself. Never a word of blame about his wife. Never a complaint about what had ever happened to him: a kindly and a brave man. A shield that caught the sneering shafts shot by Mick at Sean when he was a kid; his, Let Jack alone – he's all right, was an ever-present help in time of trouble; a knight or, at least, a man-at-arms of the illustrious Order of St Patrick.

There's always a dark feather among the coloured feathers in our cap.

> The cleanest corn that e'er was dight
> May have some pyles o' caff in;
> So ne'er a fellow creature slight
> For random fits o' daffin.

Look at Bobbie Burns himself! A hard case, by all accounts, but who, save a Catholic Young Man or a Young Men's Christian Associate, or an odd bishop, priest, or deacon, would say that Heaven was too respectable a place for Bobbie Burns to find a corner in? What was it Laertes said about the dead Ophelia when the cautious clergy were affording her a maimed burial in Elsinore? I tell thee, churlish priest, a minist'ring angel shall my sister be, when thou liest howling. And from her fair and un-polluted flesh may violets spring! Ay, Laertes, violets of the deepest blue for ever spring from poor Ophelia's gentle and bewildered dust. And maybe, from the tired and dried-up dust of Tom will spring a strident yellow, lovely sunflower, or maybe a moon-daisy disced like a cooling sun. She died a maimed death; he lived a maimed life; but why? Because his school aimed at breeding a multitude to toil and spin i' th' frost and sun to meet tomorrow's needs with the paring thrift of the day before. He learned to juggle figures to count a boss's money, and keep the figures rising; dots on a map gave him a city's vision; a line wavering a mighty river's flow; a wavy smudge, the everlasting hills; and there he saw the world. The catechism to keep him off from God; the boy stood on the burning deck to make of him a hero; and a magic-lantern slide showing hell-fire just to keep him quiet.

Nothing seemed to be able to excite the clergy. They dreaded any kind of a noise, and went about as if Jesus had never got out of the manger. Not Mr Griffin, of course, or Harry Fletcher or his brother, Dudley. But the rest of them. He himself had shyly asked a number of them what they thought of Shelley? But all he got was a hum and a haw and some daring opinions that *The Skylark* was a good poem. Not fair, he supposed, to expect a liking for him who wrote *Queen Mab*. They had drawn away from the sensitive extension of the world. So freer men like Tom ran along a brighter road into forgetfulness of what they could become. If this kind of life was a preparation for Heaven, then Heaven could go to hell for him for the saints would be but scurvy companions. Was it for all this poor assembly of insignificant things that the Word was made flesh, and dwelt among us? In what do we behold His glory, the glory as of the only begotten of the Father, full of grace and truth? Is it in the stunted efforts of the poor dead Tom? Did it flame from the squalor of the homes where the people lived? Is it in the roaring stampede into protective piety over the mention of shift in poor Synge's play? Or in the dismissal of Dr O'Hickey from Maynooth for hailing compulsory Irish in the New University? Did it abide in all the gentle and furious fairy-tales of the Bible? D'ye call this religion? No, no! Midas carries the cross.

He knocked at the Rector's door, and Jennie, his eldest daughter, opened the door. A lovely lassie she was, with her trim figure, her fair face lit up by large grey-green eyes, and a sweeping flow of rich red-brown hair falling to her waist; and a bright thrill went through his body as she shook his hand and bade him to come in. She had often made his heart go fast when he saw her in church, or when she walked some of the way home by his side when the service was over; but he had diligently driven all thought of her away from him by the calm appeal of his books, and the whirl of his work for Ireland.

—You want to see Father, John? she asked, giving a graceful toss to her heavy wave of hair that sent dancing beams of light through the hall in which they stood.

—Yes, he said, if it isn't too inconvenient for him to see me.

—He's very busy, always is now, John, since he became a rural dean. Is what you want to say very important?

—It seems so to me, Miss Jennie, and maybe more so to another.

—Stay there a moment, and I'll see; and she went into the study, returning quick to say that her father said John was to come straight in to him.

There he was, sitting at his desk, rather close to a good fire, surrounded by many papers, well within the protection of a copy of da Vinci's 'Last Supper'; not a hair astray in hair or in beard; a finely-cut alpaca coat over his suit of solemn black, the slender gold watch-chain shyly streaking across his waistcoat like a delicate sunbeam hurrying across a sombre sky: an elegant, learned, kindly, sensitive, handsome, broad-minded man.

—Come in, come, my dear John, pressing Sean's hand with a firmness surprising in a hand so slender and so white; though no wonder to Sean when he remembered the Rector had groomed his own horse in the country, and when married, with little to go on, had made a wash-tub for his wife by sawing a barrel in two, and he had done other things by hand and muscle of which he was laughingly proud. A man afraid of very little.

—Sit beside me while I finish this letter he said. John will join me when you bring me my tea, Jennie, he added to his daughter. Off you go, he said to Sean, when the tea was brought in; don't mind my one biscuit; there's cake and bread and jam for you, for you look cold, and a little tired. Take it up with your fingers, John, he said laughingly, when he saw Sean's clumsy assay to lift lump sugar in a tongs; one would want to be a qualified engineer to use those tongs comfortably, so take what you want with your fingers.

After tea had been taken, he gave a steady ear to all that Sean had to say about his brother Tom.

—Come, John, he said, when Sean was silent, we'll go now, and may God go with us.

With a warm coat over him, a dark-green scarf round his neck, his walking-stick in his right hand, the Rector marched down the street with a fine brisk step. At the Aldborough Barracks he hailed a cab, and the two of them sat silent while the mare went as leisurely as she could to where the dying man lay in his tiny room, Sean thinking of the barracks left behind where he had sometimes got a piece of liver or a kidney for the price of a pint from an Army Service Corps butcher when he was hacking up the meat for the Dublin Garrison, and when he happened to be in the giving vein.

—We could almost walk as quick, said the Rector impatiently; and that remark fell softly into the silence that had gone before it.

Silently they came to the door; almost silently knocked; and the door was opened softly by the eldest boy, for Agatha wasn't eager to come into touch with the Protestant minister; and silently they mounted the boxed-in stairs to Tom's bedroom, where he lay on his back, mixed up, murmuring phrases trickling out over his twitching lips.

—Curious dying activity in a curious room, thought Sean. In a corner the wash-stand, basin and ewer, white, with a broad blue band around both; the press with drawers to hold clothes against the wall; a cane-bottomed chair beyond the head of the bed, with Tom's clothes in a tidy heap on the seat; the window half open and half hidden by yellow lace curtains; the double bed where Tom lay stretched bonily taut and motionless, save for the twitching of the mouth; on the wall above the side of the bed where Agatha usually lay, a crudely-coloured picture of the Sacred Heart; over the head of the bed, a coloured apoplectic picture of his old general, Sir Redvers Buller, looking as he might have looked after his vain attempt to push across the Tugela river; a strip of red, white, and green oilcloth running by the bedside; a slightly-swaying twig of a sycamore tree moving gently up, gently down again, just outside a window-pane; and Mr Griffin with a stole, instead of the dark-green muffler, round his neck, looking pensively down on Tom – one of Synge's khaki cut-throats leaving the world's villainy behind him for ever.

There he was, battling for the last few minutes of life, while poor Dr O'Hickey, tired and near heartbroken, paced the streets of Rome, sent from Cardinal Billy to Cardinal Jack, from this holy office to that, talking Latin to the clerics, and finding none able or willing to reply; dying, though he didn't know it then, battling for the life of Ireland and Essential Irish in the New University, his funds near gone, and poverty asking him how he was feeling.

The Rector is bending over till his handsome face is almost touching the ear of Tom, praying that here, in this poor room, another miracle of grace might be worked for a soul's safe flight from the world, the flesh, and the Devil.

—My poor, dear man, he said softly, do you hear me? I am your Rector, your minister, your friend, come to mention the name of Jesus, the Saviour of sinners, in your closing ear. Do you hear me, my son?

Then a dead silence fell round the dying man for a few moments, distracted only by the faint sound of the little sycamore twig moving gently up, gently down, just outside the window-pane.

—Say, Lord have mercy on me, Christ have mercy on me, Jesus have mercy on me, encouraged the Rector, and his white, delicate hand softly stroked away a tawny bunch of hair from Tom's green-tinted, dewy forehead.

Silence for a little while, and then a tiny whisper from Tom of Christ have mercy on me, Jesus have mercy on me.

—Again, dear man, Jesus have mercy on me, and once more a tired and fainter whisper, like an echo of the last, of Jesus have mercy on me, came to our straining ears.

—O Saviour of the world, prayed the Rector, who by Thy Cross and Precious Blood hast redeemed mankind, save our dear brother, we beseech Thee. O Almighty God, we humbly commend the soul of this our dear brother, into Thy hands, as into the hands of a faithful Creator, beseeching Thee that it may be now precious in Thy sight. Wash it in the blood of the immaculate Lamb that was slain to take away the sins of the world. Then the Rector stood up and extended a protecting hand over Tom, holding one of Tom's in the other, a hand that was now waxy with the dignified bloom of death, saying softly as before, Unto God's gracious mercy, we commit thee, Tom. The Lord be with thee in this thy last fleeting moment on this our fleeting world. The Lord make His face to appear unto thee full of pardon and promise, and give unto thee salvation and eternal peace. Amen.

He drew Sean out to the little lobby at the head of the stairs and quietly closed the door.

—You should send for his mother, he said, for he'll last but for a few moments more, John, and his wife should be with him. Does she realize how bad he is?

—I warned her before I came for you, sir.

—Warn her again, Sean, like a good man. And will there be enough to stand expenses?

—Oh, yessir. He's insured, and, besides, he gets his full pay since he fell sick. And it won't cost a lot to bury him in our father's grave. And, anyway, he hasn't any claim on your kindness.

—He has a claim on the kindness of our Lord, John, and so much more a claim on mine. No, don't come down; stay with Tom. I'll call in to your mother's and get her to join you. And remember, if you meet with any difficulty, come to me at once, not formally as your Rector, but warmly as your friend. My deep sympathy, John. Goodbye.

Sean went back to the silent room, sat down on the cane-bottomed chair, furtively watching the hand of death quenching the last dim light glimmering in Tom's handsome face; turning now and again to glance at the little sycamore twig moving gently up, gently down, just outside the window-pane. It was Agatha's duty rather than his to be here with the dying man. He crept out to the lobby, stretched over the banisters, and called softly, Agatha, are you there? Agatha! But there was no answer, and he crept back to the support of the little chair. A strange surmise was snakily creeping into his mind: he was seeing Tom for the last time; no light shone through the darkness of departure; poor emptiness lay behind the brilliancy of the stars. Dimly he saw the clumsy bulk of Agatha come into the room, glance at Tom, and go over to lounge at the window and fiddle with the yellow lace curtains. Whisht! Tom was trying to say something. He bent down, and held his breath to hear.

—Jack there? Jack there? Must peel the spuds for the chiselurs' dinner.

—Here, Tom, oul' son; Jack's here beside you, and he laid a hand gently down on the tawny head.

—Doing me – best – Jack – to – keep – a-live.

Then Sean saw the thin legs do a strenuous stretch, and the arms outside the bedclothes go rigid; and his ears caught a sound like unto the sudden snapping of a sensitive cord strained too tight, so he knew that Tom's heart-strings had given way, and that he was now to lie still for ever. He was still staring down at the oddly silent form when the door opened and his mother, followed by Ella, came panting into the room.

—He's gone, he said; you're too late.

Mrs Casside stared at the stiff form lying prone in the bed, effectively out-braving the brazen world now. She seemed not to be able to recognize what was stretched out there, her bright dark eyes blinking rapidly to impede the tears that were pushing a way out of them, her brave humorous mouth aquiver like summer lightning in a violet sky.

—My poor dead son, she said, suddenly running over and kissing the mouth she hadn't kissed since it was the fresh dewy mouth of a boy. Ah! My poor dead Tom, my poor dear son is dead! And Sean was hard set now to keep his face from twitching and his tears from falling, for he knew full well that out of all who knew Tom, she alone it was who suffered the dearly-sorrowful agony of his going.

—I hope yous are satisfied now, said the voice of Agatha behind them; yous are all satisfied now, so yous are; and Sean noticed that her clumsily-made mouth was puckering about in strange shapes, showing she shared in the emotion that the stilly-silent, rigid favour of death evoked in man, feeling that some day each one there would be stolen away into the same silence.

—Now he's where yous won't envy him any more, so yous won't, she went on, whimpering. Bid him your luscious goodbyes as quick as yous can, for, if yous want to know, I'd liefer have your room than your company. So now yous know; for I don't want his home to be a clusther of the ragged Casside army, for the one that's just gone was the only decent specimen among yous, so he was, an' all who knew him, knows that. Me husband, me poor husband, you come of a dirty lot!

Sean silenced Ella's wrathful answer with a look. He went over to his mother, and taking her arm, said gently, Looka, Mother, you'd best go home with Ella, and leave me to do what has to be done. The Rector was here before he died. He's to read the service at the graveside, so Tom'll have an orderly burial, and you needn't worry.

—He's marble cold already, said Ella, touching Tom's forehead, as cold as cold can be.

Mrs Casside kissed her boy again and again, ran her fingers

through his tawny hair, stood up from the bed, tears trickling down a set, firm face, took Ella by the arm, and led her out of the room, forced to leave the dead Fusilier behind to make the best of it.

—So well yous may pop off when the damage is done, an' leave me here on me own to face it all! shouted Agatha after them.

Where would Tom be now in a few moments, and what would he be doing? questioned the thoughts of Sean. Shadow-hurling with the Gaels of Mooncoin, or swaggering along an empty way with the Rakes of Mallow? Strolling, maybe, through invisible groves of Blarney with Kitty of Coleraine. Watching Canon Sheehan brooding o'er the graves of Kilmorna, or sauntering, deep in thought, beneath the cedars and the stars. Listening, mayhap, to the old march-past of the Old Toughs, the Dublin Fusiliers, and shouting out the song himself, *Hurrah, hurrah for Ireland, and th' Dublin fu-u-sa-leers!* Poor Tom, he will be remembered for ever, for the hearts in dear oul' Ireland are the hearts that don't forget.

What a doughty fellow he was, all the same! No attendance in bed for Tom: doing all for himself, by himself, and with himself, till his life left him nothing but a thought or two and a wildly beating heart. A stoic, by God! An Old Tough with a vengeance. Marching to attention, gun on shoulder, to his death. Saluting death, the dark companion, as an officer and a gentleman: By your leave, sir, a pass for a few hours longer. Not in a ghostly white habit should this man be buried; but in his crimson coat, ammunition pouches full, busby firm on the tawny head, with the flaming grenade ashine in the centre. Often drunk, but never quarrelsome; whenever in a row, the tipsy Tom was ever in the centre of danger, parting the fighters. And the drunker he got the straighter he grew; his walk was a parade march when he was full to the chin. He would have made a rare Dallcassian. Though he hadn't conquered, he had died like a man. God had thought too little of him, and the active world had given him ne'er a chance. Sean was no warrior. A harper, maybe, playing others into battle; but no warrior himself. Why, even to this day he remembered with a shudder the knocking of the helmeted police-man from his horse the day of the charge in Parliament Street.

But supposing, only supposing, the rose and crown conception of Heaven be true, Tom would find it a bit awkward at first. He

certainly wouldn't run to be among the Catholic confraternities
or the Protestant associations making a round of the sights of
Sion, however grand the glories before or behind them; unless,
manacled hand and foot, he was frog-marched by the angels to
take part in the diversion. Perhaps God would conjure up in a
distant corner a radiant mirage of a cosy pub where Tom and his
Fusilier butties could for ever drink without drinking, fight for
ever without fighting, and die for their Queen and country without dying at all, and gather a harvest of glittering medals on their
chests to show themselves off to the wondering saints. Or, as
Cortez stout and all his men, standing on a peak in Darien,
silent, saw another ocean, so may Tom and his comrades see a
newer ocean of another life, and set sail thereon in a white-
winged bark, while we go stumbling on over the flinty earth,
steeling ourselves in the effort to fight and faint not, often tired,
always uncertain, many of us consigned to a kind of life lived by
the lesser rats.

—Of all th' things I hate above all others, broke in the voice of
his sister-in-law behind him, it's hypocrites. Lettin' on to pray
for him when yous wouldn't know a prayer from a pigsty!

—Now, Mrs Agatha Casside, he said, wheeling round to her, I
wish to do things, and talk as little as possible. Let's see what has
to be done: first, you get a certificate of the cause of death, and
report to the Dispensary Registrar – understand?

—I'll take no insthructions from you, she replied surlily.

—All right, then; where do you intend to bury Tom?

—That's my business.

—Look here, Agatha, you can't help being ignorant, but for
Christ's sake try to be less stupid! Bury him where you like! I
don't care, and he can't. If it be Glasnevin, it'll cost you a lot
more. Now d'ye want me to give you a hand – yes or no?

The clumsy, ill-grained face twisted about for a few moments
in resentment at having to give in to secure the help she needed.

—It would be a poor brother that 'ud refuse the last act of
charity, she muttered; but remember, I'll keep the money in me
own hands. And his Post Office friends are makin' a collection,
an' Mr Arthur says it'll come to over two hundred pounds, so it
will, see now, so that'll show yous somethin'.

—I go now, Sean said, letting all she said go by, to get Mrs
Conel to come and lay him out – give her a few shillings and a lot
of tea; and I'll send the barber to shave him; then I'll go to

Nicholl's and arrange for coffin and hearse – there's no reason to do things too expensively.

—You'll do things th' way I want! she said loudly, and he'll get th' best funeral money can buy, so he will, see now. I want all th' best coffin goin' with all th' brass that'll fit on it, an' a four-horse hearse, mournin' coach, an' two carriages, so I do. I'm not goin' to let his people give him the funeral of a ragamuffin!

—Look, Agatha, he said. The living children need this money more than the dead father. I'd go canny with it if I were you.

—Well, you're not me, see? Mighty particular y'are, now, about the children, aren't you? An' none o' th' carriages 'ill be for any of yous either, undherstand that, now.

He gripped her angrily by the shoulder, putting his face close to hers to say venomously, Go in a carriage with you, is it? Why, you yellow-skinned Jezebel, if I could I'd put a wide sea between us both, and never bathe in it if I thought you were anyway near its margin! And listen! If I hear another word from your dark tongue, Tom or no Tom, charity or no charity, I'll leave everything for you to do, though I know you can't even sign your own name! And he turned and left her alone with her dead husband, and with the little sycamore twig moving gently up, gently down, just outside the window-pane.

HOUSE OF THE DEAD

SEAN LEANED on his long-handled shovel and straightened his back. It was grand to be out in the country and close to the sea. He could enjoy it now, for he had grown into a lusty fellow of twelve stone ten, and he could feel the muscle of arm and leg go in harmony with every movement of his body, the song of the body electric. He could lift an anvil, gripping it by back and horn, as high as his breast, holding it there while another counted ten slowly. He had won a shilling from a permanent-way inspector who declared it couldn't be done, but Sean had shown him. Only one other fellow, a tall, raw-boned Tipperary man who drove the steamroller, could throw a great weight from the shoulder, or between legs, farther than he. Now every workman respected

him, not only for what his hands and shoulders could do, but
also for the ready and eloquent way he could show the activity
of his mind. Because of his enthusiasm for the Gaelic League
and for his never-ending efforts to get all whom he worked
with, and all whom he met, to join the Movement, he was known
along the line, from Dublin to Drogheda, as Irish Jack. He had
three names: to his mother he was Johnny; his Gaelic friends
knew him as Sean; to his workmates he was Jack, and when they
wished to distinguish him from another Jack, they added the
title of Irish, so Irish Jack he became to signalmen, engine-
drivers, firemen, porters, shunters, and all others who worked
along the permanent way. He was becoming famous, and he
was proud of it. He wiped the bitter teeming sweat from his face.
Satisfied with himself, and half satisfied with the world, he leaned
on his shovel to have a cool look around him, to more sensibly
enjoy the rarer sights he so very seldom saw.

It was the first time he had laid eyes on a field of growing corn,
living and rippling before him, jaunty and elegant in its way of
bending from one side to the other; gently turbulent when
stronger breezes blew, but always returning to its dignified
sway, thoroughly at home, bowing a golden greeting to all that
looked upon it with favour. Leaving aside the glory of Constable's
'Cornfield', he had seen pictures of ripe corn on calendars, or
standing stiff in pictures printed quick to teach a lesson from some
Bible story. He had heard of it too in some of the hymns sung
by Christian people – Fair waved the golden corn in Canaan's
pleasant land; and a tenor in the choir chanting, The valleys
stand so thick with corn that even they are singing; or the Rector,
padding with sighs the reading of the parable of the wheat and
the tares. Now he was face to face with it, lovelier than any
picture, fairer than any words could tell. He could fancy Ruth
standing there in that field, up to her middle in the corn, a
creamy face, rosy cheeks, and big brown goo-goo eyes staring
at poor Boaz, the kinsman of Naomi, all meant to furnish some
lesson no one ever learned. Or was it the lesson of a great con-
version? Where thou goest, I will go; thy people shall be my
people, and thy god, my god. By God! she knew who she was
after, for Boaz had more than one acre and a cow. The first
gold-digger! But a widow for your life, though it was ordained
and predestined from the first that Boaz should marry Ruth, for
from Ruth came Obed, from him came Jesse, and from Jesse,

David, the royal line ending in Jesus, king of kings, lord of lords, and only ruler of princes. Luke was set on making Him out a gentleman, so as to fit Him in with kings, rulers, and princes, who soon rolled Him out to rule themselves in over life.

But it was from a field of barley Ruth displayed herself to Boaz, and this was a field of wheat. Was it wheat now? He couldn't tell; didn't know the difference between wheat and barley, so he'd call it corn. One could easily imagine Jesus Himself strolling softly through such a field as this one on some peaceful Sabbath morning, His sensitive hand calmly plucking the ears of corn as He went along, and popping them into His mouth, chewing them slowly as He thought out some delicate parable on what He saw around Him, so that He might make remembrance safer in the minds of His disciples. So wrapt in Himself, He might well put no pass on the turbaned scribes and the phylacteried Pharisees, peeping over the hedges, on the watch, hardly able to believe their eyes at the cool way He was infringing the ritual rest of the Sabbath; hearing nothing of their whining cries of, Eh, there, eh, what do you think you're doing? Sharp and shrill they shouted then, their conscience-cry hiding the pleasant humming of the bees, thick round the scented heads of the white and crimson clover carpeting the nearby pasture fields. On He'd go, dreamily, glancing at the corncockle growing here and there among the corn, like high-born, satin-skinned ladies airing themselves among a commoner crowd. Now and again He'd touch the blooms tenderly, setting dark-rose velvety petals carefully aside so as not to soil them, their rosy petals stained with darker lines, as if they, too, had things to think of; while careless scarlet poppies like rasher ladies, flushed with wine, flaunted around the edges, the crimson of some of them fading from excess of life, puced and shrivelled now, but dying gamely in the centre of their flaming ostentation. Coloured peace was here; a gay peace; a merry stillness, undisturbed but for the ratchet-like call of the corncrake. Oh, blessed peace!

A strange smell full of sharp sweetness came to him, making him wonder, for he had never sensed such a smell before. New-mown hay, he murmured; ah! that's what it is, must be – new-mown hay. On the uplands, in the distance, he had seen the fringe of a calm sea, but from where he stood in a dip it was hidden; though when he faced towards where it was, the scent of the new-mown hay was imprisoned in the salty smell of the

sea coming in the breeze that fluttered on to his sweaty, heated
face. So he could take his choice: stand as he stood, and get the
taste of the sea; turn, and he could get the spicy feminine scent
of the hay – a golden languorous scent from the hay, or a lusty
blue-scented taste from the placid fret of the incoming tide. If
poor Up Griffith, unhappy in that he could never be what he
thought he was, if he only could be here, sprawled in the pasture,
or asquat in the shade of a rock on the velvet strand, he'd forget
his love for the golden-haired Niamh, his hate for the rival black-
haired poet, his ambition to lead where he could but follow, in
the happy, reluctant unison of the sea-breeze mixing itself with
the fragrant presence of the new-mown hay.

Christ! that was a horrible cry!

—Aw, Jack, said the grumbling voice of his mason behind
him, are yeh dhreamin' again? The mortar-board's been empty
now for ages, an' I'm idle for stuff.

—What, what was that?

—Wha' was what?

—Didn't you hear it, man? It came from somewhere over by
the sea, and he felt the sweat on his face turn cold. A cry of lost
laughter throwing itself into an icy wail that's taken the scent
from the hay, the savour from the sea, and has thrust out peace
from its tenancy of the sky. There it is again – good God!

It was an insensible burst of jagged laughter, turning into a
savage yell, that gradually declined into a long-drawn, weary,
piercing wail making him cold and making him shiver.

—Aw, that? That's only from the Partrane madhouse yeh
saw from the hill yestherday, y'know, beside the round tower;
biggest one in the land. Livin' here a little, yeh'd get used to
yells. Look alive with the mortar.

So behind this fair, sparkling, laughing curtain that Nature let
down before him many dark and evil things were lurking, or
hung entangled in the bright colours and satisfying scents like
decaying flies in the iridescent and lovely-patterned web of the
spider. Forgotten for the moment, he had already seen these
things with his own eyes, and his hands had handled them.

Out there, now, right in the centre of the corn, just where
Jesus had passed by a few moments before, floated the face of
Ella, a white face, a face of settled fear, tightened with a stony
smile that had a seed of wild weeping in it. He went back to his
work of tempering the mortar and of carrying his hod of bricks

to the mason; but whenever he turned his eyes to the growing corn, there was that damned white face, stony with fear, a swaying stem of corncockle at times empurpling an eye, or the scarlet shadow of a poppy giving it a bloodily-splashed mouth, watching him work; watching, watching him work. She had married a man who had destroyed every struggling gift she had had when her heart was young and her careless mind was blooming. He had given her, with God's help, a child for every year, or less, that they had been together. Five living, and one, born unsound, had gone the way of the young and good, after being kept alive for three years, till it grew tired of the dreadful care given it, leaving her to weep long over a thing unworthy a tear or a thought. Her home was a fanciful bastion of rags, bones, and bottles; the family hereditaments, a few chairs, a table so rickety that it seemed anxious to dissolve itself out of the life it tried to live; one large iron bedstead, rusty with shame at the beggarly clothes that tried to cover it. They drank their tea from jam-jars, and raked out the fire with a lath broken from the bedstead. Four of the children went to school, and learned a lot about kings, queens, and knights; of battles strong and flaming; of statesmen drowned in glory or a butt of wine; of all a cow gave to man; how to add, subtract, and multiply thousands of pounds without wasting much time; and all the important information necessary about Heaven, Hell, death, and the judgement; and through it all Ella helped them to master sums, to find places on a map, and understand God; helped them with a dimming eye, a dying mind, and decaying heart. Ah! faded into the forgotten past were the recitation of bits from Racine's *Andromaque* and *Iphigénie*, or from Scott's *Lady of the Lake*; the confident playing of waltz, schottische, polka, and gavotte on a piano in a friend's house; or the rich treble singing of *Come unto these Yellow Sands*, *Cherry Ripe*, or *She is Far from the Land* when the fire burned bright, the curtains were drawn, and father and mother listened to one of the sweetest voices heard by the dull ear of man. All gone now; gone into the gloom of a night hiding gifts abandoned; gone, save in the restless memory of Sean's own mind. Oh, Ella, Ella! Oh, Jesus, have pity on us! If not in harmony with Thee, let the glow of something good be in a fragment of our life!

Now she went about everything like a near-drowned fly in a jar full of water. She entertained life under a canopy of rags and tatters; a blouse warning all of its end, a skirt slit to the thigh, shattered boots, and footless stockings; and her breath of life moved faintly in the midst of it all, while her children moved round her, half perishing too, like weak and puzzled planeteens hovering uncertainly around a fast-dying sun. Her mother had helped her all she could, washing, ironing, and mending things till it became dangerous to the life of the things to wash, iron, or mend any longer. She had striven to startle Ella towards resistance to decay, but Ella murmured, My husband, it is my duty, God ordained it all; so failure was in the heart of any effort before it could begin. Her mind had fashioned a weakness too great to let her strive to save herself, and life became a maze of rotting things from which there was no escape till she lay down for the last time to crumble into dust in the midst of her crumbling property and gifts. Coughs and colds, aches and pains, came her way, but she coughed and staggered along a narrow way between them on her feet, conducting a ragged and wasting retreat from the Kingdom of Heaven.

One day a younger one had come racing to him, calling Quick, Uncle Jack, me Da's murdherin' me Ma! He med a run at her, an' we rushed outa the house, but we heard her squealin'!

Ay, and your Ma would like to change the procedure by seeing your Da make a run at me, he thought, as he went along with the youngster, not too quick, either, for he knew he was no hero, and at the moment his conscience was stirring against interfering between a man and his wife. Women who lived near Ella, when they saw him coming, ran to meet him, saying breathlessly, He's morguein' her, he's morguein' her, an' for God's sake hurry, or a short time'll have another sorrowful sight in front of us all! And when they saw he did not make haste, they caught his arm to hasten his going, though he held back as decently as he could, remembering that these two had come together for better or for worse, till death did them part, and who was he to question the grandeur of God's own ordinance? Besides, he knew his mother several times had got a shock from a push or a blow meant for Ella when she had thrust her body in between Ella and the flying angry fists of her husband; and often his mother had hurried away when a row began, too full of shameful wonder to stay and share in the violence that he was now hurrying to meet.

Coming to the wide-open door of the house, and hesitating to go in, he heard the voice of Ella whimpering, Don't hit me any more. I've done all I could. For the children's sake, don't hit me any more.

This was the price of her not doing what she was told. How he had warned Ella of her husband's odd behaviour, trying to go through walls where there was no door; leaving bed to put on his red-banded cap in the middle of the night to hurry off to work in his shirt. He had complained of his eyes at times tumbling things before him, forcing him to see men as trees, and trees as men, making for him out of a red mist. At the Eye Hospital where Sean had brought him, after examination, Mr Storey had said, Oh! drumming his fingers on the glossy table covered with silver surgical instruments, looking at Benson curiously, then glancing at Sean to say, Bring the man home; nothing here can do him any good. And when Sean had murmured, What about spectacles? Storey had pointed his grey-tinted red beard to the ceiling, craning his narrow neck to give vent to a slow sibilant laugh as he answered shortly, A pair of old boots would do as well; and he hurried away to lave his hands in a gleaming white basin between the two tall wide-spreading windows.

What the hell's wrong, Sean asked himself, leading out the silent, passive Benson, and what's this poor devil to do? And what's his wife and children to do? How the hell do I know? he answered himself. One thing was clear – he wasn't going to spend his life hawking round this poor bewildhered eejut. A thought and a fear came over him, and he tightened his grip on Benson's arm, hurrying him to Dr Wood's surgery to hear the verdict one way or another for half a crown. Visiting his mother once, Dr Wood had paused to look at, and handle, Sean's books, had smiled graciously, and had shaken Sean's hand when he was leaving; so he was a friend, and, as well, was loved by the poor, though the poor man's own state of health forced him to nearly live on drugs. When he had examined Benson, Dr Wood brought Sean into another room, standing silent for some time when they had got there.

—Do you know what's happening to this man of yours? he asked at last. He's quietly going mad; but when he reaches a certain stage, he won't be quiet any longer. Your man is developing a disease known as general paralysis of the insane. There is but one thing to do now, other than to leave him in God's hands. Has he a wife? Well, then, she must certify him so that he may be brought where he can do no harm; for any time he may become dangerous; dangerous, mind you, dangerous!

But Ella had dumbly refused to sign the form, content that her husband's creeping madness should go on bringing her in a few shillings a week, for they put a brush in his hand to keep the front steps of the railway station clean, where he'd stand for hours leaning on his brush, and gazing ahead at all he couldn't see.

And now Sean was being hurried on his way to where, in the elation of misery and want, a lunatic (after fulfilling his job of multiplying and replenishing the earth) was having his share of fun with the four last things of Heaven, Hell, death, and the judgement.

Oh, Lord, oh, my Lord! Oh, my good Lord, keep me from sinkin' down, sinkin' down; oh, my Lord, keep me from sinkin' down!

With his muscles tensed, ready for a bullish charge, which he prayed wouldn't come, he swung suddenly into the room, the neighbours clinging to the doorway; he met the glaring, red-balled eyes of Benson staring at him, his body twitching, his hands tugging to pull out a loosening chair-leg so that a solid victory might at last be won over the ragged woman cowering in a corner, whimpering softly, her stony white face, empurpled eye, and bloodily-splashed mouth appealing for a tempered mercy to the madman.

Not knowing what he was at, or what to do, or how to do it, Sean drew an arm back and swung a frenzied fist under the ear of the madman, putting him into a sprawl on the floor. Then he gripped the chair-leg the madman was trying to get, and, with an agonized twist and wrench, tore it from its socket, poised it over the lunatic's head, shouting, Bloody villain, you pig's offal you, I'll give your guts to the crows, you red-coated rottenness! And he brought down the chair-leg hard on the big skull below, dulling the glare in the eye, sending a shake through the twitching body that went limp now, and crept into a corner of the room, turning to stare stupidly at Sean, moaning hoarsely as an alto to the whimpering of his wife in the corner opposite. Sean knew by the dismal stare and the pitiful moan that present danger was past, and knew too that he must get the man behind stone walls before ever the frenzy would come on him again. Leaving Ella to the care of the neighbours, after he had seen her put her name to the form that would bury Benson alive, he took the lunatic home with him, keeping a firm grip on the chair-leg under his coat, sat up all night while Benson slept, waiting for the clutchers to come with the plain black cab in the morning.

It came towards the evening, a sunny one, with many sparrows frantically fluttering their wings on the road to clean themselves in the dust of the street, not one of them falling to the ground outside of God's attention; better for Benson he'd been born a sparrow than a man. It came slowly along up to the house, the black cab, and, when the driver stopped the horse, two neatly-clad keepers stepped from the cab, asked Sean if the patient was likely to go quiet, went in, and came out with a grinning Benson between them. One of them, noticing the bump on his head, asked Who done that to yeh?

—I did, said Sean.

—Be God, yeh hot him with somethin' heavier than a feather! Misbehavin' himself, was he? If it was us done that now, there'd be uproar in the pulpit an' Press. But you'll see how nicely he'll conduct himself with us – won't yeh, Benjamin? See how he smiles at me. Oh, he'll be a good little boy.

—He bloody well betther, growled the other one.

Between the keepers, with Sean opposite to see him safe home, Benson, grinning helplessly, was driven to the house of strident shadows, to dress in the rough grey tweed of the loony pauper, to wear the red woollen neckerchief so tied that when one became restless, a keeper could seize it, pull, and choke all movement, quench all fire out of the gurgling, foam-lipped madman; to where he would be dust to dust and ashes to ashes before he was dead, withered grass that hadn't yet been cast into the oven, to Grangegorman. Wide gates of heavy, dull, heartless lead opened to let them in, and the black cab rolled silently along the drive, drawn by a horse with a sly and regular trot as if he felt and feared anything else might entitle him for companionship with the dread life of the still-twitching dead. Dotted here and there in the grounds were the dismal brothers of disorders grey, their red mufflers making them look as if their tormented heads had been cut off, and pushed crookedly back on to their necks again. The cab stopped slowly before the building, wide and long, built like a bully that had suddenly died shrugging his shoulders. Long rows of lifeless windows mirrored long rows of lifeless faces, their silence hymning a fading resurrection of Velazquez's idiots, a

whole stonily-grinning gallery of God's images turned to dull
grey clay, the emptiness of a future age in every face. Now and
again, some of them would vent a laugh that rippled a shudder
along the walls of the asylum. The grass everywhere grew brown
and long, and fell to dust whenever it was touched; the trees
twisted their branches like limbs in pain, and grew grey leaves
that never seemed to move, a cold immortal grey, as if under the
blight of the fig tree Christ had cursed. Flowers that tried to
grow beneath the windows were slimy stalks, crawling along the
grey ground like slugs tantalizing the rim of a festering lily, lost
amid the quiet storm of lunacy distilling a sour air everywhere.
In a corner a chestnut tree dropped worm-worn fruit like leaden
balls, and riven church bells rang out a raucous angelus three
times a day, carolling rakishly mid the mindless chatter and the
rasping laugh. Only ghosts of things and men were here; nor in
the sky above was any balm of blue, or fleecy solace of a drifting
cloud; nothing but vacancy reaching to where God had gone
from. No gay bird sang, no blazoned butterfly flew through the
frozen sunlight, no gentle scent of gentler flower found refuge
in any pocket of the sour air here. No jocund dawn danced into
sight over the hills of the morning, no night came dreaming out
of the slumbering sea; no big wind ever tossed the still trees, no
tremor teased the earth, no fire blinked in the dead eyes waiting,
and no still small voice stole upon ears forgetting the sound of
their own words, maimed and bewildered, vainly uttered.

And out of the grey light and the noisy silence strutted a stout-
bellied, loud-voiced, ruddy-faced man clad in loud-looking plus-
fours, puffing stormily at a big pipe. A pair of small glittering
dark eyes were trying to climb out over the puffy lids that half
buried them; and a gay smile on his face went about endorsing
everything done by the sacred apes of God.

—Aha! he said, when he saw Benson stumbling from the cab,
here's another bright lodger for initiation into the brotherhood of
Bedlamites. Well, turning towards the keepers, what's this
novice's *tour de force*?

—Bad case of GPI, Doctor.

—Aha! Whores-de-combat, what? Well, lug him in, and regis-
ter his name in the pigskin-covered book of the lie of the living.
And you, he said to Sean, a relative, eh? Ah! brother-in-law. Well,
come along and have a look around.

—I've seen as much as I desire to see, thank you.

—Frightened, eh? Nonsense, man. Those outside are more dangerous than they who are here. The delusions, hopes, beliefs of those outside – unobtainable, man. Here every man has all he wants. Outside a man lives in worlds created by others; here he lives in a world of his own. All's accomplished here, so it ceases to interest. Come with me to a land just over the border where those who live there know nothing of their nearness – the Purple Land full of Druid moons, sleepy boughs, and voices in a fire; where all are half awake, half silent, and half a world away from life.

A commonplace-looking man, with a bullet head, bulgy eyes, and straggly grey moustache, went whirling by, head over heels, head over heels, chanting breathless as he tumbled on,

> *Here we go hurryin' home to Heav'n,*
> *Home to Heav'n, home to Heav'n,*
> *Here we go hurryin' home to Heav'n,*
> *Leavin' Hell behind us!*

—That's the holy whirligig, said the doctor, hell-bent for Heaven. He's been given three thousand years to do the journey, and he has tightened steel hoops round his belly to keep him up to it. Whisht! There's our signature tune – we've two of them. That's *Awake and Lie Dreaming No More*; the other's *Won't You Come Home, Bill Bailey?* Here we are at the entrance of the Purple Land. Stoop! Here the higher-minded muck about, a kind of limbo where they know neither pain nor joy, nor can be ever at heart's ease, for all here are heart-tight and head-heavy with brooding; though all assume in company a jaunty mysticism of life's connexion. Stoop! Mostly poets of a sort here, and fellows of lure and learning. Place of Masques. We've a long way to go yet.

Bending low, they entered through a darting screen of grass-hoppers whistling in harmony, *Has Anybody Here Seen Kelly? K, ee, double ell, why,* and came slowly into a long, long trail of never-ending twilight.

—In this place, whispered the man in the plus-fours, is all that never was – the Cover of the Sea over the Great Secret of the Tuatha de Danaan; Foam from the Horses of Emain; the Washing-place of the Horses of Dea; the Remnants of the Great Feast; the More-than-Mystifying Breath of the Dagda; and the

Four Corners of the World: so silence on your hollow head; silence on your dark body; silence on your dark brow. Make the sign of the seven-stringed harp of Aengus – it's in the air!

The colour of the place ranged from dim violet to purple that was near to jet. The trunks of the trees were dark purple, their branches a lighter purple, and their leaves a dimmer purple still. Far away in the distance, by straining the eyes, one could see the place was ringed round by dark shapes like mountains, like giant guardians watching that nothing went too far from where nothing was.

—Them dark things out there, said the doctor, are the bright spirits of the hills, where the Mountains of Dublin sweep down to the sea.

—You mean the Mountains of Mourne, don't you? questioned Sean.

—No, I don't, snapped the doctor. Nothing out of time or tune with the place is allowed to enter here. Evil things sometimes dart in to torment and disturb the brooders with such things as *Flannigan to Finnigan*, *Miss O'Hara and Her Emerald Tiara*, or even *I Want to Go to Idaho*; but they drive these evil things forth from the garden by a sacred berry tied to a sacred string attached to a sacred hazel wand.

Though they went a long, long way, they never stirred, the wide wings of numerous death's-head moths striking their cheeks and touching their eyelashes, frilling the violet air with tiny hovering skulls, squeaking out a tittering chant,

> *Come in the evening or come in the morning,*
> *Come when you're looked for or come without warning,*
> *Thought that is sky-high you'll find here before you,*
> *And the longer you stay, sure, the more we'll explore you.*

—This garden, or place of repose, or sanctuary of souls, or land of the ever old, said the doctor, stretches from where you are to the uttermost inns and outs of the earth; to where Jason, the mason, pinched the golden fleece of Colchis; to where Thor cools his hot backside resting on the Aurora Borealis; to the dark forest where Siegfried sings to keep his courage up; and down to wherever Lugh the Long-handed may be hiding. It is hedged in only where man and his mind ceases to exist. The twilight here is like no other twilight the world over.

—What, is it the Keltic Twilight? questioned Sean, in a whisper.

—Hush! Be simple, reverent, and understanding; and above all, be silent. The slightest touch or twinge of a question here provokes disturbance in the ensurance of calm and contemplation. Here has to be solved the mystery of the Pelican, the Green Dragon, the Black Eagle, Salt, Mercury, St Patrick's Purgatory, the Round Towers, Cardinal Logue's Learning, and Who Killed Cock Robin? That golden owl flying by watches over the poets; that green one in the ivy, over those who love their country; the yellow-headed one, over the thinkers; and the white owl, over those who say where there is nothing there is God. Look! Here's one of the brothers, sons of Mac Eolais, Mac Emer's son. Be silent; listen; don't question him; stand still; take it all in; you'll meet an amazing experience. There are three, though there be but one; one soul with three persons, notwithstanding – a painter, a poet, a seer.

A burly, heavily-bearded man, head bent low towards the ground, came mooching towards them, his thick, red-lipped mouth rolling out sonorous, indistinct syllables of wisdom.

—He has a puce soul, whispered the doctor, and hence he thinks life is found only where everything is perpetually purple; and he indites hymns about mystical purple dew dripping from purple mystical trees, dim in a purple twilight that ends in a purple dawn. He gives the name of Dana, Donah, Dinah to the busy earth, and believes that his place in eternity is a faery seat among a thousand purple stars. There, see! He's picking up a tiny stone and holding it high above his head. Listen to his shout.

—A Star! shouted the bearded one – I call upon the names of those Illustrious Ones who were not before I am; oh! tell me, masters, how to woo ye. Teach my bosom to reveal all its sorrows sweet unto thee, all the love my heart can feel. Oh! Layo-Tsetze, Spangler Sbungler, Confusian, Cant, and Emer's Son, the puresouled One, Spunooza, my sons, my sons, come back to your father once more and show him something exciting.

—Listen, whispered the doctor; when I call hail, he'll shout the absolute absolutum symbol of the universal wisdom; and cupping his big mouth with his thick red hands, the doctor shouted, Hail!

The big bearded fellow stopped suddenly, raised his eyes to the vacancy above, and called out to the full of his voice: Transmagnificandanbanturality!

—I heard that at a pantomime, said Sean, when I was a kid.

—Well, don't let on you did. Wait till I tell you; when I call hail again, he'll sing his symbol hymn to his mother earth; and cupping his mouth with his hands again, he called, Hail!

Opening his large mouth the bearded one sang loud and bitter and better,

> *Con*, con, with a con, *stanti*, stanti with a constanti, *no*, no, with a no with a constantino, *ple*, Constantinople!

—Sure, I heard that too, at a pantomime, when I was a kid.

—I know, I know; but listen, can't you, to his chanting?

> *Ancesthral Self, both near and far, come close and hear my song,*
> *It's only eighty verses, and it won't detain ye long;*
> *A heart-song from the mountains where the faeries dwell in glee,*
> *And pipe their mauvey melodies through lordly Tandraggee;*
> *Led by the starry soul concealed in drunken Mich Magee.*
> *For he is thee, and thou are he, and you and he are sparks of me!*
> *Ha-ha, hee-he, he's Dana's son you see;*
> *And if anyone knows a thing or two, it's me me me and Mick*
>   *Magee.*
> *But how we'll end, sure no one knows; but when we dee,*
> *We'll cock our toes in sweet repose where the lordly river*
>   *Shannon flows.*

—See, said the doctor, he's going off now, for he feels his brother, the great painter, coming. Look, the spit of the fellow who's gone! He'll steal away too, whenever he feels the third brother, the poet, coming. The three of them's Ancesthral Beings, and the only ones casting a shadow who can hear the planets sing. The dree in one. Hush, here he is! That's why he's such a great painter – the greatest ever. The first you saw was the philosopher *excelso superbum*, but he's also something of a painter and a poet; this fellow coming is a painter *supersissimum*, but also something of a poet and philosopher; and the third one, that you may see later, is a poet *miracula harmonium*, and also something of a painter and philosopher. They soar above all others in thought, see only through other eyes of dream that pierce straight through the veil of blank. Now you'll look upon the greatest painter here or hereafter.

—What, greater than Constable, Turner, da Vinci, Rembrandt, or Titian?

—Far greater, man, far greater. He hasn't an equal anywhere. Stacks and stacks and stacks of pictures he has piled up against the walls in his little grey home in the south – three hundred and sixty-five thousand of them he has, one for every day of the souler year.

—D'ye tell me that, now?

—On canvas, he has filled our vision with the micky-dazzling forms of the Shining Ones.

—What Shining Ones?

—The Noble Ones, the Beings Who Never Say Die, the Ancesthral Sylphs, the Hidden Hautboys, the Higher Hierarchies – them – you know. Here he is. Stoop. Hello, Aimi Admirabilis Aminadur!

The bearded man stopped and looked with gentle fierceness straight into our faces. The doctor waved a hand towards Sean, saying, A friend of mine, O master of mysteries. The bearded one came close to Sean, staring unseeingly into his face, his own so near that Sean felt the rapid breath of the gazer flooding over his face, making him step back as he heard the bearded man murmuring, Blue aureole, stained with red streaks: intellectual plane, but soiled with some sensuality. Godship and kingship, hidden in him, are far away from him still. How long, O Lord, how long!

—I was just telling him, sir, said the doctor, what a gorgeous painter you are, so you are, tremendous, hilla-balloo holy one.

—I paint great mysteries, he said. I bring infinity to the dotted line. I paint the twilight's dream; the star-soul of the earth, and the earth-soul of the star. Yes, I paint great mysteries, revealed to me in sleep. The gods so help me, too, coming down derry down to sit on the rail of my bed to show themselves off, so that I can see to paint them in their thrue colours, pink and light blue and dove grey; with wings sprouting from their foreheads, whence rises the Well of Indra, and plumes of coloured fire, spouting from the spinal cord, by way of the pineal gland.

—What gods, sir? asked Sean.

—O Dana, Duna, Krishnavoorneen, Ding Dong Dedero, Aghadoedo, Aeonius Pure Bolonius, and Kelly from the Isle of Mananan. Oh! be wary of will-doing, for none but the demigods can see around a corner. Goodbyee all. May the candle of candles plant a light of thought on your brows. And sinking his

massive head on his massive chest, he faded away into the twilight of amethyst, a beauty among beautiful things.

—There y'are, said the doctor, now, what d'ye think of that,
eh? Makes you feel a better man, doesn't it? Ruskin's in the
ha'penny place with him. You can hear the planets chiming when
he's talking. He's the spit of Socrates – humble, modest, retiring,
and full of himself. A flaming aego. A second Socrates that drank
water bubbling up from the well of the holy hazels, and lived on
locusts and wild honey.

—No, no, said Sean swiftly; you're thinking now of John the
Baptist.

—Socrates, Socrates, I'm saying, said the doctor loudly, his
red face growing redder till it was all a purple glow. Haven't I
made a special study of these questions?

—Maybe he did, then, said Sean, taken aback by his angry
vehemence. You may be right.

—There's no maybe about it, he shouted; I am right!

—I beg your pardon, murmured Sean.

—Well, be more careful. If you want to benefit by a visit
here, you'll have to carry on cooperation. As I was saying, after
living for ages on locusts and crowds of wild olives, for saying the
world moves, he was roasted to death slowly on a gridiron.

—That was St Lawrence, wasn't it?

—What, that said first the world moves?

—No; who was roasted on a gridiron.

—I'm saying Socrates was put to death for saying that the
world moves.

—I always heard it was Galileo who first said that, murmured
Sean.

—Ever hear anyone here saying it?

—Oh, no; not here.

—Well, then, be silent. Socrates, or Aristotle, or someone it
was who said it, standing on a peak in Darien when he was
driving the reptiles out of Ireland.

—Who drove them out? asked Sean, bewildered.

—Tim Healy did it, with the Pope's connivance.

—But you are contradicting yourself, said Sean.

—Am I now? What if I am, aself? Very well, then – I contra-
dict myself. And who has a better right to do it? And d'ye know
why? Because I contain multitudes. That's why. Fix your eyes
on the back of your head, straight on the top point of the pineal

gland, for a week or more, and you'd soon know that many
contraries are balancing each other in the psyche, up down, here
there, you see, they saw, see saw, see? The top of the psyche may
lust after the spirit, the bottom after the delights of the body,
while the centre, intellectual, may be sceptic – see? saw? Got me?
Understand? Savvy? Now quiet.

—I savvy, said Sean. Now let us arise and go farther into the
recession lost receding.

The suggestion half stunned the doctor. He stood gaping at
Sean for a long time, breathing rapidly as if his heart was
startled. Good God, man, he murmured, you don't know what
you're asking. Things in there are unimaginable to me or you.
Did you feel the earth shake? That was a shudder fleeing from
the breast of Dana, the earth-mother. This is as far as primal
clay dare go. This place isn't either the Coombe or Sackville
Street. You have to watch your steps here. Farther in's the rendezvous of the very nobbiest of the universe – princes of stars, solar
kings, and pashas of constellations and galaxies, Stoop! Here's
the third advancing, you see, head down, mind up, the poet one.
Bless yourself – *Trio juncta in lacunae, per amica violentio
lunee.*

Before he came within range of our hearing, we heard the
third bearded man singing, his red lips wagging as he sang calmly,
but with fierce distinction:

> *O swallow, swallow, swallow, follow, follow, follow,*
> *Follow me up to Carlow, and come home with me to Clare.*
> *There I'll show you sights and wonders,*
> *Till the trembling psyche sunders;*
> *Then I'll show you all the blunders*
> *Made by him who knew no meaning for the whence and why and*
>   *where;*
> *Who spent a lifetime deaving*
> *Candles, queens, and swans with grieving,*
> *Broidered cloths for women weaving,*
> *Climbing up the winding stair.*

He stopped facing us, though he still watched the ground. With
a mystic wave of the little finger, he said as if to himself, but
actually to us, A dream, a dream; I met a dream in th' forest of
the great city, a Dream of the Chiselurs. It flooded into me as I

was going down Sackville Street. Here it is for you, and for the whole world, born and unborn:

> The chiselurs, looking for berries, went into the heart of a hill,
> Saw the Shining Folk dancing like good ones, for they found it
>   damn hard to stay still.
> Their eyes burned like opals majestic, tiaras shone rich on their
>   brows,
> And flames of gigantic proportions shot up from their backs of
>   brown knowes.
> Smilin' thru the wild flame of their glory, They laughed at the
>   kids, and said, Do
> What we've done for thousands of ages, an' th' same glory'll
>   fasten on you!
> But we'll show you for just a split second what each and what
>   all of yous are;
> An' they blew with a blowin' tremendous, till each kid that was
>   there was a star.
> The kids became Spirits Ancesthral, an' towered up for miles
>   in the air,
> Enjoying with rapture uproarious all the magical funne of the
>   Faer.
> When the scintillant vision was fading, and each infant eye
>   nourished a blink,
> A far-away Voice was heard saying, you can grow up like that
>   if you dhrink!

Then the red-cheeked doctor bowed low, chanting as he stayed the way he was;

> Sir, show me the way to go home,
> My heart just longs to be there, to be there, to be there,
> Where Zeus deals out the drinks from the air, and a star is an
>   sadenease chair.
> O Friend of the Primal Fire, beneath this coloured dome,
> Let loose thy power and show us a sign and show us the way
>   to go home!

The bearded, slow, majestical dree in one paused, turned round, shook himself, and waved a little finger in the eager air. Then with a musical rumble, the distant violet sky parted like a curtain, and there, in a golden haze, a scarlet unicorn and a white lion were dancing a jig like mad to the tune of a Hungarian Rapture, while Eire's King, Lords, and Commons, all in morning-dress, bowler hats on their heads, tightly-rolled umbrellas under their arms, sat around on wool-gathering galleries of clouds, clapping applause, and singing, as they clapped, *A Nation Once Again*, guided in pitch, time, and tone by the dignified little impressario, Art Up Griffith, dawn-eyes, sun-eyes, moon-eyes, and star-eyes watching the proceedings anxiously, the Royal Irish Constabulary being strictly confined to barracks owing to insufficient mental comprehension of what was afoot. Behind all these, in a vast pit, rallied in vagueness all that flourished before, and the minor men of the present, Niall of the Nine Hostages arm in arm with Conn of the Hundred Bottles; Queen Tailte telling Queen Maeve that it was a marvellous show, and Balor of the Evil Eye replying that it was only a flash in the pan; Red Branch Knights mingling with the Irish National Foresters; and the Fenians chatting to wee Joe Devlin's Ancient Order of Hibernians; while in a far corner crouched Jamie Thompson of Portadown Loyal Orange Lodge muttering darkly, I dunno, I dunno; it dusna luk dacent to me. Over all, in a sweeping arch, hung a mighty rainbow of tears and smiles from Erin's eye, colouring themselves in gorgeous stripes of green, white, and yellow, on which Aengus Og, the god of love, was busy embroidering in letters of burnished gold Clan Vic Aengus' inspiring and magnificent slogan of Guinness Is Good For You!

And Sean turned and fled away from the happy scene; back the way he had come, through the purple twilight into the violet gloom, through the darting grasshoppers, murmuring as he ran, Oh, Lord, oh, my Lord! Oh, my good Lord, keep me from risin' up, risin' up; oh, my good Lord, keep me from risin' up!

And as he ran towards the leaden gateway, he beheld a grey circle of forms going round and round a black stake driven strongly into the darker ground. On the top of the stake sat a dazzlingly white skull, and black ribbons, tied to the stake, encircled the necks of the forms moving round it so that it looked like a maypole dance in a garden of death; and one of the grey forms was Benson grinning greyly as he plodded crookedly after the grey form in front of him.

BEHOLD, MY FAMILY IS POOR

SEAN HOPED no one who knew him would come along this way, especially any Gaelic League friend or a Republican brother. Not that he cared a lot, of course, but it was just as well to keep a few things hidden from the sneaking world. And didn't he remember well good-natured Peadar O'Nuallain catching his arm one day, and drawing him aside to whisper – what d'ye think now? – nothing less than Why don't you wear a collar and tie, Sean, and not come to the Branch with a muffler round your neck? Of course, that remark ringed his neck with a muffler for the rest of his days, for he wasn't the one to germinate into unaccustomed grandeur of clothing so that Gaelic snobs of schoolteachers, civil servants, and customs officers shouldn't shiver with shame when he was near them. When I was dry with rage, and extreme toil, breathless and faint, leaning upon my sword, came there a certain lord, neat and trimly dressed, and perfumed like a milliner. Ay, indeed, there's a lot of fretful popinjays lisping Irish wrongly. Fight for Irish – no, fight for collars and ties, and it's these boyos that have handed Michael O'Hickey to humiliation, limping lonely through the streets of Rome.

Here he was, up every morning at five, bar Sunday, home again at six in the evening, after a hard day's work with hack, shovel, sledgehammer, or hod; out again at seven to work even harder for the Gaelic League or Republican Brotherhood till he heard the bells chime at midnight; and, in between, after much agony, fear, and heart-searching, he had pulled out the jewelled pins of thought keeping together the coloured and golden gospel-pictures of prophet, saint, apostle, martyr, and Virgin singing laughingly hand in hand with the sons of the morning, so that they came all asunder, and fell into the dust and rain and cold appraisal of a waxing world, their colours dimmed, the glittering figures forced into fading, the gold between them losing its reverence, and turning an ashen grey in the red glow of all life's problems; and all this, and more, they tell me should be respectably circled by a collar and a tie!

He was leaning against a railing outside a tenement house in Summerhill on a damp November day, a cold core in the moist air that looked dark under the leaden sky that panelled the heavens. His sister, with her five youngsters, had been hunted from their home for non-payment of rent, her worldly goods had been carried out and deposited in the street just beyond the sidewalk, to do with as she would, but to take them somewhere soon, as a policeman had told her, because she couldn't be let leave an obstruction in the street to impede the passage of law-abiding citizens.

His sister's husband had died in the asylum, and a sight he was when he was placed in the coffin. Practising on him they were, said Mick. One could see the marks round his head where, said Mick, the skull had been lifted, and the brain removed, so that it could be watched for developments later on in the day. Sean had pressed his hand over the poor body, and was shocked to find nothing there but flat bone. And the knee of one leg was embedded deep in the breast just under the chin. They tried, said Mick, with a block and tackle, to get it to lie down decently, but it wouldn't budge. Sean was very glad when the pitying earth covered it kindly up for ever. His sister and her young were sheltering with him and his mother for the time being, and he had taken a day off to take care of the Benson property now collected before him in the street. He was tired and sleepy, having worked for forty-eight hours without a break as a member of a gang repairing a bridge that had shown signs of wanting to sit down and have a rest itself. Poor as the things were, they couldn't afford to let any be pinched, for they were all the Bensons had, and so he was waiting for a one-eyed friend to come with an ass and car to take them to the shelter and safety of his own home.

He glanced over them again to tick them off, for he had dozed several times in spite of a continuous effort to keep awake: a kitchen table – the one whole thing among the little heap of goods; three chairs, with slats of rough wood nailed across where the seats used to be; a sofa, with a few rags of false leather still cleaving to it, and bunches of hairy fibre oozing through holes in the sacking that vainly tried to keep it under cover; a wash-hand stand with a tin basin on the top of it; the frame and laths of a wide iron bedstead; a broken, rusty iron fender; an old dresser, with two drawers that held two knives, one fork, and three spoons; two metal saucepans and a kettle; the tin bowl of a one-wicked lamp; an iron lath to do the work of a poker whenever they had a fire; a sweeping-brush that was almost bald; a butter-box with the seat painted red, two sides white, and the other sides blue; a frying-pan with a patch on its bottom; a rug, tawny now with dirt and stains, once a brilliant thing of red, white, and blue wool, with a Union Jack in its centre, that Drummer Benson had made on a frame for Ella before they were married – and two others, of blue and red cloth, made of strips torn from old soldiers' trousers, and the red stripes that streaked each leg of them. The bedclothes, the few precious pieces of crockery, had been borne to Sean's home by Ella and the kids, to keep them safe from damp and danger, with the framed strip of purple velvet – now fading to brown – holding the crossed gold guns won by Benson when he had been best shot in his regiment, all surrounded by a spray of crewel-worked flowers embroidered by Ella out of admiration and pride – the sheen of the fading guns, the grandeur of the purple cloth, the only things left her to get a glimpse, now and again, of a perished golden sky; and a framed photograph of the statue of Luther standing in the public square of Magdeburg – treasures that couldn't be left to the chance of the wind or the rain.

—Curse o' Jasus on all landlords! Sean said to himself; and especially on this one who put me into this predicament! A boyo, too, who's all-in-all with the Gaelic League, and out for a free Ireland! If even he could only go far enough away so as to seem unconnected with this shame, aself; but the kids knocking around here would steal a cross from an ass's back, and he couldn't keep too close an eye on Ella's property. A group of them even now standing to stare at the unhappy little heap of scrap in the kennel, then over at Sean leaning against the railings of the rotting houses; for this sort of thing was to them a song, the tapping of a tambourine, or the beating of a drum in their lives. Someone in trouble, someone in sorrow, a fight between neighbours, a coffin carried from a house, were things that coloured their lives and shook down fiery blossoms where they walked.

A young woman, hatless, a jagged skirt just reaching to her knees, showing a pair of hardy, well-shaped legs, with feet thrust deeply into a man's pair of rusty rough-leather Blucher boots came unsteadily down the street. A dark-green shawl dangled from her shoulders, and a scaly basket, holding one stale fish, was hooked over her left arm. She sat down on the stone steps leading to the doorway from which Ella's furniture had been carried.

It's Mild Millie, thought Sean, and fairly sober for once in

her life. He stole a glance at her, and could plainly see, by her
torn and half-open blouse, that the line from her chin to her
throat was fine, and went curving grandly into a bosom that was
rich and firm and white. She had hips, too, that would have
made a Hebe happier. Her hair, ruffled with neglect and dulled
with the dust of the street, grew in thick clusters, and was as
black as a raven's wing. And all these feminine assertions were
jewelled with large black eyes, the sparkle of the pupils undimmed,
though the delicate whites of the iris were now finally stained
with thin wavy streaks of scarlet bloodshot. A handsome lass,
thought Sean, and well dressed would make many a fine man
long to dance attendance on her.

—You look dead tired, son, she said to him. Here, sit down on
the steps beside me, and she spread her shawl over them; sit
down, an' take it aysey, for, depend on it, God'll look afther th'
world when the both of us are gone.

There opposite was Hutton's, the coach-building firm founded,
men said, when the English were still savages, to keep in order,
and build, the delicate chariots of all the grand personages alive,
alive O, in the country. Hutton's that wouldn't look at the cab
of a commoner, cushioning the seats, making the slender wheels,
the well-balanced bodies, limning on the polished panels of the
doors the coloured, quartered armorial bearings of this lord and
that lady, argent, or, gules, azure, vert, or sable, fessed, fracted,
flanched, barry-nebuly and barry-pily; burdured and bend-
sinistered; animals combatant, courant, rampant, rampant
gardant, rampant regardant passant, salient, and couchant;
dormant, debruised, and displayed; gemels, gores, and gyrons;
ermine, vair, pean, and potens; counter-vair and counter-potens:
all running about in a show of elegantissimo, for the poor people
to see and make them wonder.

—Here, lean again' me, said Mild Millie, and get a wink or
two, for you're hard set to keep your eyes open. Your head might
easy find a worse bosom for a pillow.

Drowsy and half asleep he lay, his mind drooping into a quiet
darkness shot through at times with the gorgeous colours that
used to flit in and out through the rags and tatters and dust of the
neighbourhood. Coachmen, grooms, footmen, linkboys, and
pages, as fine, and much more forward than their masters,
strutted in and out of Hutton's to leave orders about their
master's phaetons, vis-à-vis, broughams, and barouches, their

wigged heads monstrously high in the air, sniffing at the lesser folk eyeing them all, and envying. Lord Wellington, in his sober frock-coat and his plain kind of a cocked-hat, strolled often down this street, and there is the Earl of Tyrone, Governor of the City of Waterford, having various little jobs in the Revenue, and now asking to be made a marquis, not a speck on his snowy satin trousers, arm in arm with the Earl of Shannon, owner of eighteen boroughs, well away now with a pension of three thousand a year for thirty-one years; with one friend made a Commissioner of Revenue, another a Prime Sargeant, another in Patentee Employment, another made the Surveyor of Courtmacsherry, while he himself picks up the additional little job of Muster Master General at a thousand and eight hundred a year, so we all know what way he faces.

—Aw, Jasus! said Mild Millie, will yous looka who's trottin' past now in his vis-à-vis? Oul' Lord Lifford, no less, who voted our country away from us for a five-hundred-pound livin' for his hairy oul' chaplain, an ensigncy in the 42nd Foot for a friend, a cornetcy for his son, and a thousand more in his own salary to make the weight good. Aw, Mother o' God, will you look at what's creepin' outa th' sedan-chair, in purple trews an' scarlet cape, but oul' Craddock himself, who, for his vote, was lifted outa Kilmore to be Archbishop of Dublin, with five thousand pounds a year to keep th' poor man from starvin'; an' there's Donegall's carriage goin' in to be repainted, now that he's been made the Constable of Carrickfergus, followed be Belvedere, Hillsborough, an' Clanwilliam, all havin' comfortably settled their accounts with the Castle, leavin' to a more favourable time any reckonin' they may have to make with God; with the upright Bishop of Meath, alone in his study, wondherin' why the Protestant Bible was ever written at all; an' wondherin', too, what final *pro bonus republico* would be his punishment for bein' th' one an' only mitred man who stood be his counthry, and braved fear an' favour to vote agin' th' Government.

—And there's old Rowe the whiskey man's carriage swinging in now, said Sean, whose gold made Christ's Church safe from the bend-sinister of the weather, his coat of arms, on a field gules, three swallows guardant, or, with the motto of Just a Wee Deoch an Dhorish underneath; and, look, there's a Guinness' vis-à-vis coming out, the one who made St Pathrick's fit for Christians to pray in; his coat of arms, on a field sable, a barrel rampant, argent; in chief, azure, a small harp decossé proper, with the motto of Roll Out the Barrel underneath.

—Eh, wake up there! Where d'ye think y'are? This isn't a night shelther, me man! And Sean opened his eyes to see a burly sergeant and a burlier constable looking down at him. I spoke to you more'n an hour ago about gettin' these things outa th' way, continued the heavily-coated constable, an' it's here still y'are, are yeh?

—Ay, it's here I am still, so I am, and bearing it patiently, said the sleepy Sean.

—Well, you'd bether stir yourself an' get them things outa th' sight of decent persons engaged in their lawful avocations.

—The hereditaments – that's the legal term, Constable – will be removed as soon as the pantechnicon arrives to take them where they have to go.

—Hereditaments or no hereditaments, all I have to know, an' all you have to know, is that you're legally responsible for th' removal of them goods to a proper place, for it's again' th' law to leave private property in the public thoroughfare.

—Is it telling me that it's the owner's responsibility to have them shifted, or what?

—Isn't that what I'm afther sayin' in plain words that would fall safely into anny ears but your own?

—Well, I'm not the owner, and, consequently, as by law provided, have no responsibility for their removal; so you can go your way with a quiet mind.

The two policemen whispered together for a moment, the sergeant evidently showing the constable the course of his duty in these problematical circumstances.

—Looka here, said the constable, again standing over Sean, me bucko, I reprehended you before, an' I warn you again that the law doesn't allow an obsthruction of the thoroughfare be a collection there of sundhry an' various goods an' commodities, concerned generally with residintial activity of a dwelling-house, cottage, or common room, to the possible disturbance an' inconvenience of law-abidin' citizens engaged peacefully in their usual everyday movements, necessitated be the proper carryin'-on of their legitimate business; and be your nearness, or proximity to the collected goods an' chattels, you present to every reasonable person the appearance of ownership, thereby constitutin' yourself responsible for the removal of th' same.

—If he isn't the owner, ask him who is, nudged the sergeant, after a silence of some moments.

—If you aren't th' proprietor of them utensils scatthered on th' highway, then who is? demanded the constable.

—Go and ask my Irish arse! rejoined Sean savagely.

—A saucy, fine, penethratin' phrase, said the voice of Millie, stirring on the step, a fine phrase to sink deep into their two thick an' lonely heads, an' give them a dim idea of th' way th' world's movin'.

—Take no notice of her, sergeant, said the constable, fearfully and warningly; it's Mild Millie – a terrible female, powerful woman, takin' ten men to lug her to the station when she goes wild with red biddy; take no notice, for God's sake. A fearful female would have the pair of us on the broad of our backs in th' mud of the sthreets while you'd be winkin'!

—We're sorry for you, me man, said the sergeant to Sean, but thry like a good fellow to get them outa sight as quick as you can, will you? We don't want to be too officious.

—Push off, th' pair of yous, warned Millie, hitching a porter bottle from a back pocket of her skirt, and lowering a slug out of it; push off to where there's genuine throuble, before this red biddy takes effect, or yous'll have something harder than a few scraps of furniture to shift to the station. It's you, you ignorant yucks, that breed th' throuble; g'on now, she shouted after them, for they had turned and walked away as if they hadn' laid an eye on her or heard a word she said, for a gentleman acts like a gentleman, th' way a swan acts like a swan, because it's th' bird's nature; but it's th' ignorant yucks that brew th' throuble be persecutin' decent, honest, knowledgeable, upright, innocent, an' most respectable people. If it hadn't been, she added, turning to Sean and sitting down on the damp steps again, that the red biddy wasn't stirrin' in me bowels, it's afther wipin' th' dirty sthreets clean I'd ha' been with th' pair o' them!

—You're very young, aren't you, Millie? he asked, admiring the firmly-formed, handsome, dirty face.

—I'm well over twenty-two. Me mother kicked th' bucket when I was a yearling, an' me father had to drag me up as well as he could till he hurt his spine on the quays tryin' to move a weight it 'ud take a gang to shift, for he was over six foot, powerful, an' a spendthrift of his energy. So for five years or more he dwindled away on th' one bed we had, for we pledged all we had to keep things goin'; for he got no recompense for his hurt, bein' told it was again' th' rules to do what he done.

—And didn't St Vincent de Paul's help you a little?

—Them, is it? and she cocked her nose scornfully. You'd want to be a crawler, an' deny yourself th' right to live, to get anything outa them. But wait till I tell you: I got a job at seven shillin's a week, and minded him when I came home o' nights; but one night, an' me asleep, some bright angel or another stole in an' took him, leavin' me to face th' world an' loneliness.

The one shall be taken, and the other left, he thought; then, aloud, he asked, And was it the loneliness that led you to the use of the methylated spirits?

—No, not jus' that way. Th' oul' Da, you see, was fond of a dhrop before bed, to brace him afther th' cold grip of the quays; but when he took to th' bed, we hadn't th' means to give him what his soul sought, an' he pined, though he kept th' cravin' silent. One fine day a neighbour gave me a dhrop of the methylated spirit, showed me how to spread it out, cold, or make a kinda punch of it, an' from that out, a few dhrinks changed a long an' surly night into a short an' gallant hour of thoughts, an' put a merry loveliness into all around us. And again she put the bottle to her lips and took a radiant, gurgling slug out of it.

—But you've to pay for that too, haven't you?

—I did, till th' money vanished, then I got it be force. I'd wreck th' shop if they didn't give it to me. I get me grub th' same way. I got one or two flighty refusals at first, but they were sorry aftherwards. But I never impose on them, askin' barely what I need, and they give gladly.

—But, Millie, is this a sensible way of life for one so fairly gifted as yourself?

—Show me a betther one, you, will you? Who owns the poor stuff you're guardin'?

—My sister.

—Married?

—Yes, but husband dead.

—Children?

—Five of them.

—An' why was she hunted out of th' room she had?

—She couldn't afford the rent.

—There y'are, you see. Is she any betther off than mild-mannered Millie? You daren't say she is. I wouldn't bend me

back to carry away what I see in front of me. I don't pay any
rent for my room, but th' landlord knows better than to hunt
me out of it.

—Millie, murmured Sean softly, did you never think of getting
married?

—Well, God be good to us, what a question! An' where's th'
man in Dublin would be tantamount to Millie? She bent down
to look closely into his face, and he tightened his lips to stand the
whiff of spirit that flowed reeking from her mouth; barrin' yourself, for you've a fine shape on you, a sthrange atthraction clingin'
to you, an' a melody in your voice, there's ne'er a man in Dublin
would warrant me openin' a single button to let him come a little
closer; and she took another slug of the bottle. An' who'd have
me now? But wait till I tell you, and she poked his side with the
neck of the bottle, and giggled foolishly; before me oul' fella
died, I was a child of Mary – a child of Mary, mind you, an
look at me now! Hardly credit it.

—Never fear, he said quietly, when her derisive laughter had
ceased, you're a child of Mary still, in spite of polis and the red
poteen. Righteousness isn't a badge on the breast, but a living
glow in the heart, like the core of flame in a smoking fire. The
lives we have to live are bound to stain the skin with pitch that
defileth; but one smile from God, Millie, and we are again as
Naaman was when he had washed in the waters of Jordan.

—Don't be talkin' rot! she said sharply. I know better. I
have me times of fear an' darkness till I'm lit up with th' spirit,
an' then I live where few can rise to; an' when I'm hoarse singin', I
lie down in th' corner of some dark sthreet, far from th' walled-in
woe of a room; an' tell me who has a better bedspread than the
uncomplainin' sky holdin' on to crowds of drunken stars dancin'
mad for my diversion as long as I elect to keep me eyes wide open.

He stared thoughtfully at the sweeping concave entrance to
the great Dublin coach-building factory of Hutton's, with its
great oaken gateway, and its grey-brown lion and unicorn – a
little the worse of the weather now – over the entrance. In his
long goings and comings through the streets he had never seen
this austere gateway open. Never heard a sound of hammer
falling on a nail. Never saw the flame from a forge fire. In some
way they hid all sounds away from the common people. Always
there was an ecclesiastical quietness about the place. Even now,
in its shabbiness, it showed a fading gentility.

—Hutton's is passing away, he murmured, half to himself. What a change in factory and in street since the Union led us into the shadows.

—Th' same Union has desthroyed us all! said Millie, sitting up, and staring in front of her. Didn' Grattan know well what would happen, crawling from a sick-bed to put on his black satin trousers and coat, with his black silk stocking creasing on his poor thin legs, to hurry off to sing Ireland's swan-song, sayin' as he was present at freedom's cradle, so he was present at freedom's grave. Ay, she went on, rising to her feet excitedly, an' when we got a chance to cut adrift undher Parnell, didn' th' piety-painted toughs of Ireland down him, th' envious curs, barkin' out pater-nosters, an' they tearin' at his white throat. Not that I'm one to say well done to a man goin' with a married woman, or with a single one for that matther, for I'm a decent woman that way, but Parnell was different; he wasn't beholden to us, but we were beholden to him – how much we know now, splashing about in lies, slandher, malice, an' spite, givin' Victoria, her gay son, and her son's son, with Princess May Victoria of Teck, the grand chance to put their fingers into Ireland's eye. Oh, me white blossom of Ireland's spring, cut down as you were openin' to th' sun! I'm tellin' Dublin that me own Da bruised an' bled anyone murmurin' again' him! If he'd ha' only laid hands on Dillon or Healy, he'd ha' made squeakin' ghosts of them. But what are Tim Healy and Johnny Dillon now but two shits fadin' away on a shamrock sod! Oh, me dear young Emmet an' me wise an' brave Wolfe Tone, wherever y'are, you're with Parnell today. Me uncrowned king, if you were here today it's Millie would go down on her knees an' kiss your strong, white, holy hand, an' daze your enemies with her thrue devotion! She lifted her voice into a scream: May Kilkenny, that threw lime in his bright eyes, go crawlin' down to Hell!

—Ay, said Sean, we've had our fill of woe with the whole of them, Balfour, Salisbury, Gladstone, Disraeli, who shook a shower of imperial holy water over us to drive the Irish spirit away, and save us from becoming the lost sheep of the house of Disraeli. Look at me, he says, in spotless linen and satinized suits and silken socks, an' ye in rags and weak with hunger and tired with toil; but, one day or another, our rags will glow like a burning bush, set alight by God Himself.

—To hell with him, an' his Primrose League an' all, said Millie.

—It's an ampler day we want, Millie, and not any primrose
path, though it was Randolph Churchill, and not Disraeli, who
founded the Primrose League.

—Another prime boyo for you! With his Ulsther will fight,
an' his Ulsther will be right, an' a moustache like a tidal wave
sweeping over a yellow beach; makin' more speeches than God
made men.

—We'll have our own again, Millie – one day.

—Ay, but when? It's bellied out with braggin' we all are, an'
that's what has us so low. There's nothin' for it but hard dhrinkin',
and she raised the bottle again and lowered a lot of it. Then she
rocked herself to and fro on the step, singing,

> *By Killarney's lakes an' fells,*
> *Emerald isles and winding bays.*

Isn't th' whole land an Eden of the west? she shouted, suddenly rising to her feet and extending her hands to the heavens.
I'm askin' th' question, an' let oul' Disraeli, Balfour, or Randolph
Churchill stand out there in front of me to deny it, if any of them
is men, an' darin' enough to face a poor, delicate, and defenceless
woman!

She's getting beside herself with the drink, thought Sean; and
looked long and anxiously up and down the road for the ass and
car and its one-eyed driver.

The sky grew greyer over their heads, and a misty rain, rather
than falling, soaked the street with its chilly penetration, and the
people hurrying by; soaked cold and anxious Sean and the spirit-
warmed Millie, who had slumped down on the damp steps again,
while the twilight began to darken into a sulky night. Over on
the opposite side of the street, a little lower down, moving slowly
along the gutters, came a short-legged, long-headed, oldish man,
dolorously playing on a fife, whose brown skin had lost all its
dandy gloss,

> *The harp that once thro' Tara's halls*
> *Th' soul of music shed,*
> *Now hangs as mute on Tara's walls*
> *As if that soul were fled.*

The old man accompanied the slow and mournful notes with a
slow and solemn swing of his body, keeping to the time, pausing

while he played a bar or two, facing the pathway, moving forward again, slow step after slow step, to play another bar or two, pausing again to face the pathway and play another snatch of the air. When he came nearer, Sean saw that tears were trickling down his cheeks, slowly too, as if in harmony with the slow sad air.

We all feel it, thought Sean, feel it in the deep heart's core, however poor and wretched we may be: they feel the hatred due to that which has turned Ireland's glory into a half-forgotten fable; from Hyde himself down to this poor devil tumbling patiently in misery and want.

Suddenly Millie thrust him fiercely away from her, shouting, Go an' sit on your own steps, you! It's a wet nurse you want, so go where you'll be more likely to find one! She rose to her feet, staring at the coming of the ragged bard, and Sean knew by the dangerous glitter in her dark eyes that the spirit of red biddy had taken full possession of her. Whirling the now empty bottle around her head, she sent it flying so that it broke to pieces against the lion and unicorn guarding Hutton's pompous gateway; and as the shattered glass jingled over the pavement, the one-eyed driver came up with his little ass and car.

—Hey, you, there! Millie shouted towards the ragged fifer, play up something less like the wind blowin' through the boneyard, an' show th' English lion an' unicorn that Ireland isn't even halfway outa step with life!

When he saw the strength of her body, and sensed the glitter in her eyes, the old fifer changed quick from the solemn tune to the lively reel of *The Grain of Wheat*, sending the notes out to scatter themselves gaily on the heavy air. Millie rushed headlong across the road and faced the massive lion and unicorn frowning down from Hutton's lordly gate. She commenced to dance, slowly at first, till she thought she had caught the time of the tune, then, with a sharp yell, her legs and body began to fasten fiercely into the swift time of the reel. She moved sideways to the left, then sideways to the right, gesturing her body in a way she imagined added style to the gay music; advancing and retreating with her head held high, her hands bunching up her skirts so that her firm, white legs were out of them up to her thighs. She sent a venomous spit as high as she could up towards the British arms, twirling round with frantic shakes of her head, letting a yell out of her every few moments as a condiment to the swirling notes of *The Grain*

of Wheat. Sean, eager to go, hurried the few damp pieces of furniture into the little car, unhelped by the one-eyed driver, who
stood grinning, hands deep in his pockets, watching the dancing
Millie, seconding every yell of ecstasy she gave with a piercing
yell of his own.

—Come on, for Christ's sake! appealed Sean, gripping his
arm, and let's get these things home before the rain dissolves
them all before our eyes.

—Aw, wait a second, can't you? he replied impatiently, turning
his empty eye towards Sean. It's not every day a fella sees such
a gorgeous urge in a well-made woman, an' him on business bent.
Looka th' way her skirts are up about her thighs! A little higher
ups a daisy, an' th' world is mine!

No heaviness in her clumsy boots kept her from whirling round
at the end of each bar of music like a humming-top when it had
passed from the speed of a sleep to that showing its speed plain,
its hum louder and more menacing; so she spun, stopping occasionally to face the lion and unicorn, to bring a foot down with
a wild stamp to the ground, and send another spit flying up at the
British arms. The crowd had grown bigger, and the fifer, old as
he was, danced jerkily now, and a number of men and women in
the crowd were doing spasmodic steps, sending spit after spit
on to the wall over which strutted the symbolic animals of
England's greatness, the rest of the crowd cheering whenever
any of the moisture was carried to the wall anyway near them;
pressing nearer to the gesticulating, dancing, demented woman,
and filling the woman who owned the little sweet and vegetable
shop at the other corner of Hutton's Lane with anxiety lest the
excited movements of the crowd should demolish the flimsy pile
of boxes that served for stands to show off her wares on the
pathway below the window.

Sean, leaning against the edge of the car, saw some of the
crowd edging back nearer to the boxes than the pressure of the
people impelled them, and soon, following a wild yell and a
wilder leap from prancing Millie, a wave of figures surged against
the rickety stand, and all the oranges, cabbages, carrots, and
spuds were sent rolling about the pathway and the street, where
ferrety women and agile youngsters stretched out swift hands to
gather in the harvest, taking whatever came their way through an
act of God.

—Oh! isn't it a nice thing to see me little property scattered and mangled and bruised and batthered and stolen right undher me eyes, moaned the owner, by misbegotten savages takin' advantage of a poor woman, lit up with a little dhrink, thryin' to show her love for Ireland in an innocent an' unnatural way! An' ne'er a polisman within bugle-call of the place to even puzzle them in their pilferin'!

A dark dusk fell over the street. A lamplighter came jogging along, lighting lamp after lamp standing like sentinels at regular periods of the pavement, looking as if they had stood there for centuries; waiting, waiting, with not a stir out of them, for ever hopeful that the gorgeous crimson, yellow, black, green, or blue carriages, gently holding their stately owners, would come trooping up and down the street again, pulled by sleekly-polished animals.

—What's goin' on over there? asked the lamplighter of the one-eyed driver, as he paused in the lighting of the lamp beside them.

—Some dhrunken bitch or other thryin' to get us to fight for Ireland.

—Eh? Fight what, fight who, where, when?

—Here, now, th' British, I suppose.

—Maybe it's fightin' she wants! Fightin' a feed would be more'n her line, and he thrust his long rod, topped with the tiny bulb of light, through the hinged flap of the lamphead, touching the point of the burner till the gas grew into a yellow flame. Then he hurried off at a gentle trot, zig-zagging from one side of the street to the other, leaving little dots of light behind him, staring faintly like near-sighted people peering into the gathering gloom.

—She's bet, said the one-eyed driver, coming close to the car, bet to th' world. The glitther of her eyes is glazed, and she's sunk down there – see that dark blob on th' ground again' th' wall to th' left of th' gate? That's her. What a chance for a fella if she hadn' lay down in such a public place!

Sean went over near to where she lay, and looked down on her: a huddled mass of torn clothes and mud. There, too, though, was the mass of dark hair, the white legs still showing under the tattered skirt, the firm, full breasts now rising and falling all too swiftly, the shapely hips hidden in the hunched-up skirts, the rich, black eyes, wide open, seeing nothing – or, maybe, seeing all things – and the drink-stained breath coming in painful pants from the scarlet mouth.

She loves Cathleen ni Houlihan, he thought, in her own reckless way. In a way, she is Cathleen ni Houlihan – a Cathleen with the flame out of her eyes turned downwards. The feet of this Cathleen, the daughter of Houlihan, are quiet now, but none have bent low and low to kiss them.

Her courage breaks like an old tree in a black wind, and dies.

The pure tall candle that may have stood before the Holy Rood, was sadly huddled now, and melting down into the mire of the street, beneath the British lion and unicorn.

He turned away, and mounting the car, bade his one-eyed friend drive off with his sister's salvaged goods.

HOME OF THE LIVING

EVERY MORNING, now, at five-fifteen, when his drowsy ears heard his mother's call, just after the ringing yell of the alarm clock had died down, Sean knew there was something on his mind, something he had to remember. What? Oh, yes! He must go carefully when he got out of bed, for living things were sleeping on the floor. Three of Ella's children slept in his room; the other two, with Ella herself, in his mother's. Lying there with all the old clothes that could be scraped together over them, some spared from his bed, some from his mother's, with a few old blankets lent by a kindly neighbour living below. Ella and her kids had been stopping with them for some months, were there still, and couldn't go till Ella found a room, and got a job of some kind to pay the rent of the room, and food of a sort for the children. They were watching a room a few turns away where idleness had prevented the payment of rent, and the family had got notice to quit. Ella was ashamed to apply for poor-law outdoor relief, for had she done so, her mother would never have lifted her head again, and he, too, would have sent his sister packing had she sought it. (What would it have been, anyhow, but a loaf or two, a few grains of tea, and a pound of sugar or so?) However poor they were, they didn't want that hell of humiliation. So they struggled on, his mother always aiming at sparing as much as she could from her own dish as she dared, and paring a little from his own share of bread to faintly feed Ella and her kids; and she went on darning night and day to prevent their rags from floating off their backs. It wasn't a pleasant job for him to be eating a dinner with a little army of hungry eyes watching him, so working near or far, he took his dinner with him. Taking his breakfast wasn't so bad, for they were all still asleep, though it wasn't easy always to arrange table and chair so that the legs didn't pinch their prostrate bodies; and the smell of the room from the breaths of the sleeping bodies made the air of the room thick and sluggish, even though he kept the window open, especially to him, in from a first quarter's work in the fresh and frosty air. At times, a surge of hatred swept through him against those scarecrow figures asleep at his feet, for they were in his way, and hampered all he strove to do, and a venomous dislike of Ella charged his heart when he realized that for the romance of a crimson coat, a mean strip of gold braid, and corded tassels of blue, yellow, and green, she had brought him, herself, and all of them down to this repulsive and confused condition. Sometimes his rage felt a hard desire to whip away the rags that covered them, wake them all up with a shout, and drive them with swift kicks from the house so that terror would send them flying far out of his sight; but his fury always ended in a sigh, for he knew his mother's gnarled hand would hold them there till another shelter could be found for them. Ella at last had, thank God, got a few odd jobs, scrubbing floors that would bring her in ten shillings, if she was lucky to work a full week; the room he was watching was two shillings a week, so that she'd have eight shillings to keep herself and the kids going.

He was waiting impatiently for the bailiffs to come, to send packing the people whose room he wanted for Ella. If he could, if he could, mind you, he'd give Ella sixpence a week towards the rent, though that would mean the loss of a book, or part of a book, to him. The system in the Public Library wasn't any good to him. An indicator, high as the Himalayas, with countless rows of little oblong slits of tin, coloured red on one side, shown when the book was In, and blue on the other, shown when the book was Out. After raising his eyes to the fifth or six row of figures, Sean found that they failed to distinguish the numbers, so the indicator was useless to him, and he couldn't well go on asking the assistant whether such-and-such a book were in or out. However, recently, he had bought Emerson's *Essays*; Zola's

La Débâcle; Whitman's *Leaves of Grass*, a book in which the whole world danced, even on its way to the grave; and a cheap edition of Eithne Carbery's *Four Winds of Eireann*, which he found terribly doleful, the gay, grey sob of sorrow through it all; whether she sang of love or of war, she shivered in the cauld blast:

> *A chill wind blows about my hair*
> *Where'er I go;*
> *A weeping voice is in my ear –*
> *A voice I know;*

and to Sean the voice was the voice of Eithne Carbery making her moan, though the Irish Irelanders loved her, and gave her twenty thousand welcomes; so a generous drop of sleety moisture from a leaden sky lingered on every Irish Ireland cheek, just like a tear at this moment shed, turning Eire into a woman of immemorial moaning, so that a fellow turned aside and longed for a tale of bawdry.

Now he'd have to think of Ella as well as his books. There seemed to be ne'er an end to this damned self-denial. But when they were gone, and his eyes weren't within range of Ella's misery and want, he wouldn't feel it so necessary to be generous. Anyway, self-preservation was nature's first law, and he'd have to put the other law of the survival of the fittest into practice. Why did he promise Ella and his mother, in a foolish moment, that he'd give sixpence a week towards the rent? To help get rid of them – divil a ha'p'orth else, and, if he were honest, he'd say so. Besides, weren't they all wearing out his mother? Look at the way she had to ferret out the strip of wire netting she had clumsily, but firmly, fixed round her precious fuchsia, geranium, and musk, to fend them from the chiselurs' meddling mitts. But was he really concerned about his mother? Well, yes, for it was bound to be a trouble to him, if anything happened to her. Anyhow, he had a right to think of himself. How could he read right, study things, and write, the way things were? How was he to write articles for the Gaelic League manuscript journals in the midst of this ragged, hunger-agitated commotion? How was he to think out fine things to say at meetings in the heart of this lowly caravan carrying the lees of life? The poor, he was told, were beloved by God. He didn't see any sign of His love here. *He saveth the poor from the hand of the mighty. The needy shall not always be forgotten; the expectation of the poor shall not perish for ever. The poor man cried, and the Lord heard him, and saved him out of all his trouble* – all his trouble, mind you! *I will satisfy the poor with bread. The rich and the poor shall meet together; the Lord is the maker of them all.* Oh, words, words, words! I wonder was Solomon really thinking when he said things like these, or just about to play double or quits in bed with a woman; or was he flushed with the redness of the wine? There go David, Job, and Solomon feeding you with happy phrases. Well, maybe these under my feet aren't worth saving, though no qualification is made in the declarations. The phrases say, all. Then the poor have the gospel preached unto them. They have that, right enough – God has kept His word that way. For fear one way wouldn't be enough, we have fifty different sects bellowing the gospel into our bewildered ears. Perhaps the poor were always so many; their clamours for help so loud; their need so great; their breath so bad, that God got tired, and gave the thing up as a bad job. Well, some way or another, we'd have to tackle the job ourselves. Here he was, a ripe young man, and had never yet seen the poor satisfied with bread, nor had he ever seen the purple stain of a grape on a cracking lip. Never a flower on their table, save some autumn berries he himself had sometimes brought home at the request of his mother; never more than a faded newspaper to make the bare table look a richer thing; never a safer place to lie when sickness tossed us down; never a place to bathe away the dust and sweat mottling our uneasy bodies when the hard day's work was done; by the living God! these damaging lies of life would have to go! and he tightened his teeth, and clenched his hands till the knuckles shone white. And now this added heap of misery was sleeping heavily under his feet, while by a light from a shaded, guttering candle, he tried to read, and reading, remember all the startling things in Darwin's *Descent of Man.*

Sometimes he wished Darwin had never come into the house. He had upset everything. Everything was different from what they were before he rambled in to drag him down from the thoughts of sun-tinted clouds airily sailing the blue sky, a rug under God's feet, and force him to take an open-eyed survey of frogs and toads splashing about in the sedgy wharfage of a pond or the speary bulrushes of a marsh. Brekekekesh, koash, koash! For Sean, life was to begin all over again, if he decided to think on, and who wouldn't do that? Life that had appeared, just a day ago, as simple as the soft chanting of a coloured nursery-rhyme, was now a streaming, headlong rush of shrill fifing point-counter-point, banked up by thundering or gunblasts of millions of years of life. He had been deceived by babblers ready to live, to love, and to die in the irised lure of a pretty fairy-tale. When he had ventured to ask a question or two of them who said they knew, they had stared, turned aside, and gone away from him. One, when asked if he really believed the yarn of Jonah and the whale, had looked at him in amused astonishment, had pressed a fingertip to Sean's breast, saying, See here, boy, if the Bible asked me to believe that Jonah swallowed the whale, I'd believe it; but the blessed Book doesn't ask me to believe anything so non-sensical, but only that it was the whale who swallowed Jonah.

—And quite enough, too, murmured Sean. Even dear Mr Griffin, when challenged by Sean, had sighed and said, I know, dear John, I know; the Higher Criticism has disturbed us sadly. The robe of truth has been pulled awry, and badly torn, John; but the truth is untouched. Here we see as in a glass, darkly, but one day we shall know all, and I am content to wait.

The Bible? How he had fondly thought it had been handed down from Heaven, straight from the hand of God! A day ago, here was all the knowledge, all the fear, all the hope the world wanted. Life was fashioned so that all was ordered, stately, trim, triumphant, cut out and braided as deliciously as the sacer-dotal garments of the High Priest about to enter the holy of holies, down to the last little bell and pomegranate nestling among the fringes. And poor Archbishop Ussher insisting that the universe was but a child of four thousand years of age, and Dr Lightwood, going further, light-headed with the discovery, added that it was all created on the twenty-third of October, at nine o'clock in the morning. Oh, Michael Angelo, it took more than the pointing of a Divine finger to make a man! A million of years it took to mould him into what he is today, and the job is barely halfway over. It took more than a whistle to bring a world into being. Man has tried to make things all too easy for God to do. Not the first man, but the first question the man asked, brought what the clergy call sin into the world, and all our woe. Better sin and better woe than woeful fear and bitter ignorance. Ignorance found a god everywhere and in everything, and ordered life according to its imagined whims. Knowledge had been hunting the earth and scouring the heavens for but one God, but has found none. If I ascend up to Heaven, He is not there; if I make my bed in Hell, there is no sign of Him; if I take the wings of the morning, and dwell in the uttermost parts of the sea, even there shall no eye behold Him; neither shall any hand shoot up to shade a startled eye from a sudden light. The darkness and the light are both alike in emptiness. The god Cosmogony has quietly seated himself in the vacant throne of Jehovah. Farewell, a long farewell to all His greatness. Farewell to the Garden of Eden, with all its animals, all its lovely plants, and every sweet-smelling herb of its fields, with the soft, streaming rivers to water them all. Farewell to the man himself, and his wife, clinging together between the tree of life and tree of death, the twining serpent, burnished with many glittering colours, anxious for company, insinuating itself with its roguish smile and twittering chat of knowing good and evil: they are all now as the high-painted wooden animals and green-papered garden and stiff-jointed man and woman in a little child's playroom. All the magicjestic growth of man's fall, his happy redemption, and his courtly life in Thy kingdom come have faded as a Christmas tree that has stood in a dark corner, its fairy lights and glittering gems a blaze of delight and stimulation, suddenly thrust out into the light of a fine, full, summer day to wither into a mockery, its grandeur dead, and all its jewels rayless.

He wished he had a hold of the book Donal Mac Rury had let him look over while he waited for Donal to finish grinding items in the brains of students bent on entering the Civil Service. He had read what he could of it at top speed while Donal was busy, and had begged Donal for a loan of it, even for but one night and half a day; but Donal couldn't give it, for the friend who lent it was coming that very night to get it back, for the friend's friend wouldn't let it stay any longer out of his sight. Sean had asked for it at the Library, but the assistant had never heard of it. He appealed to the head librarian to try to get it for the readers, explaining what he remembered of its scope and vision, and the head librarian had snorted viciously, saying curtly as he moved away, If it's anything like what you make it out to be, it's neither a safe nor a proper book to have knocking about here! But now Sean had something else to think of besides *The Golden Bough*.

He went along cautiously, and peeped round the edge of the

house at the corner of the street, looking down the little lane with its double row of little tottering houses. Dtch, dtch, they were there still. There was the old woman, as large as death, sitting on one of her chairs beside her tiny heap of stuff on the roadside, opposite the house holding the room he had taken for Ella. She must have been there all night, and he couldn't run over to ask her when she'd be going. Neither could he let Ella go into the tenancy while the other's furniture was staring at the house out of which it had been carried by the bailiffs. Oh, here was the married daughter coming up to the oul' one now. Whishst, she's taking a chair away. Well, that's a start in the right direction. That's what they're doing – carrying it away, bit by bit. No money to pay anyone to shift it for them. Another night'll be gone before they've finished. Better late than too late.

Suddenly he saw the old woman rising from the chair – throwing her arms into the air, shaking her grey head so that her grey hair fell about her shoulders, to shout up at the sky, Jasus, help the poor! Here I am, at th' end o' me days, bound for the poorhouse. I can't live on me daughter, can I? I can't tear down food outa th' black sky, th' blue sky, or th' grey sky, can I? I've lived nigh on seventy years with my own, an' now me few last lone days is to be spent suppin' sorra with strangers. I'll eat me skilly head bent in me belly for thankfulness, and wrestle for sleep in an odd bed with no interest in th' rest I want to take. Why don't they kill us decent an' be done with it!

Passers-by took no notice of her lamentation, keeping steadily on their way, gaping in front of them as if no voice had spoken, for to them she was already dead.

That very night, Sean, with the help of Georgie Middleton, hurried the scraps of furniture into the room, a dark room, quarter-buried beneath the pathway outside, a small iron-barred window letting a dusky light in on to the scarred walls soiled by a thousand previous tenants; and the splintery floor, showing signs of steady damp decay, exerted itself to come away from the skirting. It was a house in the lane where Massy, Ecret, and Middleton had had their battle royal, as swampy as ever, and here Ella and her clan would live a bad part of their lives in this damp gloom; but thousands were doing the same, and why should she demand any better? For the price, it was the best he could get for them, and, even so, it would cost him six golden pennies a week.

Ella said no word when she came to the room, but just went on, with glazed eyes and thoughtless face, making up the old bed on its rickety iron frame, and the other bed on the floor. Sean advised her to make that one, too, on the frame for time being, for it would be less dangerous than the damp floor, even though they all would be a little crowded. She agreed by putting all the clothes on the iron bed without a word, and so she slept at the head, with the two girls and Shawn, the youngest, while the two older boys slept at the foot – six in all in the one room, and six in the same bed. Are ye not more precious than very many sparrows? About the same value, my Lord, about the same. It was a bitter sight for Sean when he saw them tucked up for the night, but he could do no more. He had to keep himself and his mother, give a little to Ella, take an interest in pictures, books, and the National struggle, so how could he do more? His mother gave them a chair from her meagre stock, a bowl, two cups and a saucer, an old saucepan, an ounce of tea, three and a half of sugar, and a loaf, so that they might have a housewarming on the first day of their tenancy. He gave Ella fourpence, and tacked up on the wall a church calendar having a text for every day of the year, a coloured picture of the King in the middle, wearing the uniform of a field-marshal, and a portrait of Lord Wolseley, Lord Beresford, Lord Roberts, and Sir Evelyn Wood, in full military and naval uniforms, one in each of the corners. The scarlet and blue of their clothes, and the glitter of their orders and medals, gave a touch of glory to the ravelling oul' walls. Hold on a second! What's the text for today? Friday, the thirteenth of November, Feast of St Lauderdamnuss: Keep right on to the end of the road, keep right on to the end.

They had been settled in, and Sean felt that he was now done with them for good. Working from six in the morning to half-five in the evening then out to Gaelic League and National work till twelve or one o'clock, he saw little of them, and never enough to give him a worrying thought. He gave his sixpence regularly, for his mother always reminded him when he desired to forget it. He missed a jug from the dresser, and guessed that it now stood on Ella's; and fingering his mother's doss on the sofa, he saw that some of her old blanketing was gone. Doesn't give a damn how she robs herself for others, he thought with annoyance.

So Sean went on with his daily work for bread, and his nightly work for the lily, labouring to bring new things to Ireland, and safely shutting himself from Ella's poverty and her children's silent shame, misery drying up their young hearts, and leading them on to an imperfect end. They went to school in their tired and timorous clothing, filling themselves, at any rate, with the knowledge of this world, and on Sundays they went to Sunday school and church, filling themselves up with the knowledge of the next one.

Oh, God! thought Sean, looking at them kneeling in their pew at the back of the church, what in the name of Christ is the good of it all! He lingered when the service was over so that they might be gone before he left, for they filled him with rage; but Ella often lingered longer to beg a few pence from him towards the children's breakfast in the morning.

The frisky spring had developed into the more sensible summer, seeking a place in which to sit and drowse and think after her racing dance with the daffodils; and Sean was at home in bed one morning for the first time for many years, nursing three badly-bruised toes, hurt by a lump of machinery falling on his right foot while he was helping to dismantle it more than a week ago. When it had happened, like a fool, he had gone on working in agony, afraid, if he took the boot off, he wouldn't get it on again; certain, if he stuck it out, he'd be all right the next morning. When he got home and took off his boot to bathe it in hot water, his mother found his sock soaked in blood, and he saw what a state his toes were in. There wasn't a walking-stick in the neighbourhood, so he had to limp as best he could to Dr Stoker of Rutland Square to be smartly rebuked for not coming in a cab while the toes were being dressed, and a tiny splint put on one of the toes that had been broken. He was ordered to give the foot complete rest and to come again in a week's time. Not a word, though, about taking a cab home, or another about where the fare was to come from, thinking, I suppose, that it would fall down from Heaven if one waited long enough, or prayed hard enough; but Dr Stoker wouldn't let him wait or pray in the surgery, and the police would deem it rather queer should he stay to pray all night in the open street. Delayed action on the part of Heaven would make him look ridiculous, and cast suspicion on him as one who was curiously going out of his mind.

So here he was on the broad of his back, waiting for his mother

to bring him his breakfast, and reading the Everyman issue of
Prescott's *Conquest of Peru*, which he bought after reading Keats'
lovely lines on the eagle eyes of Cortez staring at the Pacific Ocean,
staring with his awestruck men, all silent on a peak of Darien
(though it wasn't Cortez who first clapped eyes on this new world
of waters). He had looked for the *Conquest of Mexico* all over
the second-hand barrow, but had to be content with the story
of Pizarro's fast and fiery bestowal of the peace that belongs not
to this world on the Incas and their people. It was odd how the
symbol of the Prince of Peace appeared so often in the midst of
fire and smoke and death and desolation! How often it brought
to black, red, or yellow peoples, not the gentle grace of God, but
the sword plunging through their bellies, and the madly-rushing
bullet searing through their throats. The cross was everywhere,
on almost every flag of every nation, and England had three on
hers to show she was holier than the others; each cross representing
a saint, one a Jew, the second a Cappadocian, and the third a
Frenchman, and ne'er a one of them an Englishman. Millions
made the sign in the air, or on their breasts, millions of times a
day. The very hilt of their sword is a cross too. Ah, that's the
real cross for the hand of a plunderer, and here it is, firmly held
in the hard hand of the murdering conquistadores. The Incas'
first taste of Christ was a bitter one: myrrh, myrrh, vinegar, and
gall for them, with their frankincense and gold carried off, even
to the scrapings from their temple doors. Had the Incas been
able to moisten the air with cries of Domino woebescums, had
they been able to darken the sky with clouds of query eleisons,
it would have profiteth them nothing, for the Christians were out
on the make.

All the labour, the building of the ship, the coaxing together
of a crew, the long tumbling trek over a salty sea, tossing them
up and down for a lark, slashing its jeering billows over the rim
of the deck, making the hardy seamen cough, and shake the stinging spume from their staring eyes, forcing them to hold with an
icy grip any beam or rope that came their way so that they
wouldn't go to Heaven too suddenly. After, the landing of
figures wan, shaken, and doubtful; then the dragging of tired and
thinning legs through knee-deep swampy slime like the primary
ooze of Hell's first flooring; then through jungles, their blistered
necks and lacerated arms entangling in the looping, twisting,
red-blossomed creepers, and tearing at the climbing vines weaving

themselves in and out of their legs; of the panting warriors, now content to be woe-mounted men, trying to save themselves with sweep of sword and hewing of axe and push of shoulders, thrusting out in pain from hollowed backs, halting to catch their breath in snaky woody webs, dropping their sweat into the luscious cups of curling lilies; halting among swarms of humming insects, blue, yellow, crimson, or purple, darting streaks of light, prodding deep stings into the frightened flesh of the sweltering Spaniards, hot curses dropping from the blackened lips of the warriors that they had ever put a foot outside the plains of Saragossa, or wandered from the sight of the mountains of Navarre. And all for gold and the love of God! For pomp and power, for riotous living, with the cross on their banners and the glory of God behind them.

Even here, in the midst of torn flesh, minds jagged with fear and anxiety, beset with hunger and thirst, the long, rough, gaunt hands of these struggling Christians were stretched out to grasp the cord that was to choke the life out of the son of the sun. Poor Atahualpa who, to save himself from becoming a sour-smelling burnt-offering at the stake, elected to be baptized in the name of Juan, for it was the Feast of John the Baptist, was received into the Church, and so holy cords pulled by holy hands choked the life out of him, as being a much more merciful death than burning. The Incas' Temple of the Sun is quite bare now; all that was worth while in it, or on it, lies safe in the bottom of the Christian sack.

They're all the same, thought Sean. Those who conquer others to use them woefully for their own poor benefit performance are all the same, whatever god they worship, whatever flag they fly. Today, the cross to the heathen is as ominous as it was to the Aztecs and the Incas in the days of the Spanish glory. The native of that day felt the love of God coming to him when the feathered shaft tore through his breast, today the fire and smoke of the belching guns sing out the same evangel. He turned on to his side from the delicious comfort of lying on his back, to shout towards the other room, Eh, out there – is that breakfast of mine ever going to come to me!

His mother brought his breakfast in to him – a cup of tea and some slices of toast. Nine o'clock in the morning, and all's well! It was grand to lie here, alone, except for the mother; to read and think and see visions. Better still, to realize that while

other poor mugs were at it hard, he lay here like a bee in a lotus
blossom. What's this it was oul' Tennyson said? Ay:

> Let us swear an oath, and keep it with an equal mind,
> In the hollow Lotus-land to live and lie reclined
> On the hills like Gods together, careless of mankind.

Like that he'd lie, careless of mankind; well, for a week or so
longer, though his mother had hinted that ould Murphy's bill
for provisions was mounting higher, for he got but half-pay now,
and ould Murphy was always hoping that Mr Casside's foot
would soon be better. He sipped the tea and bit the toast, finding
them both good, idly watching, through the open door, his
mother fluttering her brown and wrinkled, but delicate, fingers
through the fuchsia, the geranium, and the musk, fiddling them
into further bloom.

She wouldn't give her three peculiar plants for a Christian sack
of gold, he thought; she'd risk her life to rescue them from a
fire; she'll miss them and mourn for them when she gets to
Heaven. He heard someone coming into the room outside, and
then the voice of Ella's eldest girl mumbling and crying, his
mother standing stock-still to stare at her. The next minute his
mother and the girl were standing in the doorway of his room.

—Ella's dead, mumbled his mother, so Sara says; she says she's
gone; suddenly she went, in th' quiet of the night, so Sara says.

—Me Ma's dead, whimpered Sara; died in her bed in the
night in the midst of us without lettin' us know.

—How without letting you know? What are you talking about?
he asked.

—Before dawn, Sara mumbled, I felt her gettin' curious an'
cold, an' I called her, but she made no answer; so I felt queer,
an' I lit a candle, an' when I looked, I saw she was dead.

—Get up, Jack, pleaded Mrs Casside; get up like a good boy,
and don't leave us alone with this thing to face. You can't go
on lying on one bed while your poor sister lies dead on another.
Doesn't seem right she should be taken before me. Oh, what are
we goin' to do, an' her out of insurance benefit for so long! Her
face twitched, and she staggered so that he thought she was
going to fall, but she gripped the rail of the bed and recovered
a little. Get up, she went on, an' come over, for I'm not feelin'
too good myself.

—Pull yourself together, can't you? he said roughly. Her shaking frightened him a little. You go over first, and see what has really happened. What happened to her? he asked, irritably, of Sara. Once or twice I met her with part of an old shawl wound round her head. What was wrong with your mother?

—I dunno, right, she said. She went several times to the Dispensary doctor, an' he said it was only erysipelas, or something; she wouldn't listen to anyone tellin' her to take care of herself.

—Divil a much care you took of her! said Sean bitterly, or the damned doctor either. Go on, the pair of you, he added, an' I'll be over as soon as I've dressed myself. He watched them go, and felt disturbed at the uncertain way his mother walked out of the room. She's shaken, he thought, and I'll have to keep a closer eye on her. He guessed she gave Ella a lot of her old-age pension, and he often had to make her share some of what he ate himself, for he knew she went without proper food to give some to Ella and her kids.

He got out of bed lazily, lingering over the putting-on of his clothes as long as he could, so that whatever had to be done, might be done before he arrived. His face crinkled with pain as he drew on his toeless boot over his injured foot. When he had dressed, he sauntered over to the window and looked aimlessly out over the golden-headed musk, the purple-belled fuchsia, looking like a prelate hearing the confession of a golden-haired Niamh, to the railway lines beyond running down to the quays, at the long rake of wagons filled with lowing cattle and bleating sheep on their way to the boats for England, with the thick, bully-like spire of St Damnamman strutting over them like a stout jobber, wide-faced, satisfied, and silent, watching the last march-past of his treasures.

The one lovely thing about the whole place, thought Sean, is the sky. A purest blue. In it was some of the darkest blue, and all of the gentle blue of the lightest blue forming a luminous and radiant blue of its own. No fleck or frill of cloud disturbed the freshness that must have adorned it when the sky first came into being. It was as if God, in a giving vein, had draped the sky in a birthday cloak. A simple slip of it would make a rare mantle for the Queen of Sheba's shoulders; a gay shift to deck the charms of Helen of Troy; or a tempting dress for St Bridget herself to do a dance in, before her grudging hand had marred the seductive loveliness of her face.

He brought the tea from his bedroom, poured out another cup, sat down before the fire (for his mother did her best to have a fire, winter or summer) to drink it quiet, and go on reading the goings-on of the pagan-saving Spaniards in the *Conquest of Peru*. Somebody coming up the stairs now. Looking for him, he guessed. Ne'er a minute's peace, or a chance to read his fill for once! Come in! he called to a knock at the door.

Katie Kenna stood at the door, a look of reproach on her young face already getting wizened by some sort of heart disease.

—If I were you, Jack, she said, I'd leave your book and hurry over to where your sister's sthretched out dead, for I don't like th' look of your poor mother either.

He hurried on his coat, and jumping down the stairs two at a time, ran through the street, round to the back lane to his sister's shanty. There was a little crowd of kids round the door, and a few women nearby talking together who shoved the kids aside when they saw him coming. He went into the room, smelling always of damp and mustiness, now mixed with the added scent of death. He failed to see anything in the dark place at first, except the dimming blue of a sky no longer over him and away in front of him the frightened gleam of a candle stuck into the neck of a ginger-beer bottle standing on the cracked mantelpiece. Silence, too, save for timid, whimpering sounds that came from the sides of the room. Then the blue of the sky departed from him, and he saw his sister. In the midst of the whimpering, there she was, starkly stretched out on the family bed, the clothes still disordered, part of her breast showing over the edge of a coarse shift made out of a flour sack. The remnants of the old shawl were still wrapped round her head, forming a rowdy cowl from which his sister's waxy face stared like that of a nun of the higher order of destitution salvaged from it for ever at last. He recognized in the dead face his sister of the long ago, for a swift bloom of a dead youth had come back to mock at the whimpering, squalid things arrayed around it. There were the cleverly-chiselled features, tensed by death, the delicate nose and fine brow, the firm oval cheeks, the white throat curving into the breast as gracefully as a swan's neck, and the neatly-moulded hands, worn away now, resting confidently by her side. Here lay all that remained of her piano-playing, her reading in French of Iphigenia, and of her first-class way in freehand drawing. All that had to be done now was to get rid of her quick as he could, and a tough job it was going to be for him. The blue sky was a mistake: a useless waste of loveliness; a work of supererogation on the part of God. Only here, in this dark room, skulked reality, a filthy divinity that shaped our ends.

The children had pushed themselves away from the silence on the bed, and were standing with their backs pressed to the walls, the two older boys quiet and staring, the youngest and the two girls weeping in a bewildered harmony together. And there was his mother, standing against the bottom rail of the bed, staring down into Ella's insensitive face. There she stood, whimpering too, and shaking with the ceaseless delicate shivering of an aspen tree. When he looked more closely, he saw that she was breaking, that she was shivering herself into an acknowledged old age at last, while Wolseley, Beresford, the King, Evelyn Wood, and Lord Roberts, in their gay garments, watched from the wall this whining tattoo honouring the poor's natural anointing. Oh, why the hell should he torment himself with the thought of a blue robe for the Queen of Sheba, a mantle for the pert, beautiful shoulders of the charmer of Troy, or a gown of mystical blue for Bridget to dance a night away, before her ruthless hand mauled her lovely face to prevent it becoming a desirable occasion for sin!

He took his mother by the arm and led her out to bring her home, for he could see she would be useless now. He tried to think of what was to be done now, but all the images his mind could form were a medley of his sister's calmly stretched-out body seeming to say silently, Here I am, now, and the world can do what it likes with me, and whatever you like with whatever once was mine; of the steadily crying children standing like a drab and dreary guard of dishonour around the dead woman; of the coloured-paper soldiers watching from the wall; and of his mother whining and shivering in the midst of a brilliant blue sky. It was one comfort, at least, to reach home, to hand over his mother to the care of kind Katie Kenna, who set her down by the fire and planked a kettle on the fire to make her a cup of tea.

—Look, Jack, she said, as he was about to go back to Ella's, if the chiselurs haven't had breakfast, send them over, an' I'll give them somethin' hot.

—Who's to lay her out? he asked Katie. The girls are too young, and they're not much good anyhow.

—Any of the women'll do it for you. Aren't they waitin' there to be asked? They may well have begun already.

—But I've nothing to offer them for doing it, he objected.

—That doesn't signify, said Katie; someone'll have to tidy her up to meet her Maker.

He went away without thanking her, for he was full of the ordeal he had to face, and all alone, now, for his mother had come to the end of her valour. Jasus! It was terrible! A hell's pentecost to all the genteel thieves who batten on the poor! May a flame on every head eat into every brain of them, to be a soft and simple baptism of the fuller flaming life to come!

When he reached Ella's, he saw the children standing against the wall outside, and he sent them to Katie Kenna's to get a cup of tea. A woman came along with a white towel and a jug of steaming hot water, who stopped to say, You can't go in, now, for we're laying the poor creature out; and Mrs Brady's giving us the usual sheets with the brass candlesticks an' candles to put a shape on things, so she'll look decent, neat, an' ready for all she may have to meet.

—Won't she want a shroud of some sort?

—That's got; someone got it; I dunno who.

—Ask him about th' cross, Jinny, said a woman's head, thrusting itself out through a slightly opened door.

—Oh, yes, said Jinny, beaming at Sean, I near forgot. Mrs Brady always sends a cross with the sheets, to be laid on th' breast of the dead; but you an' her bein' a Protestant an' all, we were wondherin' whether it would be sensible to leave it out, or rest it on her?

—Oh, give her the fullest measure you can, said Sean; there's no reason to hide from her the sign of suffering and the badge of shame.

—Ah, then, said the head through the doorway, if e'er a one deserved it be hard work an' hunger, it's her who ought to have th' comfort of the cross; though, to even matters, we'll lay it lightly on her breast, an' not have her claspin' it in her hands.

He left the women at it, and strolled over to the wall bordering the railway, leaning on it to try to think of what he was going to do. Where in the name of Christ was he going to get the money to bury her, even in the slinking way destitution buries its out-of-benefit dead? And to only think that she had paid enough in premiums to bury herself and her family a dozen times over! Oh, these thieving, rascally, money-conjuring insurance societies! Asps on the breasts of the poor! Without the slightest garnishing, plain hearse, plain horse, plain coffin, plus the burial fee, it would come to four or five pounds, and he hadn't five pence in his pocket! And on half-pay too. Then there were other things – the fares and the tips to the gravediggers. Let the parish bury her? The common deal coffin and cart, the hurried trot to the poor-ground in the early dawn, so that it would not disturb the genteel burials that came later, with flowers, nodding plumes, and top-hatted drivers? Well, beggars couldn't be choosers. Could he get up a collection? How could he ask Catholics to subscribe to bury a Protestant in a Protestant cemetery? Anyway, they hadn't anything to give, save what they stood up in. Though a burden to him, death had been a kind favour to Ella, though it meant but carrying her from one tomb to another. No hyacinth will grow from that once lovely head, damaged by the fire of erysipelas, and turned to dry dust by the brunt of pain and the worry of want. Perhaps a burdock holding up a rusty red torch will do her some faint honour in some autumn-mirrored wasteland. The railway embankments and wasteland around them were crowded with the flaring yellow of buttercups and tall, pretentious dandelions, and the demure whiteness of the dog-daisy. The Dublin lilies of the field, flaunting the papal colours. Idle creatures doing better than those who toiled and spun. He fingered the coins in his trouser pocket: tuppence ha'penny – the price of a pint or a package of Woodbines, though he wanted neither. He must shut everything from his mind but a vision of money. A gold coin had eclipsed the sun. Nothing he had, nothing in the house would raise a penny. His books? Ten shillings; no – seven, at the most, and what would they do? And then he would be destitute indeed! Even if he had now the fifteen shillings he gave to swell the fund to help poor Dr O'Hickey to fight his case in Rome. No, no; not those. Bury her, bury himself, bury even his mother anywhere, anyhow, rather than wish the withdrawal of anything from a heartfelt fight.

He felt a tap on his shoulder, and, turning round, saw George Middleton staring awkwardly at him as he held out an envelope towards him.

—From the Rector, he said. Told me to tell you to bring it to Nicholl's, the undertaker. Says it'll make things a little easier. He scraped a foot along the pathway, stooping down to hide a reddening face. Th' envelope's open, he went on; have a look at what's inside, if I were you, before givin' it to oul' Nicholl's.

Sorry, Jack, for your trouble; hope you'll be able to manage.
S'long! And he hurried off without letting Sean get in the edge of
a word. Sean took the letter from the envelope, and read that
Mr Griffin requested Nicholl's to furnish all things necessary so
that Mr John Casside's sister could be decently, but not extrava-
gantly, buried. Pinned to it was a note asking Sean to let the
Rector know day and hour of burial so that he might officiate
at the graveside. There was also in the envelope a crumpled
piece of white paper wrapped round what Sean felt to be a coin.
He took it out carefully, and found it to be a half-sovereign. A
few words were scribbled in pencil on the paper, and looking
closely Sean read, Just a loan. Can easily spare it. Georgie.

—Cheeky boyo, he muttered, to think I wanted help from him!
But Middleton was too far away now to throw it after him, so
Sean carefully put the piece of gold in his trouser pocket. When he
found out from Katie Kenna that his mother was sleeping quietly,
he climbed the railway wall and sat down on a tussock of grass,
among the yellow dandelions and white dog-daisies, under a sky
again courageous with its blue banner, so as to calm a mind
confused at receiving relief so suddenly. However he might
change, wherever he might be, whatever he might do, he could
never forget the man, the Reverend E. M. Griffin. A faultless
man. No, not faultless, for sometimes he showed he had a hasty
temper, and he couldn't suffer fools gladly, both qualities en-
dearing him all the more to Sean, who himself had a hasty
temper and hated fools fiercely. He had, too, a puritanical de-
testation of even accidental indulgence in the claims of sex, other
than those allowed by law and regulation of the Church, and a
real sensitiveness that couldn't allow him long to look at the
effects of poverty. He had told Sean, one time, that to do so
would break him in pieces. He had, too, a curious childlike
readiness to accept almost anything said by one who, he thought,
loved and served the Church which, to him, sprang from the love
and devotion of saints Patrick, Columkille, Bridget, and Aidaun.
Once in an argument around the causes of poverty, the Rector,
laying an affectionate touch of his hand on Sean's arm, said,
Remember, John, I have been young, and now am old; yet have
I not seen the righteous forsaken, nor His seed begging bread.
And once, speaking, John, to Marcus Tertius Moses, on this
very verse, he claimed that, in his own experience, he could
confirm it in every respect. Sean so loved the Rector that he had

fallen silent rather than hurt his feelings by pointing out that a Trustee of the Church Funds and a Bank Director could hardly risk saying anything else, and that no man, banker or broker, had any authority to say that this or that man deserved to be begging bread from stranger or friend.

But what of the children when Ella had been planted? Ay, there's the rub! It looked as if his sixpence a week would have to be doubled or trebled in the future. The elder boy and the eldest girls would have to find some work to do; the rest live, or perish. Beyond what he could spare, he could do no more. Injured foot or no, he'd have to start work again the day after the funeral. He could coddle himself no longer. But he'd have to be hard. He'd have to view the kids in the calm, undisturbed way a mother robin gazed on her fledgling lying on a sturdy leaf five inches below, just having been flung out of the nest by the pirate cuckoo. There she'd sit, warming the intruder, an indifferent eye on the young of her body, helpless and alone, motionless the livelong day, save for a rare twitch of the tiny head, dozing towards death, slinking silently to its end.

He hurried off to get the death certificate, hurried to show it to the Registrar, and then hurried down to Nicholl's, the undertaker, where his tired clothes were eyed by a long, thin man, a tuft of hair on his head nicely balanced by another on his chin. He showed him the certificate, and gave him Mr Griffin's letter which he read, looked sadly at Sean, and said shortly, That'll be all right, all right; that'll do.

—Do it all as cheap as you can, said Sean, for I don't want our Rector to be asked to pay a lot.

—All right; never fear; we won't send her a coffin of copper with a silver plate.

Not much profit for him here, thought Sean, so he isn't very interested. Out loud he said, Haven't you got to measure her?

—We'll let her have a box that'll fit her, never fear, young fellow. That'll do, now; there are other dead people in the world needing attention. So good evening.

It was the poorest funeral the neighbourhood ever saw or ever heard of: a rough deal coffin, patchily smeared with oak stain, Ella's name, age, and year of death scrawled clumsily with black paint on the lid; and a small black box hearse, drawn by a scraggy mare bare of a plume. No neighbours gathered round the door, but stayed near their houses, looking from their windows or peeping out by their doors, for they attached the shabbiness of Ella's funeral to their own shamed inability to provide her with a better farewell.

On the morning of the funeral he sent one of the boys for two cabs, for one would be so crowded he was afraid some careless boot might stamp on his broken toes. Soon the cabs came jauntily along, but when they reached the place, the drivers remained in their seats, staring at the rough-hewn hearse and the meagre mare. The leading driver was a small wiry man with as many wrinkles in his face as an orange had, though its colour and texture resembled a mummified apple. He was wearing a heavy coat much too big for him, and a high-crowned, faded bowler hat. The other was stouter, taller, grey-haired, and tobacco juice oozed from a very wide mouth. He was wearing a claw-hammer coat, trilby hat, and a dirty white muffler powdered with big blue spots was wound round his neck.

—Eh, asked the man in the bowler hat, who was it here sent for us? And when a youngster silently pointed a finger at Sean, he shouted down from his seat, Eh, there, what are yous afther leadin' us into?

—How leading you into – into what?

—What a gaum y'are, he said sarcastically, his hand stretched out to point the whip at the hearse. What d'ye call that, eh? And as Sean remained silent, he went on, D'ye call that a decent thing for any decent Christian to folla?

—A fair question, murmured his friend, ay, is it; no one could ask a fairer.

—I'm askin' yous again, he went on, is it fair or is it honest to exact on any decent dhriver of any decent vehicle to promenade afther an unconcealable object like that?

—A fair question, I'd say, repeated the other, inserting a finger to scratch something under the muffler; ne'er a fairer. An' he too only afther gettin' his vehicle newly painted.

—It's the best we could do, said Sean tersely, getting the youngsters into the first cab, while George Middleton prepared to climb into the other one.

—I hope th' pair of you'll have as good yourselves when you're carried out feet first, George shouted at them. It's not a newly-painted cab, but a puck or two in the snout yous want to make yous decent!

—It's all very well, grumbled the driver, somewhat afraid of the fiery look on the pug-face of Middleton, but we have our prestige to mind.

—Ay, have we, added his friend, a long an' ancient one be now, an' valued. What'll Glasnevin people think when they see this arrangement arrivin'?

—It's not to Glasnevin, but to Mount Jerome we go, said Sean.

—Worse again, be Christ! ejaculated the first driver: a more elegant an' particular place still! He jumped from his seat and ran over to Sean, saying as he ran, I'll not keep close, I'll not do it, so I won't, not for Joe! I'll let a couple o' sthreets get between us an' that mockin' shame in front of us!

—Put the world between, if you like, said Sean, jumping into the second cab, so long as you get us there in time; and stretching from the window, he gave the hearse the signal to go.

He was silent in the cab, but thoughts swift followed one another fast so that all he saw, all he heard, all he did, appeared slantily in the mirror of a blue sky like the pageant passing through the mirror of Shalott, hurrying in and hurrying out in a continuous reel of sliding shapes, all of them headed crazily by the staggering onward of the one-horse hearse, to lay Ella on top of her husband's bones, who lay on top of Tom's, who lay on the top of his father's.

> In rags, she pray'd aloud to God,
> Who gave no answer made no nod;
> No blossom bloom'd on Aaron's rod,
> As she went to and fro.
> No angel, flying far too high,
> Came down a perch to hear her sigh,
> Or paus'd when she stretch'd out to die,
> The lady of sorroh!

Yet in the leering blue sky he could, at least, see the elegant black sleeve of the Rector's coat outstretched, and, at the end of it, the delicate, sensitive hand extended to grasp his own in the bond of friendly sympathy, as the two cabs, far ahead of the one-horse hearse, hurried on to Mount Jerome.

DRUMS UNDER THE WINDOWS

IRELAND'S LIFE of the golden, scarlet, and sable past came creeping out into the sun from many hidden corners; from Daingean, Ballyvourney, Vinegar Hill, Ballinamuck, Dunseveric, and the Islands a powerful hand had tipped out into the sea over the coasts. The hidden Ireland began to show herself to the astonished, astounded, and puzzled people of Belfast, Dublin, Cork, Galway, and Skibbereen, disturbing those engaged in the exciting job of buying cheap and selling dear, especially those who had the Royal Arms sprinkled on the lintels of their doorways; the younger King Coles of the nation, with their pipes and bowls, their fiddlers three, their jugglers three, and their drummers three, who were planted here by God and a few policemen to show the Irish how to live, and do things in the upright way, from shearing sheep, growing corn, rearing cattle, feeding pigs, telling the truth, acting orderly, and buttoning their flies properly. Astonished, too, were those who worked in docks, factories, and workshops, wearing bowler hats on Sundays and on St Patrick's Day. Ireland was giving birth to an army with banners – not the old-fashioned fancy-free ones of green cotton made in Manchester, with yellow shamrocks, wolf-dogs, round towers, harps, and sunbursts on their fields, carried usually by solid men of the Muldoon clan, Rakes from Mallow, Rattlin' Boys from Paddy's Land, Brave Sons of Hibernia, and Paddy Haggerty, in his leather breeches, from his cottage with the roses round the door; but cunning flags made from tabinet or poplin fresh from a Dublin loom, red, green, violet, yellow, and blue banners, garnished bright with speckled designs filtered finely from the Book of Kells, Book of the Old Dun Cow, Book of Ballymote, and illuminated headlines from the missal of Rob Roy MacGregor O; lovely scrolls of interlaced ornament were displayed on them, and spiralled decorations of many hues, taken from the sacred psaltery of Cahirciveen, and copied into crewel work by the fair, white, modest hands of the Lily of Killarney, Maire of Ballyhaunis, the Pride of Petravore, the Flower of Finea, Nora Creena, and the Girl from the County Clare, bespeaking a new hope and a high-strung resolution to flaunt before friend and foe things that had been deep-hidden in our history.

Ikons of the old-time leaders were snatched from the walls and flung into the first fire handy: Tay Pay O'Connor, in his muttley, criss-crossed with the figuration of the Union Jack; Tim Healy, a clever bearded oul' scut whose skin stretched tight over a portly bag of rowdy venom, who was now cursing in a corner; William O'Brien, in the centre of his All For Ireland League, like a kernel in a nut, shouting south and shouting north, but ne'er a one in an Irish class, or well away in an Irish dance, cocked an ear to catch a word; Johnny Dillon, the melancholy humbug, now no more to the people than a bleating sheep with the staggers, going about with a neat green ribbon tied round its thinning neck; and though John Redmond kept his hand held up to show the people where to go, it shook so much that it pointed everywhere at once. A busy, united Ireland was quietly weaving an ample shroud of silence for them all; and these men who had gone up and down the land, led by brass bands, under an archway of banners, through a salvo of cheering, were soon to be creeping and skulking back to hidden places in the dense loneliness of forgotten times, to sit by faint firesides, reading the yellowing records of their own long speeches, never again to notice the green liveliness of another spring; never to feel again the kiss of another lusty summer; never again to lie snug in the golden leafy lap of another autumn; never again to laugh, and run breathless with the gay earth clad in the shining armour of another winter's frost; waiting, worn out, for dapper death to carry them off, and deposit them where they'd be safe from sight and sound of men, leaving behind no damp eye to honour them, or any song for their singing.

Ireland's living symbol now was a big-headed, dark, big-mouthed man, loud-voiced, with a weighty moustache that gave a bend to his shoulders, and curtained off the big mouth completely; a man who was hilarious with everyone that seemed to matter, who was ever shouting out, with his right arm lifted so that its shadow seemed to stretch from one end of the land to the other; shouting in a strange tongue, Come, and follow me, for behind me marches the only Ireland worth knowing; in me is all that went to make the valour and wisdom and woe of Clan Hugh and Clan Owen, Clan of Conn and of Oscar, of Fergus and Finn, of Dermot and Cormac, of Caoilte and Kevin, and of Brian Boy Magee; the crooning, sad and impudent, of Piper Torlogh MacSweeny; or Sarsfield, Wolfe Tone, Michael

Dwyer, O'Donovan Rossa, and the Manchester Martyrs; of Power's whiskey, Limerick lace, Belfast linen, Foxford wool, Dublin tabinet, and Guinness' stout.

So History, in gay-coloured pageants, followed this black-haired, big-mouthed man through the streets of Dublin; and from moving lorries, drawn by ribboned horses, Dubliners saw, in costume-clad figures, Cuchullain fighting Ferdiah at the Ford, two lifelong friends slicing up each other; St Patrick, dear saint of our isle, episcopally majestic, calmly showing all the snakes in Ireland the nearest way to the sea; white-bearded Brian Boru, the brave, at prayer in his tent at Clontarf, with the beaten, bloody Brodar and his men lifting its flap, about to enter and turn him into a dream of Gerontius; Tone, Simms, and Russell on the top of Cave hill, outside of Belfast, taking the oath of the United Irishmen; Private Patrick Sheehan, gone blind serving England in the trenches before Sebastopol, and when he found that he was blind, the tears began to flow, and he longed for even a pauper's grave in the Glen of Aherlow; Reynardine, an outlawed man in a land forlorn, who scorned to turn and fly, keeping the cause of freedom safe on the mountains of Pomeroy; seven-foot Kelly of Killann, leading his shelmaliers and Bargy men to take New Ross at the point of the pike; the dark-eyed, brown-skinned, barefooted West awaking to remember again how swift before the Connaught clan, the Normans' flight through Ardrahan; the Poor Old Woman high on the cliffs of Moher watching the sails of the French fleet drawing nigh to the port of Killala; Sean O'Farrell throwing his pike to his shoulder at the rising of the moon; Geoffrey Keating writing his history of Ireland in a cave deep in a Tipperary glen, the red-coats searching for him all round about it; Lord Ardilaun presenting to the Dublin Corporation the title-deeds of St Stephen's Green for the use and recreation of the citizens and their heirs for ever; and Dark Rosaleen high on her golden throne, with a flask of wine from the royal Pope in her right hand, and a jug of Spanish ale in her left one.

And following hard after these gallant shows, marching forward through a sea of drums, a never-ending, never-ending fading into faintness, then slowly growing again, till the thunder rolled through every street, shaking life into all looking out of every window, came Guinness lorries and Cantrell & Cochrane lorries packed with all kinds of genuine things made of Irish

materials by Irish labour, whole and undefiled: a jar of Bewley
& Draper's ink as high and as big as an upright tower of Pisa;
all manner of wedding-frocks, mantles, morning-gowns, evening-
wraps, négligés and disabilities, including holy vestments, the
whole of them forming a sparkling rainbow of Dublin poplin
and tabinet; a full-rigged ship, the sails of glistening Lisburn
and Belfast linen, their whiteness sprinkled with the bright blue
of the flax blossom; an altar candle, big as Nelson's Pillar;
brooms and brushes from Varian's, each big enough to sweep
the Dublin tide out; a lorry shaped to represent a Viking boat,
the shields hanging by its side made of Bakecob's biscuits; a
papiermâché boot, big as a house, shining like a nugget, beside
a jar of blacking big enough to hide the forty thieves, advertised
Erin Go Bragh boot polish; a mountain of prayer- and hymn-
books, carefully calculated so as to keep the Irish people going
for ages, made by Jack & Jills; a cigarette, large as a liner's
funnel, beside a placard saying, Smoke Irish Tobacco, and Die
Dreaming No More; a pyramid of jars filled with aromatic
boiled sweets from Lemon's of Suckville Street; a lorry decorated
with galleries of spiders' webs, all mathematically made from
thousands of rosary beads strung together to make aheenagons,
dohagons, threeagons, caharagons, coogagons, shayagons,
shoctagons, ochtagons, neeagons, and dyehagons, each set made
by Irish hands from the primest horn from the heads of the purest
cattle of Tara, Mount Slemish, and the Isle of the Blest; enough
to make accord of prayer from that day to the one when Gabriel
would blow his blast to lift us all up to strict attention, eyes
right, and salute your superior officer.

Tableau after tableau showed Ireland relying on herself alone,
but Sean felt as he looked at the display that the show lacked a
model of a cow giving a ceaseless stream of milk, a pig manacled
in its own sausages, a sheep hidden in its own wool, and a fat
hen solving perpetual motion in the endless laying of eggs.
Lemons and oranges were in heaps outside of many shops,
griddle bread in the windows, slabs of Chester cake were in
every kid's hand, and a stick of striped rock sugarstick in every
kid's pocket, for the street sides, the windows, the pillars,
monuments, eaves, and roof ridges were packed with people
watching all the stir and gay commotion flowing by them, and
their ears were full of the roll from a thousand drums, as the
contingents marched to the place of assembly.

In front went two horsemen bearing a long banner stretching from one pathway to the other, wording a warning in red and green letters that the Irish were to Burn Everything Except English Coal. Before the warning marched a rank of drummers giving a roll every fifty yards they walked, and behind these marched a rank of trumpeters armed with barr booeys, war horns of the Fenians, who blew a flourish on them every other hundred yards, a blast that turned the call of the bucina into a squeak from a tin whistle, for their blast blew in every window, and shot in every door that hadn't been already opened. Other major and minor slogans were shouted by sections of the marching host, one crying, Ireland Divided, Ireland Down; another, Righteous Men Must Fake Our Land a Nation Once Again; another, Banish Every Whore Out of the Isle of Saints and Scholars; another – a temperance section called the Holy Thirst – Guinness Is BAD for You; the Gaelic League carried, A Country Without a Language, A Country Without a Soul. A sturdy fellow in green shawl and saffron kilt shouted, The war-cries and the slogans are here: the gun peals will follow. O'Donnell rides again in the glens; O'Driscoll rises from the waves of Cleena; Sean O'Farrell is sharpening his pike; Parnell walks the city's streets, and waits; the deer are coming back to Ireland – a stag, a doe, and a fawn; the horned stag with his head high!

And so, in the midst of the shouting, the call of the barr booeys, the insistent roll of the drums, they marched on, they stepped out together; stepped out and stepped on, as if, at last, they stepped on England, every head high, every foot firm; fixed in front was every glance, moving in a wide advance, like the deer on mountain heather, thronging men and thronging women stepped along and stepped together.

Here on the Dublin streets, in this gay and resolute procession, mingled the flowing of many streams of old, unhappy, far-off things and battles long ago – Kilmainham Treaty, Home Rule Bill, Coercion Acts, one after another, No Rent Movement, Reform Association, Land League, Cattle Driving Movement, Sarsfield's Ride, Treaty Stone, the Wild Geese, Penal Days, with minor echoes of the spirit shown at Crécy, Torres Vedras, Lucknow, the Crimea, Spion Kop, the plains of Flanders, and the battle of the Diamond; and, if one listened carefully, one could hear the yell of the Connaught Rangers, the Faug A ballagh Boys, and the wild shout of the Old Toughs, the Dublin Fusiliers:

all that had jostled each other, fighting for the first place, mingled, and flowed into one broad stream pouring through the streets of the town of the ford of the hurdles.

Gorgeous and stimulating were the costumes of the pipe bands, some with saffron kilts and green mantles, others with green kilts and saffron shawls; Armagh's beating Banagher for colour, for no one of them was dressed alike, and they took, by general consent, the head of the procession: one wore green kilt and blue shawl, another blue kilt and red shawl; one wore green kilt and white shawl, another white kilt and green shawl; one wore yellow kilt and black shawl, while his mate wore a yellow shawl and black kilt; for Francis Joseph Biggar had impressed on the mind of Ireland that that was the way the Gael usually dressed in the days of long ago, beyond the misty space of twice a thousand years, when in Erin old there dwelt a mighty race, taller than Roman spears, conclusively proving, if proof were needed, that we were on the right track, and doing nobly.

But there was a fly in the amber; a Jonah in the midst of the good men marching; one who had sinned against the consolidated spirit of the hour. D. P. Moran, editor of *The Leader*, had, in his weekly journal, argued against leaving the cult of the King to the Unionists, calling his campaign, Collar the King; and because all the young men of Irish Ireland had bitterly opposed this singular advice, which had the silent approval of the bishops and a crowd of clergy, D. P. Moran, in a bitter article, shouted that the tin-pike men, and hillmen, and give-me-a-rifle-and-let-me-away-men, and all who even gave them a pinch of salt to put on an odd potato, should be clapped into jail, to keep them out of mischief.

Another, Jay Jay Farrell, an alderman, who owned two cinema houses in the one street in Dublin, had voted, in the heart of Irish hospitality – some said he was trying to hook a title – for an official welcome to an English king; and he, too, was under the sibilant and salty hatred of the physical force party. He had received a warning telling him this act was his finale, and he would be wise to keep a safe distance between himself and the marching Gaels. But the alderman said in the papers that he defied the fretful Fenians, and that he would go, would go, and fix himself in the midst of the marchers.

So Sean felt a little uneasy as he moved about Stephen's Green, the place of assembly, helping to get the contingents into their rightful positions, his heart aglow with the colour and the life and the beating of victorious drums. Stewards, on foot and on bicycles, were rushing hither and thither, receiving instructions from Sean T. O'Kelly, a curious, quiet little figure with a calmly querulous voice, provoking embarrassment in Sean to see him among the old and new fluttering symbols of an awakened people, and he tricked out in a glossy black frock-coat, striped trousers, with a glittering top-hat on his head, the new Irish round and top of sovereignty.

Curious, isn't it, thought Sean, to see the broad blue arm-band, with Ard Mhaoir, High Steward, in gold lettering on the dark sleeve of a frock-coat? Didn't seem right. At first he thought he was dreaming; but sorra a dream it was. He noticed, too, that those already marshalled didn't like their eyes to fall on the frock-coated figure, and when they accidentally did, they turned them away at once, full of embarrassment, bewilderment, and wonder. But Shawn Tee went about his business as Head Steward as if God had created him in a frock-coat, in top-hat created He him.

—Eh, Sean, whispered the tram conductor, holding Sean by the skirt of his coat, looka that fella doin' the big with the top-hat an' frock-coat! Where did he break out from?

—Shush! said Sean. That's Shawn Tee O'Kelly, Chairman of the Gaelic League Dublin Committee and High Steward of today's gathering.

—It's queer, said the conductor, an' it gives me a pang to see th' like of that on a day like this. I see a glint of a thing here I don't like. It isn't natural. It's a dictum that's dangerous. It doesn't augur well for th' future. Sean, me son. Jasus! Looka what's comin' now!

Out of Dawson Street, into the gathering procession, surrounded by constables, came an open carriage, slowly, holding one man only, a man with raven-black hair and moustache decorating a ghastly, handsome white face, twitching convulsively with the fever of nervousness and wounded pride.

The frock-coat nodded the top-hat to the trumpeter of the day, the call sounded, and the procession was on the move. Some of the contingents had passed, when the police surged forward, breaking through the marchers, holding those behind in check till the movement of the front contingents allowed enough space for the carriage to swing into the procession, the ghastly white face of the alderman just visible through the crowd of surrounding helmets of the foot police who had mounted men prancing at each side of them, all of whom kept their eyes partly turned towards the ground, for they felt a loss of dignity by being forced to march in a procession unsanctified by Dublin Castle.

—Good God! ejaculated the conductor to Sean, is it going along we are in dumb denouncement with this Castle hack and his Castle cossacks! Didn't I tell you I didn't like the omen of the frock-coat and the top-hat? Are we goin' to let our solemn pageant of the past to be inlaid with the insult, an' drag it through a maze of sthreets to th' sound of pipe, drum, trumpet, an' clarinet, in th' midst of banners, plumes, badges, an' all manner of variegated testimonies of our hero-crowded histhory?

There was a curious hush all along those parts of the procession following, and going before, the alderman's landau and the constables. There wasn't a murmur from those in the procession or from those gathered along the sidewalk as the marchers moved by, only the tramp-tramp-tramp of feet, from which came a vision of many helmets, and now and again a glimpse of the dead-white face of the man sitting tense and bolt-upright in the carriage.

At the upper end of Grafton Street, close by the stone laid down years ago that some day was to blossom into a Wolfe Tone memorial, the uneasy landau suddenly halted; the crowds on the sidewalks fell back, for a thick column of hurlers were standing before the carriage, halting it, and those in the procession behind it, right before the great banner saying

Start not, Irish-born man, if you're to Ireland true,
We heed not creed nor class nor clan, we've hearts and hands for
* you,*

while the advanced part of the procession moved on some way to give the hurlers room to act. It was plain to all that Alderman J. J. Farrell wouldn't be let go farther on the way with advancing Ireland. It was plain, too, that the police were feeling uncomfortable. Hurleys were dangerous weapons: a quick upward jab of the boss would smash in the hardiest face; a low swing would shatter a leg-bone; and a downward swing would scatter the brains out of the fort of the sturdiest skull going – so the police were very uneasy. Those hurlers were tough guys, though some of them were civil servants, grocers, curates, schoolteachers, customs officers, solicitors' clerks, and a good many tougher ones from the farms, the railways, and the docks.

A police superintendent, dressing his face in a jocular smile, went up to the leader of the hurlers, and with a faint salute from a hand, elegantly gloved, said, We find ourselves, sir, in a very unfortunate and delicate situation, which, as you are aware, is none of our seeking. We are simply charged with the protection of a Dublin citizen who fancies himself threatened, and who insists on being allowed to participate in the public procession of a purely non-political organization; and who wishes, he says, by participation, to testify his approval of those sentiments embodied in the published aims and objects of the organization now quite legitimately and legally employed in their promotion in a most commendable manner, if you will allow me to say so; and it is very regrettable that circumstances have forced this unfortunate *contretemps* upon us both, though to you as a sensible man, and, evidently, groomed into responsibility of leading men, it must be apparent that I and my men are here but to carry out our duty; that no aggressive or provocative reason can be implied regarding our presence, and that we are here only to anticipate, and so prevent, a possible breach of the peace – ahem!

The hurlers' leader, with his stick on his shoulder, stood like a stock till the officer had ended his passionless speech, looking him fairly in the eyes; then he answered him never a word, but stepped past him through the police cordon to stand close to the open landau, where he stretched forth his right arm towards a side street, opposite to the direction the procession was taking, and said in a deadly and very clear voice to the quivering man in the carriage, That is your way, that way is your way; Ireland casts you out of her sight; Ireland casts you out of her possessions; that way is your way – go!

There was a silent few moments in which could be heard the panting heart of the frightened man, paler than ever now, with a look of timid hatred glaring in his black eyes; then the driver of the landau bent backwards from his seat, his face, too, getting haggard with anxiety, to whisper to the lonely shaking soul, tense on the blue-cushioned seat, Ara, take th' advice of a thrue man, sir, and slip out of all this savage hilarity, an' show be your ready an' dignified departure that you refuse to cock

them up with your civilized attendance. Give a cheery back of
your hand to them, man, or it's a tangled mesh of blood an'
bone we'll all be before th' day ripens into another hour!

Again the hurlers' leader stretched his arm in the direction of
the side street, and said quietly and in a clear voice, That is your
way, and the way of your Dublin Castle consorts!

In the shimmer of the sunlight the darkly-uniformed police
stood motionless, listening to nothing, but hearing all, their eyes
watching their superintendent; his eyes watching the hurler; all
calm, looking unconcerned, but constantly taking the measure
of the hurling men, and wondering how sinewy the arms were
hidden under the coloured jerseys; and, occasionally, Sean saw a
furtive hand go up to press a helmet deeper down over a vul-
nerable and anxious skull; while the superintendent stood there,
silent, watching, an uneasy smile on his rather handsome face, a
daintily-gloved hand flicking another glove against the palm of a
bare one.

The driver stretched himself farther back from the high seat in
front, getting his top-hatted head as close as he could to the
twitching face of the alderman, to say, I don't want to push me
words into your federated understandin', sir, but, looka, sir,
you're only riskin' your life an' limb without rhyme or reason.
What is it but only an as I roved out of a show, adultered cleverly
with a few drum-beats an' a canopy o' coloured banners! Say th'
word, an' be turnin' th' horse's head you can escape into a sensible an' sober world. Say th' word, sir, an' we'll be off outa this
panicky pomp; a nod, now, an' we'll baffle them outa th' row
they're seekin'. That's th' ticket, sir, he added joyously as the
alderman gave a faint nod towards the side street, as he tightened
his grasp of the reins. Get outa th' way, there, you! he bawled at
the hurler, turning his horse in a curvetting semicircle; with the
police dodging their big feet from the crunching wheels, he slid
the landau into the side street and went away at a quarter-gallop,
the constables trotting alongside, with the superintendent
hurrying after on the sidewalk in as dignified a way as the speed
allowed him. At a command from their leader, the hurlers swung
into the side street too, facing after the disappearing carriage. The
leader raised a hand; with a roll of drums, a band broke into the
swing of *Clare's Dragoons*, and the procession of Ireland's
history and resolution moved forward again, having purged itself
of a murky, stinging stain.

Here comes the carriages holding the neatly-clad forms, trim beards, set faces, sober-hatted, silently-jubilant, respectomissima members of the Gaelic League's Central Executive, the Coiste Gnotha, their whole demeanour making all men aware of their non-political, non-sectarian natures, each bluffed out with a pride of his own, for the money the crowd was giving was rattling into the collecting-boxes, the chink-chink of the falling coins loud above the methodical medley of the rolling drums.

In a leading carriage rode Dr Douglas de Hyde, with a pleasant little branch of bells in his hand, and a barr buadh a thousand times the size of a bucina on his lap, and he looking, in his innocent happiness, like a bigger Boy Blew. By his side sat a mauve-soutaned, crimson-girdled domestic prelate of the Vatican, who laughed, and slapped the Doctor affectionately on the back all the way along, calling him a jolly good fellow, and appealing for confirmation from a tinker and a flapper fairy who sat on the opposite seat. Beside them, on a prancing white horse, went Oona ni Merrily, with rings on her fingers and bells on her toes, followed by Mary ni Hayadawn, in a pony and trap, her tender voice ever calling on the Irish people to come to these yellow, white, and green sands, catch hands, and sing, The cuckoolin is icumen in in Gaedhilge. Next came the biggest carriage Dublin could supply. In it were two men, the sweat rolling off them, counting the money the collectors were pouring in on to the floor of the vehicle, with Stiffun Barrett, the official treasurer, holding an umbrella over them to keep the sun off their heads so that they could count calmly an tawn bo cooly. Then came Eoin Mac Neill aswing in a sedan-chair, carried by an Ulster man, Connaught man, Leinster man, and a Munster man, one at each corner. The grille in front of the chair was closed to keep the sun out, the panels were decorated with a profusion of higheroglyphical reports from the annals of the four musters, and a placard on each door-panel warned all whom it would concern to open the door softly. The next carriage held Edward Martyn, and a great banner went before it having on it, in mighty letters, the Martyn motto of I Am in My Sleep, and Don't Waken Me. Trudging along in a wide space by himself came Padruig Mac Pirais, head down, dreaming a reborn glory for Ireland in every street-stone his foot touched; followed by vis-à-vis, landau, brougham, and victoria, containing the rest of the Central Executive, sleek and sleepy-looking, crooning quietly to themselves, We are all nodding, nod, nod, nodding; we are all nodding, so Irish and so fey!

Oh! here we are now! Here he comes; here's the boyo, the greatest champion Ireland's language has, who hardly know a word of it himself: make way there, yous, keep back, keep back, give him space there, the one who said tin-pike men and hillmen should be clapped into jail to keep them out of mischief; who says that the influence of England's majesty shouldn't be left to Protestant sourfaces, and that the Catholics must collar the King; an eminent man, a sure sage, with almost all the priests applaudin', make way, there – silence!

Here he comes, D. P. Moran, editor of *The Leader*, in a vis-à-vis, the name of the paper on a big poster pasted round the tall-hat of the driver. Here's the champion of that Catholic Association, formed to link up in a commercial and industrial Sacred Heart Sodality for all the middle-class Catholics who had been blessed by God with the responsibility of a cheque-book so that they might go down the commercial and industrial giving-glory-to-God-in-the-highest Protestants who, too, had been blessed with the responsibility of other cheque-books. Sir Gaelahad Moran had gone forth to the battle with his lance of L S Defender of the Faith, with his shield of four beautiful green fields, with the coins of the realm, proper, superimposed on a Roman cross, gules, under the motto of *In hoc signum pinchit*. But Moran was worsted in the fight, and had to flee from the field, leaving the Protestants to give thanks to God in a special doxology for their deliverance.

D. P. Moran, proud on his seat in the vis-à-vis, wore a sober suit of Irish tweed, his head was nicely crowned in a bowler hat, and a poplin tie of a dark green gave a gayer note to his sensible austerity that went well with the look of determined wisdom on his plumpish face. On the seat opposite sat a man, crowned, too, with a bowler hat, who was nursing a Brian Boru harp on his knee, along which his agile fingers twinkled up and down the silver strings, Moran trying to appear as if he were listening to the one and only harp that once through Tara's hall was heard, now evoking again the pride of former days, that glory's thrill was felt once more, and hearts again beat high with hope, and felt that pulse encore. Fine he looked, sunk deep down into the blue cushions of the carriage, and all was sunny and all was sure, and all was happy and all was pure.

Suddenly, from the faery Land of Erewhon, appeared the damned hurlers again, who, at a sign from the leader, caught the bridle of the carriage's horse, and took it with such a sweep from the moving procession that no hesitating halt of a moment was made by the marchers, hardly half a hundred of them knowing that D. P. Moran had been juggled from their midst out of the pomp and all the glory, and but a few saw the bowler hats sticking up from the bowl of the carriage fading away down a side street, surrounded by the silent hurling men, a faint ting-a-ling-a-ling-ting of *Brian Boru's March* stealing faintly back to them as they went marching along.

So the drums rolled, the bugles blew, the banners waved as Ireland's history and Ireland's hope went along College Green, defiantly passing Trinity College with the head up and a battling swing of the shoulders; the rolling drums shaking the doors and rattling the windows of big banks, brokers' premises, insurance offices, business houses, high-class drapery, shoe, and jewellery shops, and Court photographers, all shuttered tight, and silently contemptuous of all the stir and tremble parading before them all today; opulently careless of the power germinal that thrilled the sunny air with drum-beat and bugle-call.

In that same hour, or maybe an hour or two after, the city was draped again in the colours of excitement and bristling fervour, for Dr Douglas Hyde was off to the United States to tell the great news to Texas, Arizona, Washington, DC, the two Carolinas, Virginia, Pennsylvania, New York, Salt Lake City, and, especially, that great community, happy and prosperous, who lived in a wide district called Tuxedos, the place of the elegant evening-coats, where the Doctor was to tell of Ireland's honour, nobility, and undying devotion to her ancient language; but, above all, to rake in the needful, argent and or, at all costs. The hurlers of Sean's club were chosen to be the bodyguard around the coach bearing him to Kingsbridge Station, *en route* for Cove in Cork, and thence across the Atlantic to the broad bosom of the sea-divided Gael. And so Sean, in full dress of the club's jersey, of hooped bands of alternate dark blue and dark green, walked beside the Protestant Chief of the Gael, in the midst of thousands of flaming torches carried before and behind the carriage, fol-lowed by all the hurling and football clubs of the city and its suburbs. Horsemen headed the cavalcade, carrying the Stars and Stripes, the French Tricolour, and the green banner of popular Ireland; for then the green, white, and orange symbol was known only to the members of the Irish Republican Brotherhood and their few friends. Everywhere the drums beat again their lusty rolls, making the bright stars in the sky quiver, and bands blew Ireland's past into every ear, and called forth her history of the future.

—A great man an' a fine soul he is, be God! said a hurler next to Sean. He could have papered the walls of Castle Hyde with the addhresses he got at th' Gresham Hotel before he left. Were you listening to what he said? The Gaelic League, says he, is a strictly non-political organization, and so it is the strongest political party in Ireland! Did the world ever hear a grander sayin'? I'm tellin' you, it's himself that'll make the stir for Eireann in the New Island! An Hideach abu!

On we all went slow along the mean-looking flanks of Anna Livia Plurabelle singing songs of Eireby by the dozen that would rouse up even the stone outside Dan Murphy's door. But when we came to the station, lo and behold, there was a crowd of police barring the way in to the station platform. Were we downhearted? No! So, with a roar of, Shoulder to shoulder, Gaels! the hurlers and footballers, forming a phalanx, rushed forward, swept the horde of constables off their feet, and after a few breathless moments Sean, standing beside Donal Mac Rory O'Murachadha, was beside the edge of the platform in front of a great cheering crowd.

There was the big beaming face of Hyde, topped by the globular skull, with the bushy moustache like an abandoned bird's nest, filling up a carriage window, nodding, nodding to the excited crowd, while a band outside played *When shall the day break in Eirinn* with extreme dignity and unction.

—A bit of an oul' cod, the same Hyde, whispered Donal, nudging Sean to take notice. Look at him: oh, wouldn't he like to number on the Coiste Gnotha a few dukes, earls, viscounts, barons, and a host of right honourables! For the people, maybe; with the people, maybe; but not of the people. The Fenian Brotherhood waste their time trying to trick him into being a revolutionary even for an hour. Jasus! Listen to his Deunta in Eirinn Irish! Harsh as the crow of a worn-out old cock. Listen to Father O'Leary, and then listen to him. It doesn't come natural to the poor man, and I'm afraid it never will. He couldn't be an O'Rahaille, a Donnchadh Ruadh Macnamara, or even a Colm

Wallis if he lived to a hundred. Look at him, with his arm nearly round Father O'Franticain's neck! Isn't he the one that's at home with the clergy!

—But, Donal, isn't he the one who pulled the Irish language out of the gutter and set it in the sky – a star again?

—He pinned it to the wall of a New University – or rather Hickey did – so that it could blink through the windows of Trinity College; but to set it in the sky, Sean, it's not in him to do it. That can be done only by the power and will of a free people, and your grand, gusty-mannered Hyde will always prefer having a shot at a snipe than having a shot at a Saxon.

Sean was shocked that any Gael should speak this drab way about such a man as Hyde. He couldn't understand it.

—Oh, be fair, Donal, he said. At least remember what Hyde has done as a poet in the creation of an Irish literature.

—He has created nothing in Irish literature, said Donal tersely, and he isn't, and never was, a poet. As an editor of what others greater than he has done, I'll grant you he's a pleasant and encouraging echo; then he cleans the dust of indifference from many a star; but when he signs himself, he coaxes no music into his song. Look, there! He's waving a last farewell!

The guard's green flag was waving, the engine gave a few steamy snorts, strained at the carriages, and began to slide out of the station through a storm of cheers. Hyde was high on Ireland's shoulders, and his carriage window framed the big head, the bunchy moustache, the staring eyes, draining down the last drop of the mighty farewell and godspeed, till distance hid the crowd, and stilled the stormy, sweltering roar of the gathered Gaels.

SONG OF A SHIFT

IRELAND HAD become again the Woeman of the Piercing Wail. Every wall in Dublin was a wall of weeping. Cork ran a high fever of hatred, and Galway was foaming at the mouth; Limerick was just lying down prostrate. It was awful, for the piercing wail sent flying the wild duck from the marsh, the wild goose from the bog, and the wild swan from the lake; away frantic the lot of them flew, far to the banks of the Nile, the rushes of the Euphrates, and the snows of the North Pole. It was awful, for the Virgin statues in every niche lifted their blue or crimson alabaster petticoats over their heads to hide their shame, to cover their ears, while they wept no end. It was an outrage on their innocence, their quietude, and their breathless adoration. Statues of the Holy Fathers, Martyred Bishops and Martyred Matrons, and all the golden crowd of blessed saints, strained at their clay stands, trying to lep off to Rome for a bull of excommunication against those who had stained their sense of decorum with a wild defilement. Regular Orders and Simple Ones in the Order of St Peter ran this way and that, and Father Malone lost his new Sunday hat, calling on all the fightful – and they were many, only a little less than the sands of the sea for number – to denounce and dismember, disjoint and distender, this sable-faced, lying offender, fresh, pagan-souled culture, decay in its heart, mocking all the eternities at home with our people. The streets were a thunder of boots running swiftly in and out again, vast brotherhoods, and sisterhoods too, from the east to the west, from the north to the south; Ulster men, Connaught men, Leinster men, Munster men, true-hearted Irishmen, Irishmen all, rallied round the standard of purity, led by the Vigilance Committee, led by Father Malone, led by Monsignor Malone, led by the Right Reverend John, Bishop Malone, hurried in haste to assemble and deny and assert and condemn and support the things said by Father Malone and Monsignor Malone and the Bishop Malone about this grievous and insulting thing that had hopped in among them silently, and without warning, or a second's preparation, threatening to do in an hour, or at most in a day and a half, what the British Government had failed to do in the last seven hundred years and a half, since Easter was a week old.

Hearing the alarums, the sound of the sennets, the mighty tramp of human feet in the distance, wondering a lot and frightened a little, the Viceroy poked his head out of a top window of the Viceregal Lodge and looked down on the stout police sergeant standing on the lawn below, his ear cocked towards where the noise came from.

—What's happening? who's making all that noise – d'ye hear me, you down there?

—Divil a know, sir, I know, sir.

—Well, y'ought to know. What are you fed for? No, don't

stir. Stay put. Keep your baton nice and loose. Something serious is happening.

—Be th' sound of it, I'd say, sir, the same, sir. More in it than maybe we know, sir.

—We don't know anything, man, said the Viceroy peevishly. Are all the rest of the boys on the key veev?

The answer of yessir was almost lost in the distant rumble of running feet, rising to the sound of surly thunder, and the shouting grew into a storm of anger like a forest of wild beasts growling together.

—What is it they are shouting? said the Viceroy, his face whitening. Don't you know? can't you hear, man?

—Seems like something like sing, sir.

—Like what? sing who; sing what; sing where? Be a little more explicit, Sergeant.

Yeats!

—What's that now? Didn't you hear? Weren't you listening? Don't you realize this may mean the calling-out of the military? Sounds as if they were having another fight, doesn't it?

—I wouldn't like to say yes, sir, an' daren't venture to say no, sir.

—They're not coming in this direction, are they, d'ye think, Sergeant?

—I darn't venture to say no, sir, and I wouldn't care to say yes, sir.

—Well, you gobeen, venture down to the bend of the road and find out what it's all about – quick!

The Viceroy stretched from the window to watch the stout sergeant running hard and stiff down the road, through the sad and soaking grass, by the bare beech trees, till he was lost beyond the bend of the road; then his wondering eyes turned to where the shouting came from, and where a cloud of dust showed the anger of it. And here was the big thick of a policeman back again, puffing as if his last breath was leaving him.

—Well, he asked, is it peace or war, or what?

—I dunno right, sir, for all I met wouldn't wait to tell; but one of them said that if only his fist ever comes within reach of some Yeats' bake, he'd give him a homer, an' all I could get out of th' others was a shout of sing and a shout of shift, or something.

—Shift? Shift what? shift who? shift where? Is it making fun of me you are, man, or what?

—Wait a minute, sir; can't you listen, sir? Wait till I tell you – a woman said he was a kind of poet.

—Who did she say was a kind of poet?

—Shift or sing or someone, sir; I dunno which; and they said they'd hang him on a sour apple three, sir.

—Hang who? hang what, man?

—Shift or sing or someone – I dunno right, sir.

—What nonsense are you talking? You dunno! Why would they want to hang a shift on a sour apple tree?

—Ara, how th' hell do I know? Aren't they up to any divilment when they're in the mood!

—Is there a constable behind every bush, Sergeant, as per the orders of the day? asked the Viceroy briskly.

—Oh, be God, ay, sir; behind every respectably-sized bush there's a constable concealed an' crouchin'.

—Yes, yes, said the Viceroy testily; but are they awake, on the alert, and lively?

—Ready to dive on disordher, sir, th' way a dhrone would dive on a queen bee.

—Keep them so, Sergeant. I'm going to bed now, and don't call me if anything happens; and he closed the window with a bang and shot the socket home, for one couldn't be too careful.

Sean found himself in the midst of bawling clergy, professors and students of Cork, Dublin, and Galway colleges, thousands of sacred confraternities, wide-minded boyos of the Catholic Young Men's Association, the boys of Kilkenny and the boys of Wexford, side-car drivers and cabmen of the Anti-taxi Association, brimming with zeal for Ireland's holy reputation.

Puzzled and bewildered, he was pushed here and pushed there by Muldoon and the Solid Man, the Men of the West, Ireland's gallant hurling men, and Gaelic Leaguers foaming at the mouth, all shouting

Shift!

Jostled he was by Mary of Argyle, Mother mo Chree, Willie Reilly and his colleen bawn, several fine old English gentlemen with hearts of oak, a soldier and a man, the little Alabama coon, Uncle Jefferson with his gal, a high-born lady, Dolly Gray and Sweet Marie, all yelling

Shift!

Shoved hither and thither he was by Shamus O'Brien, Kelly and Burke and Shea, Clare's dragoons, Lesbia with her beaming eye, the Exile of Erin, the Lily of Killarney, Slattery's mounted fut, Father O'Flynn, the Rose of Tralee, the Athlone landlady, Eileen Allanna with Eileen Aroon, the man who struck O'Hara, Nell Flaherty's drake, Daisy Bell arm in arm with Thora, the man who broke the bank at Monte Carlo, Kitty of Coleraine with the two little girls in blue, their hearts bowed down with weight of woe, but still keeping their tails up, all of them shrieking Shift!

Sean sturdily elbowed his way from the crowd to where the Poor Old Woman was standing by the kerb. He gripped her gently by the thin old arm, asking, What's it all about, mother?

—What's what all about, me son? she asked wonderingly, after letting a yell out of her that sent a quiver down Sean's spine.

—All this coarse shouting in the heart of the city's streets; all this running about of many hot and hasty feet?

—Aw, sorra know I know, son, what it's about. It's no new thing to see them runnin' round an' yellin' for they know not what.

—But you're running round and yelling with the rest of them yourself.

—An' if I am aself, what signifies? D'ye want me to be th' one odd outa th' many? It's a bit o' fun anyhow. She caught her poor thin skirt up in her poor thin hands, and caracoled along, shouting, The dirty-minded minstrels! Belchin' out in th' sthricken faces of our year in an' year out innocence things no decent-minded individual would whisper even into his own ear! Why don't they tell us of the beautiful things we all love so well, th' dirty, dirty bastards!

Leaving her mouthing, Sean hurried to catch up with Muldoon the Solid Man, and taking him by the plump arm, asked, Who are those there in fine array on the top of Nelson's Pillar, and who is he with the domy brow, clad in the coloured gown and black cap of some ancient and learned university, whose voice is pealing out over the green hills of holy old Ireland?

Muldoon the Solid Man looked up, looked long, caught Sean's arm, and dragged him from the crowded shouting thoroughfare into a quieter side street.

—Didn't you know who that was? He bent down and brought his fat whiskered face close to Sean's, and went on, hoarsely,

That's the greatest mind Ireland has today; though goin' back to Mount Sinai, fresh as a daisy still. Defender Fido Finnigan. Whisht, he's speakin'. Hush, silence there, th' whole o' yous, an' listen to his tale of woe! Ah, me sweet Mcgennis, a herald angel in a cap an' gown! Are yous all afther hearin' what he's afther sayin'? Help o' sinners! No sittin' on a stile for him. Up on one o' th' seven pillars o' wisdom, sayin', proclaimin', *Declanda est syngestoria et defendi senserationem Hibernicombactoerin*. Ah, me sweet yourself! Th' *vox Magennicensorensis* is a *vox pupuli*. Him an' his disciples'll sweep the counthry clean. There they are backin' him up: Coffey, with his old coat and the light of other days around him; Fearon, wrapped in the ould plaid shawl, sitting in mother's old armchair; Camac and Williams with letters afther their names; and Conn the Shaughraun, Arra-na-pogue, the minsthrel boy home from the wars, Joxer Daly, Maisie Madigan, impudent Barney O'Hea, the village black-smith in his Sunday best, Roddy the Rover, Louis J. Walsh, the Brehon, with the eloquent L. C. Dempsey, Mick McQuaid and Kit Kulkin, rowled in the seven howly ordhers, Miles-na-Copa-leen, Edward Martyn, and the Pope's brass band, all set to uproot with agitated, holy fingers every *harum maculatum* that tried to grow in the country. Ah, me pet, me choice, me soul-man, me sweet Mcgennis, Ireland's Saturday night's saviour, sure hell shivers with cold when it hears you speakin'! And Muldoon the Solid Man fell on his knees to offer up prayer on prayer for the repose of the souls of those poor Irish who had passed away before Mcgennis came.

So, unable to get more out of him, Sean hurried off to his branch of the Gaelic League where he was Secretary, teacher, and charwoman, coming early on class nights to clean the place up, light the fire, get out the books, and arrange the blackboard. He would find out there the cause of this great cry of Shift, and why the city was aflame with the thoughts of holy reprobation. When he got there, there was a great crowd waiting for him to open the door, all tense and talkative with indignation. There was his friend, the tram conductor, fretting, and forcing words of wrath on all who listened.

—Some blasted little theatre or other has put on a play by a fellow named Singe or Sinje or something, a terrible play, helped by another boyo named Yeats or Bates or something, said to be a kind of a poet or something, of things no one can understand, an' he was to blame for it all, assisted be some oul' one or another named Beggory or something, who was behind the scene eggin' them on in their foul infamity. A terrible play, terrible! There was ructions in the theatre when th' poor people staggered into the knowledge of what was bein' said! What was th' play about? Amn't I after tellin' you it was a terrible thing; a woeful, wanton play; bittherin', bittherin', th'n, th'n th' bittherest thing th' bittherest enemy of Ireland could say agin' her!

—Ordher! shouted Sean, thumping his fist on the table. Sit down, and let one at a time speak. Now what did this man say in his play to soil and censure Ireland?

—Listen, Sean, said the conductor hotly, I don't know what he said in th' play, an' I don't care; but anyone'll tell you he made a go at every decent consignment left living in th' counthry. With purpling face, he lifted his voice to shout, I tell you th' Abbey Theatre'll have to be torn down stone be stone, if it's built of that, an' brick be brick, if it's made o' that, without warnin', before one of us snatches another second's sleep!

—Ordher, ordher! shouted Sean, till we get this thing clear and straight for a fair judgement. Now where is this theatre you are yelling about?

—Didn't I tell you before I didn't know where it was, except it's somewhere near th' Liffey. For myself, I never clapped eyes on it, thank God, an' never heard of it till this outrage was flung into the face of modesty-honourin' Ireland. Where is it, is it? Stuck in some peculiar place, I'll go bail.

—Well, who is this Singe or Sinje, or whatever his name may be, and where does he come from?

—There'll be desperate work done if they don't stop this thing, shouted a member standing beside the door, if they don't banish this black thing from before our smilin' Irish eyes for ever! We don't know who this Sinje is; some foreigner paid to say th' things he said.

—And what did he say exactly? asked Sean.

—It not a matther of what he said, but of what everybody says he said, growled a voice from the right corner of the room.

—Let's get this discussion goin' in ordher, said a tall bearded man whose left leg had been crippled by an attack of Skyatica, an' pass our opinions with decorum. I propose that Aloysius McClonkey, PLG, take the chair, as this is an occasion at which

the virtue of Ireland is at question; no fitter man could be head
of the meeting, for he is specially endowed to warn us, advise
us, and invoke our antagonism to our pitiless enemies, having
each year, in wind, rain, frost, snow, thunder and lightning,
climbed, bareheaded and barefooted, up the rough, flinty ways
of Croagh Pathrick, Ireland's holy mountain, with but a bite of
coarse bread in a hip-pocket to keep life from leavin' him;
sayin' paternosters an' ave marias in thousands, head bent
down, or head held up; takin' off his trousers when he got within
a mile of the top, th' wind blowin' through his thin cotton shirt,
devastating all th' parts that modesty keeps covered, so that when
he got to where th' real devotion started, he was only fit to think
of th' three last things, death, judgement, an' Hell, open for
sinners, shiverin' away from all thought of earthly things, fires,
hot soups, balls o' malt, mulled porther, or th' hot presence of a
desire for a woman, so that his groans could be heard all over the
fields of sweet Mayo, shaking the little houses in Connemara, and
waking up the deep sleepers in the house of the square of Galway
with his singing of Oh day of mourning, see fulfilled the prophets'
warning, Heaven an' earth to cash is burning. Who then could
be better adopted to enunciate the way we are to think in this
great world crisis, and tell how to overcome this threat to all
near and dear and clear to us, by these vultures, these waggas
sagas, who scent out and feed gluttonously on corruption of
mind and morals; these waggas sagas who rave in a row and
jabber in a chorus about freedom of self-expression and art for
art's sake: so says the *Irish Rosary*, a magazine pregnant with the
grace of God, with knowledge, and with good feeling to all
men. I call on Aloysius McConkey, our learned and beloved
poor-law guardian, to tell us how to comport ourselves in the
fight against this Synge or Sinje, about whom, thank God, we
know next to nothing.

A little old man, oh, so old, a hundred and more if all was told,
was carried up to the head of the hall and gently set down into
the chair. His face was the colour of a shrivelled and well-faded
lemon. His little eyes saw no more than the shadows of men, and
his ears heard little more than a misty memory droning a last
lullaby. He rapped his bony knuckles on the table, and his
squeaky voice mumbled, Now boys an' girls, be quiet till I tell
yous, for I'm really here as a delicate delegate of the Young
Men's Catholic Christian Cross Association—

—Who kept his bloody public-house open on St Pathrick's Day? shouted a voice from the hall's centre.

—Ordher, ordher, there! shouted the bearded man. No politics, no politics!

—Never mind, went on the poor old man, bouseys will be bouseys. Well, as I was sayin' – what was I sayin'? Aw, yes: I was asked to speak to this Rich and Rare Branch of the League to put before yous the exthreme case of necessity of doin' something, all we can, what we must, if we're to be loyal to the principles of faith, hope, an' charity, here and now, without hesitation, not countin' the cost, takin' the blame, full-hearted, steady-willed, and clear-minded men, firmly resolved to counter with all our energy, force, an' world-renowned Irish courage, famous from Dunkirk to Belgrade; an' always an' ever prepared to face fearlessly the enemies at home and abroad, who sedulously, seditiously, and seductively endeavour, be night an' be day, to asperse, slandher, and generally defame that honour and fair pride and sweet modesty, thriple stars of effulgent illuminants shining from the forehead of Cathleen ni Houlihan; so, having said so much in explanation of the why, the wherefore, and the wherewithal for which we have come together, as thrue Gaels should, and do, and must, proceed to banish from our virgin verdant shores the anglis in herba that have crawled from the Keltic Twilight, when no one was lookin', to spit from the air their venom into our enchanted eyes intent on gazin' up to where Gabriel, no, no, Michael, slew, no, no, overthrew th' dragon, the father of lies, enemy implacable of Eve's poor children, lost so long, asthray so often, an' flung them, no, no, him, into the outer darkness from which there is no returning, and no hope; so now that you all understand the thrue position, and are primed with the knowledge of what is, and of what is to be, I declare this meeting open—

—Who kept his bloody public-house open on St Patrick's Day? shouted a voice from the back of the hall.

—Their myrmidians are even here, the old man went on, but we'll shift – I refuse to say shift, for we are here to shift the word shift from lips and ears of decent people – we'll remove them as we'll remove the others. Now I call on a member to voice in a resolution the irrevocable determination of all assembled to condemn, from first to last, the terrible things said be, be, what's-his-name, though it doesn't matter much, not at all, in face of the desperate audacity of what has been done to knock about our world-admitted sanctity, exemplified in the one fact that an hour ago today I and my donah celebrated our diamond wedding in the Church of the Twelve Pathrons, so that me and my wife, Jemima Mary Jane, being the proud parents of twenty-five children, two hundred and eleven grandchildren, and one hundred and twenty-nine great-grandchildren, making a great grand-total of three hundred and sixty-five souls, having body, shape, substance, and feeling, movement, density, and opacity, mingling with time, and measured in space, enjoying, without any speed limit, a gay and delectable journey towards ethernity, declare that we shall end for ever this feast of horror, indecency, blasphemy, and smut.

The bearded man lepped up on his sound leg and shouted, Let's get this thing goin' without any more waste o' words, for God's sake! I propose the followin' resolution, that this Rich an' Rare Branch of the Gaelic League—

—Who dhraws the rents from th' houses of the whores of Montgomery Street? shouted a voice at the window.

—For pity's sake, whimpered the wizened old man, let's have unity in the face of a common enemy. Can't we remember, he added imploringly, how Father Guffney reminded us that we are a noble people in a noble movement, and mustn't let any low, sordid, or unsavoury thoughts into our elevated minds.

—Besides, it's a libel on the Irish Race, said a young man from Rathmines, and I protest, he went on roaring, I protest against this tirade of sulfurious infamity, for the fact is there isn't a single what-you-may-call-them from one end of holy Ireland to th' other!

—And whenever he draws his monthly salary, whispered Donal O'Murachadha, a boy from Tourmakeady, he makes straight to where the ladies are.

—Remember, will yous, what Mcgennis says about the ten commandments! whined out the old man in the chair. Will you move your resolution, an' be done with it, man, he said to the bearded one.

—I propose the following resolution, again went on the bearded man, that we, unitedly, of this Rich and Rare Branch, in ordhered assembly, do hereby, without any further posthurin' of words, or any additional *sine qua non*, declare, assert, assume, avow that this day forward we shall allow no maiden to wed, leave every harvest unreaped, every eye unshut, every mouth unopened, every ear cocked, till this vile thing is driven from the Abbey stage, from our dear city, from our verdant shore for ever, immediately, and as quick as circumstances will allow; acting according to, and always within, the canons, rules, and counsels of the astute and solicitudinizing bishops of the Church, so that those refusin' to keep step with the pilgrims on the march to Heaven may be set aside, so that we may go forward, like Christian soldiers, canons to the right of us, canons to the left of us, volleyin' an' thunderin' out th' thruth, led be Roddy the Prover surrounded by a steel-clod cohort of Holy Romans that came, in the long ago, in a ship that sailed too soon, singing his Romewards song, chirping away though pushed about by the Irish Press; seeking the hidden Ireland, even at the canon's mouth, ready to defend the faith of our fathers in rant and rhyme, against the culture taking delight in obscene literature or stage blastphemy; the relics of oul' dacency under his arm in a silver box made to the pattern of St Patrick's bell, and he smoking a cigar presented by Professor Tim, an' leaning on a walking-stick made from the wood of a tree from Mr Tchehkov's cherry orchard that he had cut down because it was poisoning the fresher fruits of Ireland; Nell Flaherty's drake as sign on his shield – a guyde to us all, he marches, and we march with him, *in signia sommnia, dimnia, domnia*, amen; and he sat down, exhausted.

—I beg to second that sound resoluton, Sir Chairman, said a pretty girl on a front bench, and to regesther me own personal abhorrence of these people's poisonous approach to the dauntlessly chaste womanhood of Ireland; for the world knows, and I speak here hyperbolically of course, that wings grow from the shoulders of every thrue Irish lady.

—All in favour say ay, said the chairman sleepily, an' hurry up, for I've got to go to bed.

—Before we move to denial, said Sean, let's know what the man has said.

—I don't think a thrue Irishman should ask such a question, said the bearded man hotly, seeing what's bound to be imbedded in th' answer given. There are pure-minded, innocent girls at this meeting.

—As a writer, and as the Lad from Largymore, said a wild-looking young man with long black hair trickling into his eyes,

a flowing black bow, and a wide-brimmed black hat on his head –
One o' th' ones who copy Yeats, whispered O'Murachadha –
I move we move that ye move the resolution without further delay.
Isn't it enough that our priests have said the thing is to be con-
demned holus-bolus, *in toto*, without reservation, and aren't they
supported by Up Griffith, Up Thomas Davis and the valiant
D. P. Moran, editor of *The Leader*. We condemn Synge and all
the works and vanities of his Abbey Theatre.

—Wait a second, fiercely spoke up the O'Murachadha, his
tawny moustache flapping like a banner. We are Gaelic Leaguers,
and as such owe no silent reception to what the priests or the
politicians say. Let's hear, and then judge for ourselves.

A few stalwart members pulled the old man to his feet, and
for a time he swayed about, pale with the terror of what he had
to say; but gripping the table as strongly as he could with his
bony hands, he opened his pallid lips to say, as a delicate delegate from the Young Men's Catholic Association of the Cross, I
burn with shame at the job I have to do. In this play of Synge's,
about the middle of it, before everyone, mind you, without
puttin' cap or cloak on it, the principal character shouts out the
word Shift!

—He said worse than that, if worse there could be, went on the
oh so old man; for he made out, I'm told – for mind you, I
wouldn't go near the place for love or money – he made out that
the blessed saints sthrained their necks to get an unholy glimpse
of the wanton Helen o' Throy, an' her sauntherin' round Heaven
with a nosegay in her golden shawl!

Within the frightened murmuring of the Miserere by most of
the members, the Lad from Largymore jumped to his feet,
foaming at the mouth, shouting, What more do we want to hear!
We'll make them feel the sacred animosity of Catholic Ireland, feel
it sharp an' sudden an' always! This pagan-minded, anti-Irish
ravisher of decency, Yeats and his crony Synge; ay, an' that oul'
hen behind them, Gregory, with her pro-British breedin' oozin'
out of everything she says an' does, must be taught a lesson!
This fella Yeats, in particular, with his ribboned eye-glasses, his
big-brimmed hat, his flowin' tie, this so-called poet who isn't a
poet at all, must be made to feel the force of our Catholic indignation!

The young man from Tourmakeady sprang to his feet, the red
glow of anger on his face, pouring out burning sentences in Irish

that no one, bar Sean, understood, then into a fierce flow of
English with, You stutterers in the life of Irish Ireland, what do
ye know about th' joys and perils of poetry! He who denies to
Yeats the name of a poet is a liar in his ignorance. You all
shouted another way when you listened to his Cathleen ni
Houlihan. No one has sung a finer song about Cathleen ni
Houlihan than Yeats; no one has fashioned her into a holier
symbol:

> The yellow pool has overflowed high up on Clooth-na-Bare,
> For the wet winds are blowing out of the clinging air;
> Like heavy flooded waters our bodies and our blood;
> But purer than a tall candle before the Holy Rood
> Is Cathleen, the daughter of Houlihan.

Let any of you do as good as that, and you can be licensed to yell
that not this man, but another, shall fill his place and guide us
where we want to go! Yeats is a flame in the sword of light, a
radiant wing on the shoulder of Aengus, a flash from the spear
of Lugh of the Long Hand, a banner of song in the midst of the
people!

—This is a Catholic counthry! shouted the bearded man, an'
we want no pagan symbols here.

—Didn't this same boyo write a play not long ago about an
Irish queen who bartered her soul for gold? queried the Lad from
Largymore, and didn't the great Cardinal Logue condemn the
thing without even havin' to read it by a snap of his ecclesiastical
finger an' thumb that sounded in a Catholic ear clear like a clap
o' thundher?

—Come on, Sean, exclaimed the young man from Tourmakeady, and let's get out of the crowd, for Christ's sake!
When they got to the door, he wheeled about to shout savagely,
Cardinal Logue! A big, stout, stupid, lumbering mind, more at
home with a dish of bacon and cabbage than with a book or a
play. But in a question of this kind, no cardinal, no, nor even
the Pope himself, with his counts, knights, chevaliers, and mon-
signors fifing and drumming behind him, will make me draw
back from a play they say should be banned, or a book they say
should be burned. To hell with yous that would burn a crimson
rose that had a spot of honest dust on it! And, followed by Sean,
he turned on his heel and hurried away. They hadn't gone far

when they heard the clatter of heavy boots running towards them, and soon the tram conductor was panting by their side.

—What yous two think, I think, he said, in the main; not altogether, mind you, but in th' main. The clergy were always in th' sthream of things goin' against Ireland. They fought men of Forty-eight, the Fenians, and then Parnell. I'm with yous right enough.

They journeyed down to where the Abbey Theatre was standing, surrounded by a multitude of people forcing themselves to hiss, blast, and boo the building. A tiny building for a theatre, thought Sean, two-storeyed, a circular-topped window on each side of a circular-topped door, and three narrow, oblong windows on the upper storey: a glass-roofed awning jutting from the main entrance over the pathway, and, between the storeys, THE ABBEY THEATRE in bold letters on a panel stretching from one end of the building to the other. The three of them went into a pub opposite and furnished themselves with a bottle of stout apiece.

—There'll be ructions here before the night is out, said the conductor.

—Let them rave, said O'Murachadha contemptuously; let them shake their throats into hoarseness till their raucous shouts smite the ears of the saints with a protective deafness.

But supposing, said Sean, a little ill at ease, that what this man said in his play was a deep and bitter insult to Ireland?

—Yeats will never let a thing be said that will be either a bad or bitther reproach to Ireland. He is one of Ireland's incantations, the Irish logos of the day, a singer of rare songs to Ireland's honour – Tara's harp is mute no longer, but the people are throwing dust on its golden sthrings.

—But, insisted Sean, it's said that this man is proud and pompous, ever standing stiff before an opinion other than his own, telling, like those cries that are as the clash of cymbals, that the voice of Yeats is the voice of God, and not that of the people.

—The voice of the people, Sean, is the voice of God when it shouts against oppression; it is the voice of ignorance when it shouts against a song. Yeats is proud, sometimes pompous; and his words at times are like sounding cymbals, but the cymbals are always silver, and his sensitive hands bring them together with great cunning. Listen! he went on loudly, turning to those

who were in the place, no shouting will frighten Yeats. Holding
his glass of stout high in the air he recited vehemently,

> *He who trembles before the flame and the flood,*
> *And th' wind that blows through the starry ways,*
> *Let the starry winds and the flame and the flood*
> *Cover over, and hide, for he has no part*
> *With th' lonely, majestical multitude.*

Listen! he cried, listen all of you – a toast to W. B. Yeats, Ireland's greatest poet; a mań, too. Fit to keep company with the
Shining Ones, Aengus, or Lugh of the Long Hand; fit to kiss
the cheek of Cathleen, the daughter of Houlihan: I dhrink to the
poet and the man! He drank till the glass was empty, and then
he flung it to the floor, smashing it into foamy fragments, and
no one murmured. Then they went out, and stood watching the
crowd swaying to the left and right, its spearhead swaying towards the theatre entrance. All those seen before were there
again, flooded now with those who had hurried from Lanigan's
Ball and Finnigan's Wake, all kinds, civil servants, clerks of all
kinds, schoolteachers, a few workmen of all trades, and many
woman, haggard and soiled, long shawls covering their jaded
skirts and blouses.

—Aha, said O'Murachadha, there's throuble inside too, for
from the entrance a young man, struggling in the arms of two big
policemen, was carried out, shoved headlong into the crowd with
a parting slap on the jaw from one of them, the two policemen
remaining at the entrance, grinning provokingly at the crowd.

—There he is! cried the man from Tourmakeady suddenly, pointing to a stately-looking man with long black hair, a lock of it half
covering an eye, who had come to the entrance, and, in the light
of a street lamp, stood looking dreamily at the agitated crowd.

—That's Yeats, Yeats the poet, the best poet Ireland has,
went on O'Murachadha in his impulsive Tourmakeady way. Oh,
me choice man chucked into an unharboured life of ignorance,
and a piety that makes a tabernacle of a till! Jasus, will you listen
to that! as a great cloud of booing gathered stormily round the
head of the wondering poet. There's th' voice of Ireland for you –
hoarse, hollow, and hasty, from the mouth of gobeens, sure anything they can't understand is smothered in the smoke of Hell!

—Oh, you're there, are you? screamed a fish-hawker when she

saw Yeats by the theatre door. An' proud yeh look, yeh long-haired throubler of decent people, fleerin' in ecstasy at every-thin' we hold to be holy, or that's sanctified be th' testimony of well-robed scholars, in writin' on scrolls no ordinary man can scan, held in awe be all th' scarlet-clad cardinals, walkin' wisely in th' sthreets of Rome. Pipe late, pipe early; pipe sad, pipe gay, you'll not pipe tauntin' tunes in th' holy city of ours. Learn to chant a tune we all understand, or you won't chant at all. Let me get a grip o' you till I sthrangle you with the ends of your own tie! Come out here an' I'll gut you th' way I'd gut a Liffey gurnet!

A policeman, pushing his way through the crowd, touched her on the shoulder and motioned her to go away. With a shrill, nervous laugh she jigged a way through the people, who made a wide path for her, singing as she danced a bawdy song to an air very like that of Whiskey Johnny.

The police manoeuvred the rest of the gathering away, and Sean O'Murachadha wandered to the quayside to lean over the parapet of Butt Bridge, and gaze up the river, going swiftly now to the sea, for the dark tide was ebbing. Sean wished he had seen Yeats' *Cathleen ni Houlihan*, so that he might know more about the man; but a shilling was too much for him to spare for a play. He wished he could see this play by Singe or Sinje, so that he might know more about him too. He lifted his eyes and saw in the distance the naked tremble of a leafless tree set dogged on the pavement, waiting for the spring. A gleaming star, low down in the sky, seemed to be entangled in its delicate higher branches: like Yeats and Ireland, thought Sean; Ireland, naked and quivering, waiting for the spring, and. the glittering poet caught in its branches.

—I'd dearly like to have a quiet talk with Yeats, murmured O'Murachadha, the young man from Tourmakeady.

LOST LEADER

SEAN WITH a group of comrades, all naked to the waist, was wiping the sweat off his steaming body after a rough and racy hurling match, each hurler criticizing the play of another, and grumbling that but for this or that hesitation the match would

have been won, and, at the end of the Hurling League, a gold
medal would hang from the watch-chain of any hurler having a
watch, when they caught sight of a comrade cycling furiously
over the sward towards them.

—Dhress yourselves! he shouted, while he was still pedalling;
dhress yourselves, an' quit arguin'. He flung himself from his
bicycle to run into their midst: Ireland calls again!

—She's always at it, grumbled a back, forcing a damp body
into his shirt; what th' hell's she want now?

—The Standing Committee of the Hierarchy in Maynooth has
declared against Irish as an essential subject in the New University; and we're all wanted for a meeting at once.

—The bishops again! growled a lusty forward. I guessed as
much, for they were always in Ireland's way when she went
forward. But let them look to themselves this time, for we are not
now what we once were; and raising his hurley over his head, he
shouted, Who's with Dr O'Hickey? Irish in the University – or
else! . . .

All their hurleys flew into the air, and all shouted together,
Irish in the University – or else! . . .

—There's more to come, said the cyclist excitedly. Wait till
I tell yous: Dr O'Hickey was summoned before the Committee,
ordhered to resign, and when he refused, was dismissed from his
Professorship of Irish in Maynooth College.

—They've gone a little too far this time, said the full-back
vehemently, raising his hurley again into the air; we fight till
Dr O'Hickey, deafened by Ireland's cheering, marches through a
lane of bowin' bishops, back to his Chair of Irish in Maynooth
College in the county of Kildare!

They all raised their hurleys together and shouted with one
voice, Irish in the University – or else! . . . O'Hickey abu!
Then they all hurried into their clothes, those who had bicycles
pedalling away, those who hadn't formed fours, and marched
down the Park road in quick-step time, to get the tram at the
gate and hurry to where they had been called.

Dr Douglas Hyde was going round and round, beseeching the
consent of the University's Senate to Irish becoming an essential
subject, Cardinal Lug, with a nod at O'Hickey, commending to
others the coy manner of Hyde's advocacy of the language,
worthy of a gentleman; while Eoin Mac Neill went another way,
lullabying his language so that a new-born lamb wouldn't hesitate

to nudge his knees. All this time the bishops were hitching up their chasubulleros bullen a laws to make short shrift of them, helped by their clerical coadjutants among the many curates looking to be parish priests, parish priests longing to be vicar-generals, many of these aiming at being bishops, and many a bishop believing the world well lost for a cardinal's hat. Short shrift they would have made of these tame talkers had it not been for the energy and valorous scorn of Dr O'Hickey who raised up a storm among the plain people for the proper recognition of Irish by the Senate of the New University. The breath of his mouth became a big wind blowing off biretta and mitre, and sending their chasubulleros bullen a laws flying over every Dublin chimney-pot, while cheers for O'Hickey went rippling from one end of Ireland to the other. O'Hickey made no fancy, polished pattern of words, telling the University Senate, including the Archbishop of Tuam and Monsignor Mannix, President of Maynooth College (who afterwards blossomed out into a full-bosomed patriot), that if they voted against the Irish National Cause, they would resolve themselves into recreant Nationalists whose act of treachery would ever be remembered by the Irish people.

Forced by the roar of the plain people (most of whom knew nothing, and cared less, about the language) to make Irish an essential subject in the University, the official clergy were furious. Realizing they couldn't hit the people, they determined to strike hard at O'Hickey, so a College Mandamus was shoved under O'Hickey's door, ordering him to appear before his betters to answer a charge of want of respect to the holy, high and mighty bishops of Ireland. Without any demand for an apology, without even a chance to defend himself or to take counsel from an advocate, or even from a friend, there was just a charge levelled, a plea of not guilty by O'Hickey, and then the sentence: Resign, or be dismissed. As he refused to resign, he was dismissed. Armagh got him by the scruff of the neck, Tuam caught one arm, Cashel the other, the rest of the episcopate pushed at the back, and he was shunted out through the gates, which were shut, locked, bolted, barred, and chained against him for evermore: banished from the good cheer, sacred associations, from chapel, refectory, infirmarium, lecture room, and Chair of the College, and from all paths therefrom and thereto, garden, playing-fields, cloisters, theological continuities, in compliance with, and in consequence of, a *nullo tremulato antea profundi craniumalis omnibusiboss episcopalitis.*

So that was what Dr O'Hickey got for criticizing the bishops, though he hadn't done so; only a possible action of criticism of the members of the Senate of the National University, some of whom happened to be bishops, but whose position as Senators had nothing whatever to do with any office in Maynooth College. But it was determined to show O'Hickey that the mitre would prove to be the Cap of Death for him. Sean was filled with a great bitterness, and he resolved to do what in him lay to fight this sanctified coercion, this mitred tyranny, this malicious resentment; so he ran around asking questions, and wondering what the Gaelic Leaguers would do now. So he rushed round asking all whom he met, Coo Ulla, cocky Sean Tea O'Kelly, Birch Aar, Finnan Hadde MacColum, Nora Greeno, Paddy Daly, and all the boys and girls of far away and long ago, but all vouchsafed the whisper of, It's up to Dr O'Hickey himself, now.

—Don't yous realize, he kept shouting, that on this question of Essential Irish, were it not for Dr O'Hickey, Hyde and Mac Neill would have been left sitting on their backsides, some more kindly bishop, when he knew they'd got cool enough, giving them a hand to their feet again? Can't yous see it was he frightened the Senate into compliance? He led the fight, he fought the fight, and he won it for us; and are we going to leave him to fight his fight alone? But all the answer he got was a whisper of, If we once get the bishops against us, we're done.

So he ran round again, asking questions of Cunnin Mwail, Micky Free, Harry Lorrequer, Louis J. Walsh of Killebook, the Vicar of Bray, Charles O'Malley, Luke Delmege and his new curate, a lad of the O'Friels, and found them a centre of silence. Accidentally coming across Edward Myrrhtyn, looking longingly in at the windows of Kildare Street Club, he put the question to him; but Edward set off at a gallop from Dublin to Galway, never stopping till he staggered through the doorway of Tillyra Castle, flung himself into bed, singing for all to hear, *I'm asleep, and don't waken me.*

He journeyed to Republican places, asking this Fenian and that, taking in Arthur Griffith, what were we going to do to help O'Hickey in his fight.

—What do you expect us to do over a question that is plainly one for ecclesiastical juridicity? asked a Sinn Feiner who had plussed himself into a Republican, while the massive-minded Griffith robed himself in the stillness of the strong, silent man.

—Was compulsory Irish an ecclesiastical question? countered Sean; and as they stayed silent, went on, Well, then, that's what he fought for; that is why he has been damned: he defeated the proud bishops, and that defeat was gall and wormwood to their voluptuous souls. They say he has been sacked because he treated the bishops with improper respect, and thereby broke the sacred Statutes of Maynooth College. Well, hasn't it been demonstrated that it was the Trustees of the College who pushed him out, so it seems the act of dismissal wasn't an exercise of ecclesiastical jurisdiction, or connected with ecclesiastical authority of any kind. And why? Because the body known as the Trustees of St Patrick's College isn't an ecclesiastical corporation in any sense of the word. These Trustees were incorporated by an Act of Parliament of Great Britain and Ireland; so it seems they have stamped the cross of Patrick over the lion and unicorn (bringing the British symbol up to date), and have thrust out O'Hickey for daring to say that Irish should be an essential subject in the New University; adding a memo to the effect that this professor and fellow priest had said boo to a few bishops who happened to be members of a secular Senate of a secular University.

—I have to go now, said Griffith to his fellow Sinn Feiner, for I have important things to think about; and off he went.

—As for the famous Statutes, continued Sean, isn't it true that the College has been ransacked from roof to cellar without a copy being found? Nor, it seems, does anyone know anything about them. So O'Hickey ups and writes to a Cardinal Log for one, who writes to say that he had read the paragraph on the Duty of Professors from the College Statutes, and that O'Hickey could read it himself in any of the printed copies; O'Hickey replying that he never had a copy, and couldn't get one. The Cardinal made reply that that surprised him, now, so it did; but anyhow he had written to Monsignor Mannix (who subsequently became an Irish patriot of purest ray segrene) to send O'Hickey a copy at once. But as none came, O'Hickey wrote again to point out how necessary it was for him to have a copy of the Statutes he had infringed.

The Cardinal then wrote to say that Mannix had promised to send O'Hickey a copy, and the Cardinal was sure Mannix would send it still, adding that the Cardinal thought the Cardinal himself had one, but found that what he had were but extracts for the students in English. Aha, me boy, aha: so Cardinal Log condemned O'Hickey for infringing a rule he had read out of a book he hadn't got! This was the enlightened boyo who put an end to W. P. O'Ryan's art-and-industry community in the Boyne valley; this was he who bawled shame towards Synge, and who condemned Yeats' *Countess Cathleen* without bothering his red-hatted head to read the book of the play. The hetman of the Catholic Church in Ireland imposing his will on far better men than himself. The Christian way of life!

When the famous Statutes were at last bored out of Mannix, it was found that they were ten years old, and had expired long before Dr O'Hickey had been dismissed. After that, the Cardinal sent to Dr O'Hickey a pamphlet, printed by Browne and Nolan (good references given in *Finnegan's Wake*), entitled *Statutes of St Patrick's College, Maynooth, 1897*, whereas the reference in *Official Record of Facts* was to Statutes published in 1907; and this pamphlet bore on its cover the half-erased word of Draft, while the reference made no mention of the chapter so that it was not possible to know with certainty where Section VIII. 1. 4 was to be found (under the Cardinal's hat, maybe). So Dr O'Hickey had been condemned by the Cardinal and his sub-equals from a bunch of Statutes of which no one in the College had any knowledge; which, as far as could be made out, had never been promulgated; and of which the President of the College, Monsignor Mannix, couldn't ferret out a copy save one poor specimen labelled Draft.

—What does Sean O'Casside suggest we should or might do? the Republican Sinn Feiner asked, a patient smile curling his lips.

—Fight for him as he fought for us, said Sean excitedly; march into the grounds of Maynooth College with drum and colours to tell the authorities there, under their very windows, that Ireland wants Professor O'Hickey back in his Chair of Irish.

—Mob law? said the Sinn Feiner.

—It is no more of mob law to demonstrate against the bishops on an Irish National question than it is to demonstrate against the Castle gang for the same reason.

—And what do you imagine the police would be doing? asked the Sinn Finn Republican.

—We have faced the police before, we can face them again.

—We can't afford to have the bishops against us, said the Sinn Fein Republican, and, besides, Dr O'Hickey himself would never give permission for such an action.

—Oh, no one suggests he should be asked, retorted Sean impatiently; and as for the bishops – shall we, who have nothing to lose, run away from them, while O'Hickey, who has everything to lose, be left to face them alone?

—We're with him in spirit, said the Republican unctuously. Now I have work to do for the Sinn Fein Bank, and I must be off, so slán leat, he said, speaking the only Irish words he knew.

—So-long, said Sean; go behind the curtain to work hard for your nation of bishops and bobbies! I can see now that there won't be even a stick rattled along the railings of Maynooth College.

On the advice of a friend, Dr McDonald, DD, a Professor of Theology at Maynooth, Dr O'Hickey decided to take his case to Rome, and to put something of a faint flush on their white cowardice the Gaelic Leaguers started a fund to help defray his expenses, Sean handing over ten shillings that he had saved towards a new coat, and, in addition, a shilling a week till he had given fifteen shillings altogether; so that a tint was added to O'Hickey's childlike hope of finding a soft spot in the petrified piety of Rome. So this blameless priest, fine professor, everything he did done from a keen sense of patriotic and religious duty, set off for the City of the Boccaneros, Don Vigilios, Monsignor Nanis, the red-hatted Sarnos, and Abbé Trouberts, amethyst rings, pop-eyed papal counts, Swiss guards, and noble memories of Raphael and Angelo – an *athanasius contra junta episcopolician hibernica*. His fellow professors – all but those near the orbit of the President, Mannix – admitted the harsh injustice of the punishment, though not a soul of them, bar McDonald, lifted a hand to help him. Selfishness and fear dominating the teachers of the Irish Catholic world! Safety first for them: eat, drink, and be cautious, for tomorrow we live.

So with a pamphlet of thirty pages, composed into fine Latin by his friend Dr McDonald, Dr O'Hickey found himself in that city which some say is the front door to the gates of Heaven, the keys hanging from a nail over the Pope's bed. They got going in June of 1910, and the Sacred Rota summoned the Trustees of the College to answer for themselves; but did they come? No.

O'Hickey's advocate wrote for the copy of the resolution appointing him to the professorship, and the minutes of the meetings that were held to deal with the case; but autumn came, all the leaves fell, but none came. The Promoter of Justice attached to the Court said they were necessary, and off went an order demanding them within forty days, but after these had fled, the papers still lay, warm and snug, under some bishop's blissful pillow. Then what was called a peremptory order was sent, but sorra care the bishops cared – letter post, pigeon post, telegraph, cable, courier, or Morse code couldn't coax the letters from under the bishop's pillow. They refused deliberately to comply with, or even to take any notice of, the order of the Court. Instead, after another peremptory order, Cardinal Log sent the decree of removal, adding that he had no other documents to deliver. His Eminence, apparently acting as the mouthpiece of the bishops, refused to send on the minutes of the proceedings demanded repeatedly and peremptorily by the Court. They were in existence, but the bishops, each of whom was something more than a pope in his own diocese, refused to deliver them, alleging that there were no documents to send, other than the decree of dismissal – they sent that post-haste. A year and five months after the start of the case – the ecclesiastical law's little delay – the President of the Court said that provision had been made for the delivery of the documents, and then Cardinal Log landed in Rome to complain about the slow way the case was going. It wasn't till February 1912 that three of the documents were handed in, which gave the Cardinal and the bishops a fairway of time to get things going their own sour way. In the document giving an account of the Trustees' meeting only the vote was given, and no word of what had taken place at a previous meeting of the whole episcopal bench. And when the harassed O'Hickey demanded this, it was said that he wanted to keep the case going till Tibb's Eve, with, in the view of their lordships, a malicious intent to weary them out.

The reinforcements were sent, and more of the Irish bishops began to trickle into Rome; and while O'Hickey was pressing for documents bearing on his case, rumours began to be sent round that O'Hickey was incompetent as a professor, that he had been insubordinate, arrogant, ill-tempered, disloyal; that in fine he was, as the Trustees represented him afterwards, an anti-clerical wholly dependent for support on anti-clericals too. Is it likely he would have been hustled out of a Chair in Maynooth

if they didn't know something about him which they couldn't
publish without causing a scandal? They hunted in tame places
and in populated quarters seeking anything they could to murmur
against him. So his advocate hurried to him, saying, Get someone
to write that you were a good priest; and poor O'Hickey had to
say he couldn't, except some who were on the white list, and
their testimony would do him more harm than good. Before
going to Rome, he had asked a testimonial of the Bishop of
Waterford, but that fine fellow contented himself with saying
that O'Hickey was an exemplary priest when he knew him, but
didn't know anything since O'Hickey went to Maynooth; and
the greater Walsh, Archbishop of Dublin, who had been in close
touch with him on the question of getting Irish into the common
schools, satisfied himself with the remark that, as far as he knew,
Dr O'Hickey was free from censure and irregularity. Maynooth's
staff was sounded, but only two were ready to come to the fore,
and, when they had heard that no one else would, they hid
themselves in silence. Is there no just man here to speak a word
for another just man? None: most of them were in the hunt for a
purple or a scarlet biretta.

Then the advocate decided to have evidence taken in Ireland.
Then began the cooking of the questions to be asked of the
witnesses – put in a form, says a brother professor of Maynooth,
notably different from that in which they had been previously
handed to O'Hickey; distorted in substance, and formulated in
wretched and almost unintelligible Latin; while, as regards his
having or not having given occasion for reprehension and
admonition, the added clause – *in any grave matter* – was whipped
away.

One of the Auditors of the Rota, Monsignor Prior, an Englishman, was appointed to be President of the Body for taking down
the evidence, but as such men rarely act in person, someone had
to be selected as a substitute. The names of three Irish clergymen
working in England, all of them domestic prelates of the Pope,
were suggested by Dr O'Hickey and Professor McDonald;
but out of a sweet tenderness for the Irish bishops' feelings,
Monsignor Prior, who had business in England, said he would
come over to Ireland and take the evidence personally. But the
bishops knew a thing or two about setting up a court in holy
Ireland, for if Monsignor Prior came to Ireland he'd ask for the
journal of the Trustees, and then the minutes, so long hidden

nicely away in the darkness of their bottom drawer. However it may have been manoeuvred, O'Hickey got word from his advocate that the bishops had protested against the appointment of an outsider, and so the bould Monsignor Prior had nominated as Judge Instructor Delegate no less a genius than the boulder Cardinal Log himself. No opposition on the part of O'Hickey could alter this, for Prior couldn't do otherwise in face of the protest that had come from all the bishops; and it was even said that the protest had flown in through the Pope's window, so that he, in the interests of justice and fair play, had interfered in the right way when tackled by the Irish bishops, equally athirst for justice and fair play for all; and O'Hickey lost his case, leaving this to be said by Dr McDonald, Professor of Theology at Maynooth for forty years: I regret to have to say I regard the Auditors of the Rota as having judged, or not having judged, this case on prejudice, and not on evidence, and that they have, by the decrees they issued in connexion with it, confirmed what those who distrusted the Holy See had often told us – that it is but a fool who would take any action in a Roman court against the body of bishops of any country. I did not, and would not believe it of the Roman Rota; now I am convinced of my simplicity.

And no cry of shame came from any Irish Seneschal, Taoiseach, or Tánaiste standing angry at the gates of Maynooth College, beside the dismantled castle of the Geraldines.

They took his living from him, says Dr McDonald, and prevented him from getting justice, nay, a hearing in Rome; but he hasn't been injured with the Irish people, except, indeed, with those who think any man a fool who sacrifices his own interest for anything on earth, or, almost, in Heaven. It is a class that has become more numerous, especially among the clergy, many of whom – those who either have got preferment or are on the lookout for it – regard Dr O'Hickey as a fool. Only the other day, the Bishop of Waterford wrote to him urging him to give up the struggle in Rome, and saying, There is not and there never has been any imputation on your priestly character. It's a pity, adds Dr McDonald, that the Bishop didn't summon up the little manliness that was needed to tell this truth when asked by Dr O'Hickey for a testimonial to his character as a priest.

Later on, Dr O'Hickey sent a memorial to the Pope asking permission to take the case to the secular courts, and, to Dr O'Hickey's surprise, received a note telling him the Pope was sending the case again to the Rota – a favour O'Hickey had in vain begged before. O'Hickey, because of the great expense involved, decided to refuse the favour; but before he could find the pen and ink, he was told the Holy Father had withdrawn the case from the Rota, at, it is said, the insistence of Cardinal Vanutelli (welcomed with thunders of cheers at a Gaelic League gathering with Edward Martyn and Hyde hurrying to touch his hand), primed by Cardinal Log. What a host against O'Hickey!

So he came home, and when he had managed to get a better suit of clothes, he called on his bishop, who asked him what he intended to do and what were his intentions. O'Hickey said he had none, save to serve on the Mission in any office to which he might be sent, living in the meantime with his brother in the town of Carrick-on-Suir. No offer of any kind ever came to him, and at last he died, his friends believed from a broken heart. Not the first heart the Irish bishops have broken. And some say that at times a mitred will-o'-the-wisp flickers over his grave in Carrick Beg whispering in the sigh of the wind the honoured name of Mannix.

What a loneliness there was in the silent burial of Dr O'Hickey on that cold, damp day in Carrick Beg! A few faithful friends were there to honour a death that had a sting, and a grave that won a victory. How lonely compared to the stir and vivacity around the burial of a Father O'Growney a few short years before. What a flutter there was when *his* body was brought all the way from California to be buried in Maynooth College. Hyde and Mac Neill left their beds at five in the morning, clapping their hands and blowing their cold fingers, hurrying into their flannels when the alarm clock crew, to be down in Cove in time to honour the homecoming of the dead man. All the Gaelic Chiefs from Cork and Kerry were there, with Oona Fearally and Edward Martyn, freshly toninsured, broadly belted with holy beads, his little boxed-up soul safe for the time being in the midst of the clerical cargo present on the cold quay. Out they went in the jumpy tender to watch the coffin being lowered from the great *Campania*, a rich affair – as Hyde tells us himself – costing a couple of hundred pounds or thereabouts. Carried to Cork, in goes the costly coffin to the Cathedral; me Lord Archbishop taking Hyde and his friends out to dinner, and back to the Cathedral again, where a rousing sermon was given eulogizing the quiet-minded, harmless dead man for compiling five wee

books of cuckoo Irish for beginners which all too frequently
made them enders too. When they were done in Cork, off they
hurried to Dublin where anna lividia plurahelle Irish was spoken
on all sides, and into the other Cathedral with them, where they
said the Rosary, and left Father O'Growney there by himself
till the morning. Then at the crack of dawn, off they went in
stately procession through the principal streets of Dublin, Dr
Hyde and Major Donovan in front standing out from the rest of
them, Donovan to the right of the hearse and Hyde to the left
of it, the mass bands playing the *Marseillaise* to a funeral step,

> An' we're all trottin', trot-trot-trottin',
> An' we're all trottin', so happy an' so gay!

to Broadstone Station.

It was a gorgeous procession, as Hyde tells us himself, taking
fully fifty minutes to pass a given pint; and seven packed trains,
running side by side, and one after another, carried the quick and
the dead to Maynooth, there to meet a splendid coach, drawn by
four great handsome black horses, with Dr Hyde walking bareheaded by its side; followed by six hundred, the noble six hundred, students in their brightest robes, led on by Bishop O'Dea
and Monsignor Mannix, President of the College. When the
coffin had been laid down on the green sward, a Father O'Reilly
ran out to give a roaring, rushing sermon in praise of the dead
man, giving the College the devil and all for their indifference to
Irish, adding that Father O'Growney, the did man, was wiser
than they all; ending up with them all singing, *And so say of all
of us, and so say all of us*; after which, as was quite natural, they
had dinner in the College, Hyde sitting between Monsignor
Mannix and Bishop O'Dawn O'Day, while a tenor of a student
sang, standing on a high stool, *An Irishman's glory shines brighter
than gold* while they were having their whack of good things.
That night, Dr Hyde slept in a room presented to him by Dr
O'Hickey.

But they weren't done yet; oh no, for when the first sign of the
morning came, they hurried into their glows again, hurried into
the church again where Requiem High Mass was said, after
which the cortège wandered its way around the grounds, Dr
Hyde, barefaced and bareheaded, marched again by the erse side
of the hearse, tears in his eyes, clenching his fists while he recited

his own Irish Prayacawn Dove Donah to the calm and keen edification of Monsignor Mannix, O'Day, and the swarm of justickilogical, rustickological, buyological, and sellological students that followed trenchantly behind. At last the costly coffin was laid to rest in the chapel. Hyde gave it a last chaste kiss, as did many of them, for the glory of God and the honour of a poor dud man.

None of these things for Dr O'Hickey, who fought for Ireland in a far, far firmer and finer way than the timid, gentle O'Growney. Ay, and died for her too, as many had done before him, done to death by a far cuter foe. When he was put under the sod, there was no Hyde, Mac Neill, Oona Fearally, Edward Martyn, in freshly-made suits of mourning marching down to Carrick Beg to murmur a last farewell to one of Ireland's greater dead. They stayed at home. No mitred Dawn O'Day there to see the last of him: that they saw in Rome when an iron heel, shaped like a cross, stamped down on him. No drum taps beaten, no last post sounded; only the caw-caw of many a crow flapping a dark wing through a grey sky. No sermon; no band of students chanting sad melodies; no banner of Waken up your Courage, O Ireland, for banner, staff, and spear-point had been cast with O'Hickey into the grave; nothing here but a tiny band of friends, shivering in the centre of a cold, damp day, a little in from a lonely road alongside the noisy sullen Suir, led by the courageous Dr McDonald, to see their comrade safely sheltered in his last home.

O'Hickey's name is never mentioned now. In the fight for the Ireland of his vision he collided with the bishops and got his death-wound. The hounds of Banba had hunted again, and had brought down their quarry. So he is never mentioned now. In a well-known Catholic annual there appeared, under the title of *Taoisigh Gaedheal*, the pictures of those who had served Ireland well, clerical and lay, soldier and politician, and there in the gallery is the long, retiring, rather sheepish face of Father O'Growney; but none, no, not even a silhouette of Father O'Hickey.

Here is one who remembers you, O'Hickey. Here is one who, when you died, had but a flitter of a coat on his back, who walked on the uppers of his boots, who hadn't the penny to buy the paper telling of your death; here is one left to say you were a ray in Ireland's Sword of Light – a ray then, and a ray still, and no episcopal pall can hide its flaming. Though there be none to speak out your name, here is one to utter it in the same breath, with the same pride as those who speak out the names of Ireland's fair and finest sons; for you are one with her they call Cathleen, the daughter of Houlihan, though you have not been remembered for ever; one with her as is yellow-haired Donough who's dead; who had a hempen rope for a neckcloth, and a white cloth on his head.

GAELSTROEM

SEAN STOOD on the borders of doubt again. He was a bit bewildered about the essences in the freedom they were struggling to gain. Was this freedom within the circle of the fight they were making, or was it merely a vision floating about the rim? Strange things had happened that put an ugly look on the face of the freedom they thought so beautiful. Look at what had happened to Parnell when he was breathless with extreme toil, and leaning on his sword before having another bout with the wily foe. Stricken down he was by those he led so well within the circle of what they all aimed at achieving. Hadn't Dr O'Hickey been dismissed from his job, and disgraced by a covey of screeching bishops for saying a few edged words in Maynooth College on a National question? Ay, had he. Could such a thing have happened at Trinity in Ireland, or in Oxford or Cambridge in England? No, it couldn't. Then there was the case of the Rory O'Moore branch of the Gaelic League at Portarlington, whose officers had been hushed, banned, blackguarded, and some of them beggared because they had insisted, against the obey-or-be-damned orders of the local clergy, on holding mixed classes for the teaching of Irish. The clergy had discovered them, and all of them withered away. The fig tree had been cursed for bringing forth fruit. He saw this odd thing himself in Moycally where he had gone on Sundays to teach Irish with a comrade, the two of them giving up their whole day of leisure to hasten the day of Ireland's deliverance. There the girls were forced to sit in the lower room of the local school, the men in the upper one, a local priest always present to see that this canonical rule was flagrantly obeyed, assisted by a Mr Caocaun, steward of the Eire Gobrath estate, a stout, tall man, built up by nature to resemble a lusty pig gradually assuming the shape of a man, all dressed in a Sunday suit of rich black broadcloth, lightened by a gold watch-chain flowing across the wide, bulging belly, like a streak of summer lightning astray in a black and sullen wintry night. There he stood, pretending to listen to all Sean said, but with a keen ear cocked for any stir below that might suggest the girls were leaving; for among them was his daughter, Julia, a dashing and very handsome lass, the fear of his life in that such a sweet girl aflower in the fortunate circumstance of having a well-off father might, if his eye closed for a moment, make a fool of herself for the sake of some of the hardier and handsomer men of Kildare. When the lessons were over, they all hurried away, girls in front with quick step, the boys behind, with slower pace, pretending indifference, but sending long, searching glances after them, the priest between with a walking-stick, looking like a drover keeping one herd of cattle from mingling with another.

The Branch Secretary, full of fire for Ireland, strolled with Sean, the hectic skin on his face almost cut through by the sharpness of bone in nose and jowl; wasted by consumption he was, and his tense eagerness seemed to be born of a need to do all he could before he was pulled out of the play. He led them to where they would get their dinner, talking of Ireland, Ireland leading the world when she gained her freedom, turning his face away at intervals to cough into a handkerchief that Sean saw was bright with tiny spangles of brilliant blood. When they came to the cottage where they were to eat, he held out a hand to say goodbye.

—Come in and have a share, invited Sean.

He glanced around, hesitated, and coughed again. I'd like to, he said, but can't. We have to keep guard on ourselves here. The eyes of our soggarth aroons are everywhere, and they don't like us to be long with the Dublin Sinn Feiners. There's either an eye or an ear behind every bush around us, for all words here, save paternoster and ave maria alone, are secular and dangerous; and with a Gaelic farewell he left them at the door.

Then there was the row over Tennyson's *Voyage of Maeldune*, done into Gaelic by Torna, which was to be sung by the Gaelic League Choir at the annual gathering of the Gaels in Dublin. The choir had rehearsed it long and ardently, and were ready to sing

it in great style, when up jumps the Reverend Father Francis
Joseph Ignatius Polycarp Dominicjerome Sebastian O'Callaghan,
to shout that this poem slandered Ireland of the Virgins; and
away goes the Gaelic League Executive in a panic to beg the
choir to give the poem up, which they did, but not before there
was a split that ruined the choir completely.

Then there was W. P. O'Ryan, with his Boyne valley enterprise
in his arms, along with his journal *The Irish Peasant*, forced by a
pope-eyed cardinal to work and sing no more by the beautiful
banks of the Boyne, to bury his paper, and to leave Ireland a lot
lonelier by leaving it himself. Look at the gush of pious venom
that was splashed over poor Synge, Gaelic Leaguers firing stones
through the stream – save only that queer fellow Pearse, who
ventured a trenchant word or two on behalf of the playwright.
And don't forget what that thick of a Cardinal said about Yeats'
Countess Cathleen. And didn't the clergy fall flat with the weight
of the denunciation they heaped on the proposal to send a caravan of artists round Ireland playing Irish plays in towns and
villages, fearful of what would happen when the sun had set, and
the artists were all asleep under the cedars and the stars. Hadn't
he himself organized, in all innocency, Sunday evening summer
gatherings between St Margaret's and the Drumcondra branches
of the League, each body marching halfway from their clubroom
to meet at a pleasant crossroads, there to sing and dance an hour
or two away to the sound of fiddle and fife; and on the second
evening of the gathering, didn't the St Margaret's curate come
tearing on his bicycle, sent as courier from the parish priest, a red
light on the top of his biretta, to tell them that these strange ways
of men with maids wasn't, and never would be, recognized in
Ireland; that it was an occasion of sin; that their conduct would
embarrass the Irish saints above; and that they were showing a
froward example to the Royal Irish Constabulary, the Royal
Irish Academy, Trinity College, the Dublin Fire Brigade, the
Grand Loyal Orange Lodge of Dublin, the Anti-taxi Association,
and all those who constantly thought of the four lust things. So
the fiddle was locked in its case, the fife thrust into a deep pocket,
and all trotted home without a word, like sheep that hadn't
gone astray, leaving Sean staring at the curate, and the curate
staring at Sean. Soon he departed, and Sean sat down on a grassy
slope to think it over. Even the Drumcondra members, all city
folk, hadn't murmured a word. Had it been the Lord Lieutenant,

they would have hooted and hissed, would have gone only when pushed away be a serried rank of police. But a few words from this insignificant man had sent them slinking home. St Patrick had sent a hot wire to the parish priest to stop this tickling jock. And a number of the men who had withered before a word were Irish Republican Brothers. Sean hadn't believed it before, but now he had seen it with his own eyes. It was a stingy republicanism that wouldn't fight for the right to dance with a girl in the open light of day.

Again, didn't the bishops every Easter, in their epistolals, denounce the Fenians, insisting that it was a mortal sin to belong to them; and the Irish Republican Brotherhood had been losing so many members who had been infected with religious scruples by this insistent and effective attack, that the Supreme Council was forced to hold a meeting of the Circles in the Clontarf Town Hall, whose caretaker, Mick McGinn, was an old Fenian. The meeting was pictured as a lecture on Brian Boru. A number of young priests were on the platform, and these, one after the other, told their audience that love of country was a paramount Christian virtue; that no Irishman loved his country better, or as well, as a Fenian; that it was no sin to be one, and that they mustn't mention it in confession; for if any man confessed that he belonged to a secret society, the confession revealed a scruple, and the father confessor could only order him to leave it immediately. But to be a Fenian, far from being a sin, was a Christian honour, and so no matter whatsoever for confession to a priest. Cheers and the roll of drums ended the meeting. Everyone was satisfied except Sean: he felt there was a twist in it somewhere, though as a non-Catholic who paid no guarded or unguarded honour to the clergy's yea or nay in politics, it was no business of his. So the leakage was caulked for the time being, though there must have been an ecclesiastical spy present, for shortly afterwards the young priests were packed off to a distant mission where there was neither room nor need for a Fenian. Christ only knows how many other instances there were in which things were hushed or throttled silently, without a sigh escaping to whisper the tale into a listening ear. These were enough to make Sean pause amid the riches of Sackville Street, or the squalor of the Coombe, to ponder them in his heart, and to make him wonder why the leaders of the Irish Movement kept their Irish mouths so tightly shut about them all.

They could move when they wanted to, like the damned non-sense of the League Executive forcing a group of Protestant enthusiasts, Seumas Deacon, Ernest Blythe, George Irvine, himself, and others, to abandon their special efforts to get the Protestants interested in the League's work, because, the fools said, it was bringing insectarianism into the Movement; though all it sought to do was to bring the League into touch with those who opposed, or were suspicious of, it, by sending to Protestant parishes enthusiasts of their own persuasion to put the objects of the Irish Ireland Movement plainly before the Protestant people. Some of them had spoken in parish halls where Ireland was emblified by a Union Jack, those honouring it forgetful that the flag bore the cross of St Patrick as well as those of St Andrew and St George.

Dean Bernard was asked if he'd give St Patrick's for a service in Irish on the Saint's festival. After the Dean had recovered out of a bud swoon by swallowing a big dollop of warmed whiskey, he asked, Is there anything else you'd like? of the deputation that went to see him. Then he burst out laughing, shook his hide, and frowned with kind malignity, saying, Erse? What! have a service in Erse, and in St Patrick's? Not in Erse, surely? Yes? No, no, gentlemen, it can't be did. It couldn't happen here. We don't want our church to be filled with Conn the Shaughrauns, like a Wicklow wedding. Besides, Heaven is used by now to the English language, and it would be a nuisance for them to have to become bilingual, so that they could make some sense of what a few might say. St Patrick spoke Erse? So he did; but it was we forced him to it. It's his one great handicap to this day. Let me tell you, gentlemen – privately, mind you – that infra-information from above has kindly let me know that the poor gentleman sits in holy isolation there because he knows no English. Wah? Tristan and Isolde spoke Erse too? I didn't know that before this. Well, we don't speak it here. We can't afford to be Isoldationists any longer. God, gentlemen, has become a thorough old English patriot, and we're not going to let a few frantic Gaels disturb Him now with their teareasonable aspirations. With all your persuasiveness, it's no go, for such a thing isn't up our street. Be jabers! gentlemen, yous ought to have more since! Erse! Sorry I can't *noblesse oblige* you, so so-long, gentlemen all; and a footman beadle pushed them far out into the night to tell Sean, who was waiting in the garden under a yew tree, not being suitably clad to be fit to appear before a dean.

Off they went to see the Reverend Phineas Hunt, Rector of St Kevin's, George Irvine and Seumas Deacon taking the Rector, and Sean holding fast to his lady, a pillar of fire in her desire to evangelize the Irish. Sean testified to his belief that if the Irish would only flee the Pope, and throw themselves into the arms of Sankey and Moody or Silas K. Shocking, all would be well; and to make it sure, the two of them sang softly together a verse of a hilarious hymn:

> *Sankey's as high as the Pope in Heaven –*
> *Higher in fact if the truth were known –*
> *For the Pope's at the gate, a mere mean porter,*
> *While Sankey's well away on his own;*
> *And weighted with wings, like a big cyclone,*
> *Flies round and round and round the throne!*

When the murmured song had ended, Mrs Hunt hurried to her husband to convince him of the truth, to turn his hesitation into hasty agreement, so that for the first time in many years a service in Irish, according to the rubric of the Church of Ireland, was held in the house of the Lord and of Phineas Hunt; and once again the deers' cry went up to Heaven on behalf of Gael and Gall-Gael, making Patrick cock his ear and wonder what was happening.

In an effort to keep the good work going, Sean went himself to Gaelic Headquarters where the Central Executive was in session. He opened the door softly, and went in to where the mighty ones were sitting round a round table, discussing whether the organizers should wear the kilt or stick to the trousers. The Secretary, waking out of a doze, rushed at Sean, gripped him by the hair, asked him what he wanted, adding that this was a private meeting that wasn't to be disturbed. When Sean told him what he wanted, the Secretary gave a frightened squeal, rushed Sean out of the room, down the winding stairs, shoved him into the road, closed, locked, and chained up the heavy hall door to make things safe. Then Sean tried to persuade his comrade Protestants to damn and defy the League Executive, but the timidity of their leaders had so nullified and dullified them that they slunk away from a fight and allowed the whole thing to dissolve into a forgotten memory.

What a difference here from the stand of his own Rector, who had joyfully promoted a debate on the Irish language between Sean and the schoolmaster. Later, the Rector wanted Sean to let him cancel the discussion, for Sean had spoken badly and brokenly at a previous meeting in the part of appointed speaker; and the kindly Rector was afraid Sean would make a show of himself in the debate, a thought troubling him more than it troubled Sean. Determined to go on with what he had set himself to do, Sean refused to back out; and to this day he could see the delight on the Rector's handsome, spiritual face after he had spoken eloquently for three-quarters of an hour; he could see the white graceful hands applauding vigorously when he sat down to give place to the schoolmaster who had been upset by the fire and vigour of Sean's talk, and his few hesitant objections were passionately disposed of in a reply, amid the smiling appreciation of the Rector. To this day he had the Irish Testament the Rector gave him in honour of his fine fight, a book that carried the escutcheon of the Rector's satisfaction in its inscription of To John Casside, with all good wishes. E. M. Griffin. 1905.

All the time, the indomitable Dr Hyde splashed and spluttered a way through the foaming, swift-flowing, swirling Gaelstroem, saying again and again the things he had said again and again before; striving to make the Gaelic League a force to be proud of and fiercely respectable, keeping the vision before him of the wonders in the old Irish Hierarchaeological Society of 1842, in whose bosom were embedded a duke, an earl, a viscount, and a baron, while flowering in the Society itself were three dukes, five marquises, fourteen earls, ten viscounts, seven barons, one archbishop, eight bishops, a big fistful of baronets, and an un-countable crowd of right honourables. Though the Society that followed, to Hyde's sorrow, had no gigantic people to guide it, wasn't Standish O'Grady the uncle of a lord, and wasn't his father an admiral? So Hyde went about, gathering into the League what he could, including a host of civil servants whom the law prevented from touching politics.

—Looka Birch aar, said Hyde, Paddy O'Shea, Shaun O'Cahan – customs officers all who wouldn't have had an earthly, but for the League, to toil for Ireland; but might have spent their lives weaving daisy-chains in a summer field, amusing themselves with green thoughts in a greener shade. Yes, shouted Hyde, every-where we have brought into friendly comopinionship people who before wouldn't walk on the same side of the street!

—No, shouted a priest into Hyde's ear, not till the day of judgement will it be known how much the Gaelic League has done to bring the quarrelling Irish into the way of a sweet unity, and a refresher peace among the Gaels!

All this, and more, the undaunted Hyde said in a long letter to the editor of the American *Irish World*, who, in leading articles, was accusing the Gaelic League of butting its head against the Irish Parliamentary Party. Reams long, the letter was, and so remarkable that Dr Hyde kept a copy of it; but one night, when he was in a deeper sleep, the little mice crept in and ate up every scrap of it. The three blind mice, maybe. Hyde, by keeping out of politics, drew all the Irish together into the bonds of an uncommon love. But, blast it, it didn't last! Over came Father Yorke of San Francisco, to give a lecture before the Central Branch of the Gaelic League; but as Hyde had no personal acquaintance with this gentleman, and couldn't tell beforehand what he'd be likely to say, he kept at home – enemies staying in a locked room, made safely dark with all the blinds drawn. Well it was he didn't go, for when Father Yorke came, he saw the way things were, and a right anger seized him. He put a point on his tongue, lashing out at Members of Parliament, the Press, priests, nuns, managers and teachers of schools, fathers and mothers, not sparing anyone, so that Dublin shook, saying things, says Hyde, that badly needed saying, that he himself would like to have said, were he not afraid that it might make matters worse. There were ructions the following morning, the *Freeman's Journal* letting roar after roar of anger out of it, for Father Yorke had plunged a knife up to the haft in its hiphurrahypocrisy; and Hyde, naturally, was delighted that the paper couldn't say he had aught to do with it; for had it been otherwise, they would have lost its help, and an attack on Hyde would have damaged the cause. Some defended the *Freeman's Journal*, and Yorke answered with a letter that shoved the knife still farther into the bowels of the poor quivering journal.

After that, came a shot from that bounder D. P. Moran, editor of *The Leader*, who wrote a leading article entitled *We Want a Man*, causing another rent in Hyde's temple veil of unity, and another roar to break the quietness, for many ran hither and thither, shouting, This is meant for Hyde; the article clearly implying that there wasn't enough of the man in Hyde to fit him to be head of the League. Hyde didn't believe it himself, for he had always been great with Moran, and sometimes wrote for his

paper, so that the article was best forgot. But, damn it, there was
Arthur Griffith screeching in his paper that there was a plot to
oust Hyde and all gallant Gaels from the League, and hand over
control to the King's men, desirous that the Pursuivants Sorroy
and Norroy should be the chief officers of the Gaelic League;
but, Griffith went on, if these people persisted in their evil work
to disrupt the unity of the Gaels, they'd be cast out, stricken
down, knocked silly, and burst to bits, so that the joy of unity
might be held in the bond of peace.

While that thunder was still grumbling, Dr Hyde and Norma
Borthwick, an official of the League, culled out a holiday and put
on their best attire and set out for Donegal to help in the un-
veiling of a new cathedral, built by the Bishop O'Donnell; and
who d'ye think they ran into on the white steps of the new church
but the bould John Dillon, and he dressed up to the nines for the
great occasion! And what d'ye think, without by your leave, or a
ha'p'orth, but Farella from Dublin must rush up to him, clutch
a hold of his coat-tail, haul him back a bit, and shout in his left
ear, Eh, you, about this question of the Irish Movement – if
you're going to give it a miss, and refuse to reckon with it, it'll
reckon with you, me boyo! We've a man in Ballyvourney, and
we've only got to say the word and he'll be elected!

—Do you mean, said the Dillonock, nonplussed for a moment,
you'll put a man up against the Member who has fought in the
House of Commons for Ireland, without thought for years of his
own needs and necessary emolument?

—That's exactly what I mean, said Farella.

—In that case, if yous do, retorted the Dillonock, jabbing a
dint in the steps with the point of his umbrella, and pulling his
coat-tail out of Farella's grip, I'll fight yous while I've a leg to
stand on!

—Now boys, boys, boys, murmured Hyde, the pikeman of
peace; no quarrelling in the shade of the Cathedral.

—Shade of a cathedral or shade of the old apple tree! shouted
Farella, it's all one to me – we're going to keep leatherin' away
with the wattle O!

—What bottle O? asked the Dillonock, puzzled. Leather away
with what bottle O, man?

—Not what bottle O, man, answered Farella derisively; wattle
O, not bottle O, man. Aren't you even acquainted with the order
given by Ireland herself, and she in the form of a beautiful young

lady steppin' stately through the streets of Dublin, or the green plains of County Mayo, your own homeland? Listen, man alive! and he caught the Dillonock again by the tail of his coat:

> *Last night I strolled on a hillside bare,*
> *And sat me down to hear the birds;*
> *A wonder came to me unaware,*
> *For their singing changed to mighty words.*
>
> *A lovely damsel, tall and fair,*
> *With clusterin' hair that shone like gold,*
> *An' a tiny mouth like a cupid's bow,*
> *That open'd wide to shout out bold,*
> *Leather away with the wattle O!*
>
> *We'll rout the English bucks, says she,*
> *With showers o' shot, an' our harbours free,*
> *If yous only listen right to me,*
> *An' leather away with the wattle O!*

What sort of a survival are you – giving a tug to the coat-tail – of your glorious ancestor, General Dillon, who fought an' died for Ireland on th' field o' Fontenoy?

—You're becoming quite personal now, said the Dillonock, so we'll part: I'm not accustomed to such aspersions.

—Aren't you now? Well, you soon will be, for th' threes of Kilcash are growin' again!

—Here, now, me good men, stand aside an' make room, said a constabulary man, shoving them to the side of the mighty flight of steps; are yous all blind that yous can't see the clergy comin'?

—Leggo me coat, leggo, leggo! snarled the Dillonock, twisting the tail of it from Farella's grasp; and then the golden wrangle was lost in the jangle, mangle, and tangle of the bell-ringing, as the clergy, led by the Bishop, carrying his closure, led by the cross-bearer, came slowly up dem golden stairs, chanting *Deo dubilin-laddi*, followed by canons major and minor, priests secular and regular, and the renowned Orders of Laurestinians, Holy Hards of Eireann, Vigilantians of the Clean Mind, Sacred Sodality of Ruddy Roverians, Standardarians, Universalists, Catholic Timerians, Bellopatricians, Crossoconglians, Monasterboiceans, Holsomlititurians, the Most Primitive Order of Ancient Hibeer-

nians, led by Weejodavlin; Catholic Heralangelists, Green-
flaggregorians, Knights and Squires of Honestogodians, the 1872
Company of Griffithians, Cullenites, Macabians, Breenboru-
vians, Tirnalogians, Banabanians; the Black and White Assembly
of Censorians, Sleevenamonites, the Knights of Columnbannus
with their blazon, on a field sable, a dove with a money order in
its beak, all proper; the sacred choir of Micuirmick, chanting
the palacestraina of *Rome Sweet Rome*; the united Confraternities
of Bancorians, Investorians, and Brokerians, their banner of
white, holding three gold balls, with holy emblazoned on each
of them; the poor Sodalities of the Guild of Matthewisons of
Talbuttamia, all clad in holy rags, roses of Sharon mingled with
their hair, and tight bands of rusty steel round their pinched
bellies, and they chanting, Religion is the only d'hope of the
workers; stalwart members of the Architects of the Treasurrec-
tion, heavily cowled, all earnest students of the things written
round the angelic life of A. Job; then in slow and solemn step
came the Gulled of Dreamy Jerontius, chanting in slow time, *Oh
for the wings of Above*; while the procession was closed in by the
spirited Confraternity of True Maltaterians, displaying their great
banner, the colour of liquid gold, having in chief three swallows
perching on a red cross, silver star in each bird's beak, incrested
with a dancing baby bottle of aqua vita, inscribed with the gullant
knights' inspiring motto of Neamh na Neul – the Heaven of the
Clouds.

Donal Mac Rory O'Murachadha was grumbling about it all
to Sean, the pair of them standing, hands in pockets, under the
Grecian portico of the Post Office, staring at a sharp slash of rain
pelting off the tops of the trams assembled at Nelson's Pillar.

—Hyde's always blathering about the League being non-
political, he said, but forgets it's sectarian too, hurrying off to
every Catholic gathering where he hopes to meet a bishop.

—Parnell went after the clergy too, Donal.

—No fear, he didn't: the clergy went after him. They didn't
like it, so they sat silent, blinking on their benches like horned
owls, waiting their chance; and when it came, out they flew,
hooting, to help the wolves in the rending of Ireland's grandest
son. They'll never do that to Hyde, for he has a bend in his back,
looking at episcopal rings.

Poor old Hyde, thought Sean, out of one dilemma into
another! There's the Tory *Daily Express* for ever aiming venom

at him; and look at Father Barry of Oldcastle, a Royal Meath
townland of a handful of frightened and scattered people, look
at the malicious lunge he made at Hyde, writing in a Meath paper
of the filthy insolence of Hyde, mixing the poor man up with the
careless, conceited covey responsible for the quarterly called
Dana (which Sean longed to have, but couldn't afford), the name
of a kind of prehistorical, mythological Mother MoChree to the
older Irish gods, though Hyde never read a line of the journal,
never spent a ha'penny on it, and had nothing whatever to do
with it, so he said. The same courtly priest came down on Hyde
for mixing the clever Munster poem called *The Illbred Child and
His Mother* among his Connacht sacred songs and soulos. Then
the Kilkenny branch of the League staged Hyde's little Nativity
play, several priests joining in it, and delighted at the bare idea;
but the Church waxed indignant that she hadn't been told about
it, and down comes the Bishop with a train of clergy to put the
kybosh on the venture, and to teach the Gaelic League of Kilkenny something more than manners. Dr Hyde, of course, made
haste to make it clear he had had no knowledge of the idea,
neither had he any acquaintance with a single person active in
putting it into practice.

The passion to be all things to all men is too strong in him to
allow a leadership bringing the people into the promised land,
thought Sean, sauntering along Sackville Street, passing Chan-
cellor's, optical-instrument makers and Court photographer, with
its three-faced clock swung out before its façade, and a gilded
bell on the top of it. Something like this bell Hyde was; Ireland's
heavily-gilded tin bell, chiming the hours sweetly away, but never
hardening into a tocsin to call the people to a battle. Sean went
over the road to lean on the river parapet, looking over at Butler's,
seller of everything musical, with its window festooned with oboe,
clarinet, drum, and trumpet, with a gorgeous model of a uniform, dazzling in its blue-and-crimson facings, its gold-and-
green collar, shoulder-strap, and epaulette, ready-made for any
Dawn of Freedom or Erin's Hope band and Irish town might
think of forming. Hyde played the accordion in Ireland's brass
band, keeping the turmoil in tune.

Hyde had a hard furrow to plough. There were rocks everywhere threatening to knock the share to bits. After all, the Movement was strictly non-political and non-sectarian, though Donal
had asked why a special invitation to be at a gathering should be

sent to a Catholic cardinal, when no similar one was sent to the
Protestant Primate of Armagh. It was plain that Hyde had to be
cautious, though that wasn't a hard thing for him. He was no
fool. He had had a narrow escape, though, when he went as
prime speaker to a dinner in Sligo given by the Association of
National Schoolteachers, where he sat next to the local Member
of Parliament whose statue, one of Connacht's wonders, stands
in a public place to this very day. Hyde's bum hadn't warmed to
the seat when he noticed that something was wrong, for numbers
were standing up, sitting down, standing up, sitting down
again, as if an invisible force was tugging them two ways at once.
One of them slid from his chair, crept under the table, pulled
Hyde's trousers, and thrust up the menu card to the tip of his
nose, and there on the back of it, in letters of purest gold, was
The Toast to the King.

—What are you goin' to do? queried the man from under the
table.

—What am I going to do? Eat my dinner, what else, said Hyde.
And eat it he did like a man, till he was full up, and the time of the
toasts appeared in the land. Then he thrust a hand into his bosom,
groped round for a moment, and drew it out again empty.

—My soul to glory! he exclaimed, if I haven't left my cigars
behind me! Excuse me; leaning over towards the chairman,
till I rush back to my hotel and get them. Then off he went with
the speed of Master McGrath after the hare, dawdling about till
he felt the coast was clear; came slowly back to find that the
toast was a thing of the past in time and space, and all serene, and
danger over, and hope renewed, and freed from blame. Ah, me
sweet yourself, me cunning gayboy, me witty now-you-see-me-
and-now-you-don't conundrum, me cameo cumonora nah
erreann, one of the faithful, one of the phew!

Look at the row there was, too, over the proposed International
Exhibition, held, some said, to ruin the few hen-picked industries
in Ireland. So the true-hearted Gaels were all for a National
Exhibition, where only the home products and native manu-
factures would be helled up to honour; and at a meeting held to
uphold the International Idea, Mac Neill, Alderman Cole, Edward Martyn, and some of the descendants of Brian Boru
spoke so trenchantly against it that the audience lost its head, and
led by the solid men of the Muldoon clan, the three hundred
men and three men, the Boys of Wexford, Erin's hope and pride,

the young men, and the men of eighty too, some of the noblest
peasantry on God's earth, and the boatman of Kinsale, helped by
the wind that shakes the barley, broke up the meeting, and everyone said that gall was over. But the people behind the International Idea, nothing daunted, went their way, got Pembroke
Park, and in two twinklings the Exhibition was there in substance
and in fact. But wait till I tell you: no sooner was its flags flying
than, before one could say Jack Robinson, Danny Boy, Kelly of
Killann, arm in arm with Kelly from the Isle of Man, Peg o'
Me Heart, with her bonny bunch of roses O, the peeler and the
goat, Brian O'Linn were flocking in to it; and at their heels a
crowd of Gaels, blocking up the entrances, keeping each other
out by trying to get each other in, striving to be the first to see
the sights, to purchase bargains, and to get a tasty lunch at a
reasonable price, served by the prettiest girls from Clare; Flowers
of Finea and Roses of Tralee, with many Shan van Vochts,
were there too, among others who, on bended knees, had sworn
they'd never set a foot inside; indeed, some said but two persons
refrained from having anything to do with it – Sean O'Casside
who hadn't the money to pay to get in; and Dr Hyde himself,
though the story went round that he was often seen there as large
as life, running around, eating and drinking his fill, though he
says himself he never never even as much as looked over the wall.

—Listen, said a member of the Keating branch, as he, Sean,
and Donal were walking out to view the shamrock plains of
Finglas, listen till I tell yous how Hyde made a cod o' poor
Johnny Redmond – yous'll die laughin', Affther Redmond made
his speech in favour of Irish and again' th' Education Board,
didn't Hyde discover that him an' he were stayin' at th' same
hotel, an' on th' way home he let out that he was to speak at a
dinner in Oxford in honour of St Patrick, a few days before the
festival, an' nothin' would do Johnny Redmond but to make
Hyde promise to be at the great dinner of the Irish Party on the
night of the festival itself. An' then it flashed on Hyde that, if
he went, his tour of America might be mixed with a roar of
derision from start to finish. In a nice fix, wasn't he?

—It takes Hyde to pull out of a fix, growled Donal.

—Sure, I know. He done it all right; but wait till I tell yous. He
wrote out his speech for the Party dinner, an' sent it to the
Freeman's Journal; then what did he do in th' evenin' but rang
up the paper, tellin' them to hold back th' printin' of the speech,

for he was ill in Oxford and couldn't go to the Party dinner! He told his Oxford host he wasn't well, an' poured himself into bed, an' indeed th' poor man had a pain in the head brought about by the breakfast and lunch he had had that day; an' in bed he stayed till St Patrick's Day had dwindled away to the morning after, when he went back to London, and that night sallied off with Lord Monteagle's daughter to an Irish concert in the Queen's Hall; an' where d'ye think did he sit but plump between Johnny Redmond an' his wife – Tow-row-row, Paddy, will yeh now sit beside me, silent, silent, I'm all right!

—That's th' sort he is, said Donal.

—Redmond believed him, said the Keating member, for after some singing, when he was givin' a gorgeous speech, Hyde gave his throat an odd squeeze to bring about a whoarse-son wheezing so as to give Johnny Redmond the benefit of a doubt. Clever, wasn't he?

—I'd say he was mean, said Donal. He wouldn't do it to a bishop. Look at the way he glows telling us how an archbishop put a grand, costly dinner before him, with the company of twenty guests around the arrogant table, who, he tells us, must have been together worth upwards of fifty million dollars. Ireland's Chief and a follower of the lowly Jesus find everything bright, generous, and lively in the midst of wealth, with lashin's to eat and drink to make it all livelier still.

—Be fair, Donal, said Sean, and don't forget that a letter written in Irish, by Mary Spring Rice, Monteagle's daughter, converted important persons by showing them that the Gaelic Movement had the support of elegant and most respectable people.

It's far more important that Irish should be written by Mick McGilligan's daughter Maryanne, responded Donal fiercely. If all the Mary Spring Rices, daughters of all the Monteagles, spoke the Irish, and none of the Maryannes, daughters of the Mick McGilligans, spoke it, then the Irish would be dead. Hyde's arm's round everyone's neck. All things to all men. A volgayno smothering Ireland in a smoke of empty words. A king with a cushion for a crown! Keep cool, says Hyde, Keep cool, says Arthur Griffith, and cool keeps Eoin Mac Neill. To ask Ireland to keep out of politics is asking her to keep out of life; and the only politics for Ireland today is animosity to England, shown by word of mouth and blow from fist!

And keep cool, whispers St Patrick, through his successors, to them all; you knights of St Patrick especially, for a lot depends on you, and cool you must keep if you're to hang on to those fifty million dollars. They weren't in this Club for the sake of fame or honour, or for the sake of their money, nor for their own personal gain, but only and alone for the good of the country at large, said the chairman; and Hear hear, says the saint, we know that well; and don't forget the boy in the biretta when yous are jottin' down your wills. So give all yous can, for yous are all sons of the Church, an' good sons too, though it's I who say it who shouldn't. Your outlook is a natural one, says Hyde, and you do well to keep out of trouble.

—Be God, he's after takin' th' words out of me mouth, remarked St Patrick to St Bronach and she chanting the *Star of the County Down* to herself. A nice little group, these friendly sons o' St Patrick, he went on musingly; all rich men and good Catholics, th' one an' only organization the Irish rich would touch, for they found that in the others there were too much deceit, disunity, and quarrelling; or, to use betther-known phraseology, too much envy, hatred, an' malice, an' as these had all the contrary virtues, it was very wise not to go where they would be condamninated; so here, in moneyastic serenity, they could eat lunch and dinner without any untoward thoughts disturbing their contemplation of divine things. He leaned over and stretched out, hanging on by his toes to a twinkling star, so that he was near enough to ding advice into Hyde's ear: Keep your head, he said, and go warily, but not warrily; don't let them go off the rails, for that means I'm up all night sendin' therms to the bishops to get them spruced an' spined to birch it into any elementary idiot who, to make himself poplar, leads people to where their barks may be beeched, to the treemendous loss of their souls, leavin' them in the larch, tremblin', like aspens, when they find themselves with a horn beamin' from their bums, an oakasion yew never want to view. I know it's not easy keepin' them in bounds, for give them an inch an' they want a hell. You made a slip when you sung about young men with the pikes on shoulders, an' I had a time explainin' it was an innocent way you had; for well we remember the tense time we had when that freethinker Tone an' his French fleet in Banthry Bay was only a few yards off from our holy isle, the sweat pourin' off us, an our hearts burstin' raisin' th' wind to blow him an' his back to France. An' whisper, listen, will you tell them not to be givin' so much space-time to a St Ignatius here, a St Aloysius Gonzaga there, an' a St Pether of Alcantara yonder; with St Anthony of Padua worn out attendin' them, an' his poor eyes dim with the glare of the candles lighted to him, when we have enough an' to spare of our own, like meself, Columbus, Bridget, Kieran of Kilkenny, Finbarr of Cork, Codalot of Queery Isle, Damawluvus of Sinisagoner, Tatther Jacwelsh, patron of hoboes, Corruckther, patron of dancers, with his sacred companion and martyr, Kayleegoer, Feckim-gumoy, patron of seelots, Janethainayrin, patron of factories, Sheemsa, patron of marrymakers, Sullisanlay, patron of slums, Hillolureus and Ardalaunus, brother patrons of free-drinkers, Willogod, patron of workers, Ellesdeea, patron of employers, and money more who are a credit to our native land.

There the saint stood, all alone in his glory, surrounded by a wide frame, thickly gilded, over the broad fireplace of the Jolly Topers, the happy pub in Finglas for bona fides; there he stood in his grand green chasuble, quivering with embroidered sham-rocks, harps, and round towers, a golden mitre covering half of his flowing white hair, a crozier in his left hand, his right stretched out, pointing a way to the sea, for the information of the swarm of green and yellow snakes who were, in a frenzy of fear, gliding swiftly by the crimson slippers of the saint, eager to hide them-selves under the waves lest a worse fate befall them.

—Ay, said Donal, taking a swig from his frothy-headed glass of stout, there he is – a man who for centuries has done our country more harm than good.

—Ah, I wouldn't say that, now, murmured the member of the Keating branch.

—Frightened us all into a fear of thought, went on Donal, and Hyde is one of his forth-rate agitant-generals. Well, he exclaimed suddenly, here's to all the unfriendly sons of St Patrick, the best sons Ireland ever had, and he raised his glass high over his head.

—I join you, said Sean, clinking his glass to Donal's.

—Ah, I wouldn't say that now, said the member of the Keating branch; no, I wouldn't go as far as that now; and he watched them emptying their glasses at a gulp.

HORA NOVISSIMA

SEAN WAS growing tired. He saw how few had gathered around Eire. His eyes, too, were aching, and forget them how he might, he'd the feeling that they weren't as strong as they had been. Dry bones everywhere. Owen Mac Neill brooding over the Brehon Laws and wondering when he'd lead the people back like a shepherd, green-ribboned crook in hand, to the Arcadian Gaelic State. The Irish Republican Brotherhood thinking always of tomorrow when the rebels would be on the hills, red coats and black coats flying before them. James Connolly for ever assuring himself that his Irish Socialist Republican ten commandments, beginning with the nationalization of railways, canals, banks, and braes, would be observed by the common people, too busy keeping themselves in good standing with saints, angels, and parish priests, by a gallop every Sunday morning to the entrance of the Pro-Cathedral, to stand, bareheaded and silent, for short twelve Mass, so as to show they were to the fore when needed; to show God that they wouldn't be behindhand when the bell tolled, when the world was gone with the wind, and nothing was there to do, save sing the song of Bernadette while the stars looked down.

Who would be the first to make an army out of these active and diligent dry bones? Who the first to breathe into them a breath from the flame of endeavour and strife and defiance? Whose lips would first be touched by a red coal from God's altar? Who would be daring enough to snatch a flame from the burning bush and light the land with it? Not Arthur Griffith, for all his words were cold and common; not any of the Republican leaders, for though brave and terribly sincere, none could show a light brighter than a dark lantern; neither Hyde nor Mac Neill, for though the one whispered while the other bellowed, no one of the common people caught a flake of flame from anything they said. Certainly not Bulmer Hobson, Protestant Secretary of the IRB, editor of *Irish Freedom*, and head bottlewasher of all National activities, with his moony face, and bulbous nose, long hair half covered by a mutton-pie hat, a wrapped look on his face, moving about mysterious, surrounded by the ghostly guns of Dungannon:

Ireland awoke when Hobson spoke – with fear was England shaken.

Once, leaning over the counter in the little tobacconist's shop to speak to Tom Clarke sitting in the corner, Sean had said, Why don't you get an editor for *Irish Freedom*, a betther and brighter man than Bulmer Hobson? You ought to know, Mr Clarke, that our members read the paper, now, not for guidance or for inspiration, but merely in a sense of duty. Hobson's articles are nothing more than hundreds of dead thoughts on thousands of cold, leaden slabs of words; and Tom Clarke, who had been nodding in a doze, sprang to his feet excitedly, fire flashing from his remarkable eagle-like eyes, and said hotly, Get out of my shop if you came to talk against Bulmer! D'ye hear, I'll listen to nothing against him. I love Bulmer Hobson as I love my own son!

For a joke, some seraph must have touched the lips of De Valera with a chilled coal from God's altar, to laugh henceforth at the sturdy mouth's efforts to blow it into flame, to turn it into a song of derring-do for everyone to whistle o'er the lave of it. Though Sean knew not even of De Valera's existence, there he was walking beneath the gentle clouds caressing Dublin's streets: a young man full of the seven deadly virtues, punctual, zealous, studious, pious, and patriotic, cautiously pushing a way through crowds of queerternions, stopping occasionally to put them through their paces, numbering them off, making minus double exes of them, forming them into plus fours, and sending them forth in a hurray of feshelons so that one day they might make Ireland a nation of restraints and scollars. In love with a clever and beautiful lady he was, too, who yearned deeply to make her isle a nation free and grand. So De Valera hurried about – for such as he never sauntered, or strolled, or took their ayse in a walk – unknown to all but those to whom an Irish word unheard before was another rung in the Gaelic ladder up to Heaven.

Yeats, the poet, wandered, lonely as a cloud, through the streets, singing his lovely songs into his own ear, wailing at times to his own psyche, *Romantic Ireland's dead and gone, It's with O'Leary in the grave*; the wind for ever rustling the reeds around his feet; wild, white swans for ever flying in a blue sky over his head; and a black-and-gold theatre curtain for ever rising or falling before his eyes. No; he would not kindle a flame in the eyes of the common people, though he had kindled one in the eyes of Cathleen, the daughter of Houlihan; though in a strange, deep way he loved the common people more than Griffith, Mac Neill, or De Valera did, or ever could. Hard at his heels followed

the stout, lumbering George Russell, watching figures, featured
with fire issuing out of their petuitary glands, streaming from
every chimney-top and every smoker's pipe; jumping hilariously,
when on a holiday, from peak to peak of the Wicklow Mountains, the planets for ever chiming the advent of an avatar who
would lead Eire back to her old gods; believing that the world
was buried in a purple glow; staring fixedly at every person newly
presented to him, so that he might see if a red, a blue, or a golden
aura bathed the body, telling him on what plane of spiritual
achievement the newly-presented person stood. Then there was
Patrick Pearse, unknown but to a few, sitting at a desk editing
the Gaelic League's *Sword of Light*; a dreamer pulled separate
ways by two attractions, for one hand held on to St Patrick's
robe, and the other stretched out to grasp the Spear of Danger
held out to him by the singing, laughing, battling boy, Cuchullain. None of these would do. The people still waited for a
Prometheus to bring down a brand of the divine fire and set
the leaden hearts of the poor aflame from one end of Ireland to
the other.

Sean knew them all. He had served in the secret IRB and the
open Wolfe Tone Memorial Committee. He was their Press
steward, and was in charge of all publicity for concert, anniver-
sary, and procession. He was ever at them to put more colour
into their activities. He had persuaded them to fix the Republican
green, white, and orange flag at a saluting-point just before the
grave of Wolfe Tone was reached, so that the marching contingents could give eyes right to the flag and to the dead leader
when they assembled to honour his memory. Then he had gone
to Mr Jamieson, proprietor of the Rotunda picture house, and
had induced him to promise to make a film of the march past the
flag, if the Memorial Committee agreed. Sean had long arguments
with the members, for they were afraid that so much publicity
would give too much information to the police, though Sean
knew full well that what the police didn't know then, wasn't
worth knowing. The delegates of the Wolfe Tone clubs voted for
it; the film was made; and for many nights the Rotunda was
crowded out by the members of the IRB flocking to it to see
themselves taking part in the Bodenstown procession. But the
Committee or the Centres wouldn't hear of route marches with
meetings at different places, when the march ended, to get re-
cruits. It was a secret organization, they said, and so it must

remain. He couldn't get them to see that such activities wouldn't allow the police to break into any inner secret that mattered. He couldn't get them to see that their fight would be tougher than a rough-and-tumble with the police, and that they weren't preparing for this fact. At Centre meetings he tried to put before them some of the problems they would have to face: digging sudden shelters; a slow come-together, a quick get-away, or the opposite; the use of signalling; the problem of provisions; and the care of the wounded. But the meetings of the Centres solely engaged themselves with the collection of this and that levy, or the sale of tickets for one thing or another. It was maddening to him. No important matter was ever discussed unless he himself thrust it under their nose. Few of those whom Sean knew could handle a pick or shovel, tie a knot, do a bandage round a serious wound, slash a gut-way in a hedge, light a fire and cook a simple meal in a wet field with a keen wind blowing. About these things they knew next to nothing.

Once in an effort to be mysterious, to keep him quiet, and to show how wide-awake they really were, a prominent Centre had handed him a British red-covered *Manual of Military Drill*, full of trivialities, useless and out of date, such as the way to slope, port, and shoulder arms, dig shallow trenches, and skirmishing; the guards and thrusts of an infantryman facing a mounted soldier, one, two, three, how to shield a head from a sabre-cut, how to drive a retaliative thrust, how to pin down the cavalryman when he fell from his horse, how to make it a sure thing by a twist to the bayonet as the thrust was made, and a contrary twist when pulling the bayonet back – old stuff, and useless; so he flung it back at them, saying that he'd gone through all this with a broom handle when he was ten, from an identical book given to him by his Dublin Fusilier brother.

They were all lost and dreaming in the romantic ecstasy of Thomas Davis':

Oh, for a steed, a rushing steed, on the Curragh of Kildare,
And Irish squadrons skilled to do what they are ready to dare –
A hundred yards, and England's guards
Drawn up to engage me there!

They were immersed in the sweet illusion of fluttering banners, of natty uniforms, bugle-blow marches, with row on row of dead and

dying foemen strewn over the Macgillicuddy's Reeks, the Hills of
Dublin, and the bonny blue Mountains of Mourne, with the
Soldier's Song aroaring at the dawning of the day. All guns and
drums, but no wounds. Not a thought, seemingly, about the
toil, the rotten sweat, the craving for sleep, the sagging belly
asking for food; the face disfigured, one eye wondering where the
other had gone; an arm twisted into a circle or a figure-of-eight;
the surprised lung, bullet-holed, gasping for breath; or the dangling leg, never to feel firm on the earth again. All these thoughts
he forced before them, asking them to think of ways now by
which they might be made less terrible. All your singing is but
glittering tinsel, coloured balls, and green ribbon. A song is a
fing thing so long as the arms in your hands are as good, or
almost so, as those in the hands of the other fellow. Our methods
won't be dashing cavalry charges, or daring and irresistible
charges by massed infantry. It will be a modified example of the
Boer way of fighting; not those even of Cronje, Joubert, or
Prinsloo; but rather of Botha, Delarey, and De Wet. Sean had
always had a bent for criticism, now it had been sharpened by
Shaw, and those who heard it resented the disturbance of their
dreams.

However, he had persuaded them into selecting a Committee
from the Supreme Council and the Centres to see how the IRB
could be brought into closer touch with the militant Labour
Movement. They met in Seamus O'Connor's house in Clon-
liffe Road, and he and Sean Mac Dermott were chosen to visit
Jim Larkin, to get the *Irish Worker* to record their activities.
They found a hearty welcome, and a direct promise that the
paper would do all it could, which couldn't be much more than
it was doing at the moment in support of the National Movement,
which Sean knew to be true; and a firm request that *Irish Freedom*
might, in return, pay a little attention to the cause of the workers.
This, said Sean, will surely be done. The next meeting of the
Committee was to be held in the *Irish Freedom* office, so that
what had happened might be recorded, and when Sean got there
on the tick, he found Tom Clarke sitting on the counter, waiting
for the others to come. None of the rest, S. O'Connor, S. Deakin,
Bulmer Hobson, Peader Cearney, author of the *Soldier's Song*,
came. Nor did any send a reason for their absence. They just
ignored the whole thing. Both Sean and Tom Clarke waited
for some time. Then Clarke slid from the counter saying, They

can't be coming. I must get back to the shop. So in silence Sean saw him lock the office door, slip the key in his pocket, heard him say, Well, so long, Sean, and saw him go without breaking his silence by a single word.

Clarke knew they wouldn't come, thought Sean as he walked homewards through the once aristocratic Gloucester Street, past St Thomas' Church where his sister's children had been baptized, standing sentinel at the top of the street, keeping back the poor from pressing into the richer part of the city. So they have decided against bringing the rough energy and virile splendour of the workers to the definite aid of the National Movement. Well, to hell with them then! Why should he give up all his energy and the little money he had to spare to a movement that left almost all the people out of it? They didn't seem to know even what they would have to face. Any shelter they might need, they would have to build it with their own hands, hands that wouldn't know how to do it. A shelter, strong, but to last through the time of danger only. Any permanent sit-down in any place wouldn't do; it would be surrounded, and dissipated in smoke and flame. Their vantage points would have to be the deep ditch, the bramble hedge tangled with the dog-rose, or the street corner leading from a maze of turnings. They couldn't hope to stand upright in the battle: they would have to come crouching, and, crouching, get away again swift and foxy. And there would be no green flag for a wounded man to wrap around him; he would be lucky to have a bandage to stay the flow from his leaking body.

Few of the Republicans were of his kinship. Here, in these houses in the purple of poverty and decay, dwelt his genuine brethren. Why shouldn't he fight for them against the frauds that kept them prisoners there? Sean had seen and felt the force of the corrupting hand stretched out for profit, sometimes from the sleeve of Christ's coat itself. A foreman where he had once worked, a highly respected churchwarden, and a good fellow in a lot of ways, had a club from which the workers had to buy what they rarely wanted, costing four times the market price. All earned by overtime went to pay what they owed. Sean refused to join, gathered the men together against it, and the club was dissolved; but from that day he had been a marked man, and found peace only when he returned to idleness and hunger.

In another job a number of arches to carry a big building had to be constructed by a Dublin firm of Jim and Jerry Dilish, and Sean was selected to watch that the job was done according to contract. He had been told smilingly that the Dilishes were a reliable firm, and that he needn't put himself out watching: immediately, Sean felt suspicious. Like Sir Boyle Roche, he said to himself, I smell a rat; I see him forming in the air and darkening the sky; but I'll nip him in the bud. When he got to the job, the foreman, a carpenter, ran to him, shook his hand, said how glad he was a Gael had come to him; that he had heard Sean speak splendidly at Gaelic League and Sinn Fein meetings; said he was a good Gael too, and that they were bound to get on well together; and asked Sean out for a drink. The rat was growing bigger. When he saw Sean poring over the specifications, the saucy grin on his face weakened, and he came close to whisper, This may mean a fiver for you; and it's well to know that the firm's friendly with the engineer, wines and dines with him.

It was a hard fight for Sean. What good would any opposition be from him? The loss of another job would be God's own reward for honesty: that was the hard fact, coupled with the soft one that a fiver would be the reward for a closed eye, a shut mouth. He had never seen a fiver, much more owned one. For one of them he could buy ten fine second-hand books he needed. And by putting himself in the way of getting them, he linked himself up with a new pair of trousers, and a new skirt for his mother that she badly needed. By accommodation, too, he linked himself with greater men, the contractor, the engineer, and the foreman. Who was to pay for the job? A crowd of shareholders who'd never know anything about it, so that, as the Church would say, there was no individual soul against which to sin. Neither would there be a betrayal of trust, for those connected with the job were all rogues, bar the workmen, who were honest because they hadn't the chance to be anything else. So what or whom would he betray by taking the fiver? He'd suffer a sense of shame for a short time, that was all; though he couldn't stop the thought that never again would he be the same man he had been before he took the money. To hell with them! he thought: God or no God, I'll be as straight as I can. So the contractor's foreman paled with anger, and cursed when Sean held him to the bond.

—Dilish's a boxer, he remarked one day, and I shouldn't like to be you if you upset him.

—I can do a bit of rough-and-tumble myself, replied Sean, and tell him that from me.

One day, high up on the plank of a scaffolding, along came a tall partner of the firm, trim in a fine navy-blue lounge suit, cream embroidered waistcoat, soft hat, and natty tie, till they touched the rough garments of Sean, and the stalwart figure bent down to whisper in his ear, though he looked straight in front, as if not noticing Sean, I understand you're giving a lot of trouble here, interfering, holding the work back, and making yourself a nuisance.

—I? whispered Sean back at him, staring frontways too. Oh, no, not at all; I'm an amiable fellow really.

—The likes of you make me sick! said the blue lounge suit venomously; for one pin, you conceited, third-class ape, I'd knock you off the scaffold!

—Oh, you would, would you? whispered Sean, tensing his muscles, still standing side by side with the lounge suit, his cheeks flaming; then you'll come flying with me, and if there's any kind of a God at all, you'll be the underdog when we hit the ground!

But the lounge suit turned away, leaving a bitter curse stinging Sean's ear, walked across the plank, slid down the ladder, snapped at the foreman when he got to the bottom, and stalked away from the job.

It was all useless: it made Dilish surly with the foreman; the foreman surly with the men; and the job a worse one. They began to work overtime, and when Sean told his own foreman this, he was told sharply that he needn't bother to stay; that a good job would be done; and that the engineer had full confidence in Dilish. So what they couldn't do in daylight, they did at night, rushing the poor men to make up for lost time. When the arches had been built, one of them began to sink on bad foundations, and when the big building began to be piled on them, it sank quicker; it began to crack, in spite of all the frenzied patches applied; and, to this day, a wide crack from floor to ceiling can be seen, testifying to the foolishness of Sean. He might as well have taken the fiver; a better job would have been done if he had; and many times afterwards, whenever he put a hand in a pocket, he flamed with regret that he didn't feel the rustle of a five-pound note there. The angels in de heabn gwinter write my name, write my name, write my name, yes, write my name with a golden pen. Sean laughed silently at the poor fancy. To fight well, there must be a crowd beside and behind you to fight with you. Dilish would be blessed by bishop and priest. They didn't know; why the hell didn't they know? The workers must be rallied to the fight.

It would be a hard job to drag them from their rag-warmed stupor. Middle Gardiner Street and Lower Dorset Street on their knees before the rich and lordly Jesuit church of X Xavier's; Cumberland Street, Marlboro' Street, Nelson's Lane, and Gloucester Street, with its Diamond, lurching and rotten, leaning for succour on the precious Pro-Cathedral; Dominick Street and Upper Dorset Street bowing their rags before the St Saviour's Church of the fair-robed Dominicans. Jesus! the poor were everywhere, crowding the value of their Christ out of existence; their real *lux mundi* the glitter of mirror and bottle and glass in the nearest beckoning drink-shop, where all their gods dissemble. There they were safe and snug for the nonce. There they could crawl and climb away from their dung and destitution to a more exalted state of joyous misery. There they could play wild games and sing many a wild song with a mad Beethoven and many a crazy Shakespeare. Jesu, mercy! Bind up their wounds! Let Tennyson sing outside to soothe them; or David quiet them with the tinkling of his golden harp: psalm, boys and girls, calm. John the Baptist dances, and Salome's on her knees in prayer. Hush; let her alone – she isn't the worst. Strip tease, and take the consequences. Juggle me into jeopardy.

As far as countries go, Ireland's no worse now than she was before she was as bad as she is now. Whatever happens, the colour round the throne of the Man above is an emerald green, let the orange Ulster idiot yell as he will that it's orange and blue. We had God's sky over us, and St Joseph's Free Night Shelter for homeless women, so that the few who could be crowded into it couldn't forget that kind hearts were more than coronets. And if it went to that, there were Ulster's own grain-carriers, on their own orange quays, each of them carrying two hundred tons of grain on his own back from the hatch to the ship's rail as a fair day's work, and no shinnannican, so as to keep the other fellows in the suffocating hold from the sin of idleness, bare-footed, half naked, coughing the dust out of their lungs, and keeping pace with the Protestant tubs swinging down on them, or going up, making the men's muscles creak with the strain of keeping them full. Then there were the women and children in their Protestant mills, fined for laughing, or stooping to smoothe down their hair; and the little children fined when sick twice as much as they could earn in the same time, using the quickest speed their little hands could know. Christ Himself would find it pretty hard to do this kind of work. Carrying two hundred tons of grain on a back each day, without a hope in their bowels or a thought in their minds of any ease in the future, was a heavy cross for any back to carry. And not a one of these girls, like the sprightly Pippa, the silk weaver, would spring out of her bed when the whole sunrise, not to be suppressed, rose, reddened, and its seething breast flickered in bounds, grew gold, then over-flowed the world. Not a one of them would spring from her bed to rush into a Lurgan or a Belfast linen mill, murmuring, God's presence fills our earth, each only as God wills can work. Stretch and stretch, it would be, sigh and sigh, dole and dree, oh, sour and bitter first hour of the morning!

Work? Ay, work's all right; but is this work? No; it's the ripe robbery of life from the very young and the little older. Browning, Browning, you make too much of almost everything you say. Your Pippa never passed through Lurgan or Belfast, nor did she ever see a bobbin spinning on a spindle there. Enjoying the grace of only one holiday in the year, Pippa had to turn the few hours into a dance and a song, a sweet song; one of sure faith and reasonable hope enduring. May God forgive her.

> The year's at the winter, the days are still-born;
> The workers are restless, while others, bepearled,
> Sing God's made us the one wonder-light of the world!
> The workers sweat dumbly, while others are dancing,
> Their meekness forsworn, bewitched and begirled,
> Singing God's in His Heaven – all's right with the world!

If Pippa couldn't, it was Browning's yearning that she might, that she should, touch the conscience of the selfish and the sloth-ful; make the heart of the young to see strength and fair promise in darkling things; fire the heart of the wealthy young man to strike for human freedom and a just survey of man; and stir the pulse even of a monsignor to lift himself out of his own fear into the courage and love free and firm in the singing heart of a maiden. It is a fairy Pippa who passes, a fairy who would like, for an hour or two, to walk the way of all flesh. She is Browning

forgiving and excusing his own certainty and comfort by dreaming
a little mill-girl into singing a song of God's good management of
man. A noble fellow, loud-voiced in his lusty loneliness. The surge
of a trombone's song through the still sad music of humanity. A
clever singing simpleton straying through an uninspected isle.
A red moonbeam streeling through a dark sky. With all his gay
talk, his hilarious, comfortable clothing, he wore an eagle's
feather in his hair. And when the day comes, Browning will see
our joy, and hear our laughter.

But it is well that Pippa has passed by for ever, singing her song
of forgiveness to us all. The Pippas now need a new song and a
new hope; the women, side by side with their men, assaulting the
castle, the big house, the boardroom, till the walls are breached,
the doors down, and the song of life is heard in their halls. And
in the song will be the unfolding of the final word from the
evolving words of the ages, the word of the modern, the word
En-Masse.

GREEN FIRE ON THE HEARTH

A STRANGE fellow in every way he was, and his name was
Kevin O'Loughlin. Relatively to the rest of the members of the
O'Toole Gaelic Club, he was rich, for he filled out a good job
in the Civil Service. He was very thin, except for the shoulders
which seemed to be trying to climb to have a look over his head,
so that the eager, alert face appeared to look out on life from the
upper part of his shrunken chest rather than from the top of a
neck. This slight deformity, added to a royal flush on the tips of
his high bony cheeks, indicated that he had been ordained to
end his days in a gale of coughing. Rather large, sloppy ears
stood out from his head, and he could flap them at will like the
way a fowl flaps her wings; and the muscles under his scalp
were so strong that by a quick quiver of them he could throw a
book from the top of his head some distance away on to the
ground. He had a fine high forehead, a long, thin, aristocratic
nose, and large, critical, luminous, beautiful brown eyes. Indeed,
had he been of a very small stature, he would have looked like a

rather handsome gnome. His lungs weren't able for a hearty laugh, and any he tried to give, and he tried to give many, for he had a caustic sense of humour, ended in an eerie sound like a moistened hiss. He was sharply intelligent, and highly respected, and a little feared, by the other members of the Club. He had the history of the Gaelic Athletic Association – at that time the finest in the world – on the tip of his tongue, and he was something of an authority on the tactics of every Gaelic game. He was a pious fellow, critical of the practice but not of the theory of his Church, a weekly communicant, broad-minded, and a sincere member of the Third Order of St Francis. He dreaded smutty stories, and liked Sean because he hated them too, unless they were salted with wit or illumined and purified with humour. Kevin had two passions, the one something of a vice, the other something of a virtue – he loved betting, and however ill he'd be, he never liked to miss the Grand National; and he worshipped the writings of Bernard Shaw. Whenever a Shaw play or preface appeared in print, he wasn't to be seen that night at the Club, however important the business happened to be; and for nights afterwards the laugh like a moistened hiss was loud in the land.

—Shaw, Shaw! Sean would say petulantly; you're for ever shouting that fellow's name in our ears. Who is he, anyway?

—The cleverest Irishman the world knows, Sean. A wit of wonder. A godsend to men who try to think, who's creating a new world out of new thought. Read *John Bull's Other Island*, and the Ireland you think you know and love will vanish before your eyes.

—Well, that's a damn fine recommendation! I don't wish the Ireland I know and love to vanish before my eyes, thank you and Mr Shaw. So talk sense, Kevin, and tell what this Shaw is doing, or has done, for Ireland.

—The best thing possible by helping to make Ireland plain to her own people.

—He hasn't done that, for any Gaelic Leaguer I've asked up to now says, Shaw? Is it that fella? Him? A dangerous gazebo, hot-foot after English money, that's what he is, making game of his own people – that's your Shaw.

—Don't mind them, Sean; they've never read the man. You can get a paper-covered copy for sixpence.

—Paper-covered copy of what?

—*John Bull's Other Island*. It'll make a new man of you – I'll get you a copy if you promise to read it.

—Thanks, said Sean; but I'll buy a copy for myself if I want one; but I don't, and before he could say goodbye, Kevin had to race for the last tram for Rathmines, leaving the Pillar, and, through the lighted window, Sean could see him panting as he sank heavily down on his seat.

He failed to get that green paper-covered book out of his head; so one week, when payday came, instead of hurrying home to change out of his dungarees and go to the Gaelic League, he went straight to Jason's, where the decorous, trimly-dressed assistant stared at him when he asked for the sixpenny edition of the play, handing it out and taking the sixpence as if she were sure Sean was making a mistake. At tea he began to read the green-covered book, the play first, then the preface; the clock ticked, the time passed; the Gaelic League forgotten, he read on till dawn was near, and had but a chance for a few hours' sleep before he rose to begin another day's work.

From that day, for quite a while, Sean seemed to see Shaw everywhere; his tall figure, in his Irish homespuns, marched in front, and whenever he looked behind him, there was Shaw following quick to overtake him. He replaced Nelson on Dublin's Pillar, standing there with a questioning smile on his roguish face, looking cynically and sadly over all the Dublin streets, slum-poisoned and square-pampered. Sean saw him peeping from behind the fluted columns of the Bank of Ireland, whispering to Sean that lots thought the building the Temple of the Holy Ghost, but that this was all bankum, and that it was a mighty den of highly respectable, and greatly honoured, thieves. The figure of St Laurence O'Toole towering over the top of the Pro-Cathedral had changed the head of the holy man for the head of the smiling sage. Sometimes, when Sean was swinging his pick, the red beard came close to his ear and the musical voice said – Take it easy, man; don't kill yourself for any employing exploiter. Wait till I tell you, and the voice whispered, Blackguard, bully, drunkard, liar, foulmouth, flatterer, beggar, backbiter, corrupt judge, envious friend, vindictive enemy, political traitor: all these an Irishman may easily be, just as he may be a gentleman (a species extinct in England, and no one a penny the worse); but he is never quite the hysterical, nonsense-crammed, fact-proof, truth-terrified, unballasted sport of all the bogy panics and all the silly enthusiasms that now calls itself God's Englishman. England cannot do without its Irish and its Scots today, because it cannot

do without at least a little sanity. – Then the musical voice went
into a laugh, and added, Idolatrous Englishman and fact-facing
Irishman are proved today, for though I shock you, you are
fearlessly facing me, aren't you? Of course you are; and a lot the
better for it – eh? But don't be too cocky, young fellow, for though
the Irishman refuses to be a subject of England's, he is proud to
be one to the Vatican. Oh, yes, I know you're not; but all the
rest of you are. And though Sean had heard that Shaw was a
strict teetotaller, in every pub Sean was in, he seemed to see
someone very like him there, arguing with bartender and customers, and lowering pint after pint with the worst of them. Up
on the tip-top of Tara's hill, there he was, looking for all the world
like the statue of St Patrick, his gay green cope tucked around his
knees, poking his crozier about the ground to turn up the elements of ancient Gaelic culture and shouting at the bottom of his
voice to all the villages lying around, I don't see any signs of
glory knocking about here. If the Gaels would search the slums
as diligently as they searched Tara, they would be doing wiser
work.

—A man without a soul, said the Gaelic Leaguers; nothing is
sacred to him – not even the slums!

Shaw showed an Ireland very different from the lady Yeats
made her out to be, peasants dancing round her to the sound of
tabor and drum, their homespun shirts buttoned up with stars.
Shaw's was rather grimy, almost naked, save for the green flag
draped round her middle. She was grey with the dustiness of
flour mixed with the dung of pigs, and her fair hands were horny
with the hard work of turning stony ground into a state of
fertility. The look on her fine face was one of unholy resignation,
like one once in agony, now at ease in the thick torpor of murphia.
Inconsequence stared from her eyes, and leaving her at ease at
home telling her beads, or telling small coins till they mingled and
became one, throwing some of both to jingle on a street in Heaven
in the way of a priesthood for one of her boys so as to endorse
a claim to a rookery nook in a respectable part of Paradise. No
fool, she was sure of her place in this world, and surer of one in
the next. So she stood in front of what was the most powerful part
of England, Broadbent, in the shape of a breezy mountain of
bombast, dressed in a motor-coat, goggles, and gauntlet gloves, a
fat purse dripping largesse, golf-sticks on his back; full of pom-
penduring confidence, ready to take away even the green flag

round Ireland's middle and turn it into a gilt-edged security. There the jovial fellow stood, surrounded by some of Ireland's sons, the butcher, baker, and candlestick-maker, headed by a practical priest with an eye fixed on the bulging purse; a priest who was as ignorant as the Englishman of Ireland's close kinship with nobility; ignorant even of the piety that had sanctified every sod, so that God Himself could walk out anywhere without soiling His holy feet. Near naked, Ireland stood, with the one jewel of Keegan's Dream occasionally seen sparkling in her tousled hair, attaching poverty to pride; a shameful figure, but noble still, though her story was hidden and her songs unsung. Hewing wood and drawing water ceaselessly with the thoughts amurmur on her cracked lips,

> Waste no time on paltry things,
> Life would have us queens and kings.

Two elements fought each other here, back to back: a dream without efficiency, and efficiency without a dream; but with this tense difference: that from the dream efficiency could grow, but from the efficiency no dream could ever come.

And now in every Roscullen throughout the land, still with the green flag for a hope and a battle-eye, the long, long brooding was at last becoming pregnant. The dreadful dreaming was being hitched to a power and a will to face the facts. And this Irishman, Shaw, was helping us to do it; this strange Irishman, no stranger to his kin, warm-hearted, and arrogantly Protestant, who had had an Orangeman for a great-grandfather, whose sister had been an abbess, and whose uncle had been hanged for a rebel: these few details giving us the queer *status quo*, the life, the soul, the dream; the unending change, the temerity, the eternal jubilate that are known as Ireland, Eire, Banba, the Poor Old Woman, Sheila Nee Gyra: Orangeman, Abbess, Rebel – three in one and one in three, and there is Ireland.

One of the reasons, says Bernard Shaw, why the Abbey didn't do my play was because it wasn't congenial to the whole spirit of the neo-Keltic Movement, bent on making a new Ireland out of its own ideal, while my play was an uncompromising presentment of the real old Ireland. – No, no; not quite. No more uncongenial than was W. P. O'Ryan's Boyne valley enterprise, both of which left behind them a deep and unquenchable growth towards reality in the minds and hearts of many Irish people. And part of the Gaelic Movement, coloured and glossy though it was with many poetical and political symbols, was a trend towards realism in thought and act; a proving of most things, and a holding-fast of some that were good. The Irish were beginning to look into their own lives, not through the distorting mirrors of Westminster; nor yet through the flattering ones in the Old Parliament House of College Green; but through the reflections given from city and town, from farm and dairy, from field, factory, and workshop, from Church and State, though the Movement, maybe, too often draped its realism in coloured shawls and kilts and fluttering flags, and flavoured it with the music of pipe, trumpet, and drum. Neither did the play show the real old Ireland, for that went further back than the coarse, quick, and common mind of Doran; the harassing anxiety of Haffigan over his five-acre meadow; the sober and settled acceptance by Corny and Judy Doyle of things as they were and ever will be; the forty-pounds-a-year magnificence of Nora O'Reilly; nor was it the common honouring of holy things by Father Dempsey, whose vision from Mount Carmel was the surety of a plump chicken for dinner and a plenitude of candles in his church; nor was an Ireland further back, a Patsy Farrell, meagre and barefooted, harnessing himself in a humour of silliness against persecution, and trying to ease his misfortune and misery by giving an occasional cheer for poor ould Ireland. The Ireland further back was more like Fadher Keegan, banished from the altar, hinging himself more closely to his breviary than ever, torturing himself delightfully with the vision of a country where the State is the Church and the Church the people; three in one, and one in three; where work is play, and play is life; where the priest is the worshipper, and the worshipper the worshipped; three in one, and one in three; carrying the vision around with him to pour it into the loneliness of a round tower: the dream of a madman, but the dream of an Irishman too.

Sean was now in bad company constantly. Not a week passed but he was found hobnobbing with Shaw, Darwin, Frazer, and France, and the volubility and loudness of their positive talk were having a dangerous effect upon him. One day, having honoured, in Bodenstown, the memory of Wolfe Tone, as he was coming home on a lovely late summer evening through misery-crowded Marlborough Street, he saw a crowd of Barney Dorans,

Matt Haffigans, Corny Doyles, and Patsy Farrells gathered round
the Church of the Immaculate Conception, known to all Dubliners as the Pro-Cathedral, staring up at the figure of St Laurence
O'Toole gesticulating with his crozier, standing tiptoe like a
ballet dancer on his pedestal, and sometimes leaning down
towards the street so that you were in fear he'd come tumbling
down any minute. Shouting away the saint was, to the crowd
below, and Sean, when he had pushed his way forward, found it
was a tirade against Shaw, while Professor Mcgennis in his
acodemnical gown held on to the saint's skirt to keep him from
falling.

—I'm tellin' yous, shouted the saint, that Shaw said there
wasn't a single creditable established religion in the world. An'
they say a sayin' man said it. He's mad, an' unashamed of it!
An' he follows this up with the asseveration that we've only to
read the folk-tale of John Barleycorn to get a clear idea of what
put redemption by the sacrifice of a Saviour into the mind of man.
That's what he said here when he clambered up after I had climbed
down to run and get a quick one in the DWD to thry to quench
the drouth destroyin' me. An' Pathrick over there on th' opposite
corner never lifted a finger to stop him. So busy colloguin' with
scribes and Pharisees to put Armagh to the forefront at the
expense of Dublin that was thrivin' before Armagh was thought
of. I tell Patrick to his face, here an' now, that he was what he
wasn't, an' is what he shouldn't have been, possessin' enough
ignorance of letters that ought to have kept him from being
anything above a rural-tooral dean, a dimestic prelate, or a
vicarago-general. He pooh-poohdled the danger of Darwin,
tellin' me it was all a stunt, sayin' that man was too sensible to
let himself be associated with a monkey; and so that bounder,
Hoaxley, spread the good news all over England, an' a hint of it
came over here, to be made into an elegant and humorous story
by this Shaw fella in preface an' play. He comes along to upset
things just when we've got yous into the teetotalarian order of
being happy in misery, and safe in your poverty; th' glow of hell-
fire dazzlin' your eyes so that yous would, without a murmur,
toil up th' slopes of our highest holy hill, with joints crackin' and
feet bleedin', never thinkin' of singin' the song of *Take a little bit off
the top for me, for me*; content that the hill might get higher an'
higher so as you'd be climbin' an' climbin' till the praties were
dug, the frost was all over, and the sumer was icumen in.

Wasn't I glad to see in *The Universe*, the other day, a reply to a query asking what was Adam's and Eve's surnames, and when did the rite of marriage begin, tellin' the inquirer that there weren't surnames then, and that marriage began with them, an' that the book which questioned it was both silly and dangerous. Now, went on the saint, stretching farther down over the parapet, so that Mcgennis found it hard to hold him, I'm tellin' yous that Shaw's books are both silly an' dangerous too. Th' Garden of Eden's as far as yous can go. There yous stop. An' don't thry to look over th' wall, either. Yous must all ask questions that can easily be answered, see? What is it to you, or to anyone, if one of the apostles tells of the flight into Egypt, and the others don't? Or that one apostle said the birth of a Saviour was told to Joseph, and another that Mary heard about it first? Things like these are neither here nor there to yous. Or that the crowding of Mary out of the inn, an' th' sudden filling of the sky with angels bursting their lungs with a rhapsody in the blue for the benefit of ignorant shepherds, was Luke's story, and his alone, the others seeming not to have heard a word about it. There's such a thing as wanting to know too much. Hasn't Luke a perfect right to be romantic if he wanted to? You just keep tight to the dogmas of your faith an' yous'll never know a poor day.

Suddenly Sean saw, at the back fringe of the crowd, the tall, lithe figure of Shaw standing, and he looking up with a smile at the raging saint. Raising a hand and his hat, he caught the eye of the saint, and said in a quiet, steady, harmonious voice, My dear man, Christ harped, not on creeds or catechisms, or sacraments, but on conduct; harped on conduct, fifed and drummed on conduct, and, were He here today, He'd saxophone on it too.

—Away with you! bellowed O'Toole. You're like the witch of the rock of the candles whose smallest glimmer when seen brought death to all who saw it; so your wizard rashlight of knowledge will bring spiritual darkness to any heyeball that catches a glampse of its gloom; but with the help of SSSSSSS, Barra, Beccan, Coman, Dima, Dalua, Flann, and Garvan, we'll down you, an' shut your sayin's out of every free library livin' in th' land.

—Still him, spill him, kill him for his bad books! roared the crowd, raising handsome sticks into the air, sthrike him down for malingerin' us! But Fadher Dempsey held them back, saying,

Patience, patience, boys; not just yet. Leave him to the saint for a few minutes longer.

—You go about everywhere, Shaw, mutterin' that miracles are poor things to depend on; but what d'ye say to the saint, who in a brown study of the gospels, never felt a pair o' birds buildin' a nest in his outsthretched hand, which, when, what the dear saint saw, sat without a stir so's not to disturb them till they had mated, the eggs hatched out, and the young birds able to wing it for themselves. Was that miracle a poor dependage for the bards who have sung of it often? No, Shaw, it won't do. Many brave hearts are a-yell down in Hell; so beware, beware!

—Let him think, shouted Mcgennis, peeping from behind the saint's cope, let him think of

> The ghost of John, James, Christopher, Benjamin Binns,
> Who was cut down right in the midst of his sins;
> Now his home is down below;
> Though he gets out for an hour or so,
> When the cock begins to crow,
> It's farewell, Benjamin Binns!

—Aha, yelled a man, full-dressed in green coat, white breeches, polished top-boots, and plumed hat of the Irish National Foresters; aha, wiping the creamy froth of a newly-lowered pint from a flowing moustache, now maybe he knows what's in store for him before long if he doesn't mend his way o' thinkin'. If he wants to understand things above our poor fumin' minds, let him go an' ask poor Benjamin Binns about them.

—Shut up, and go home, you! the saint rebuked, shouting down at the plumed hat. Go home, an' look in the glass to see if you're there at all; and if y'are, keep it a dead secret. And let the rest of yous all remember, includin' the man under th' sin of conceited knowledge, that St Uiskebaha has taught that the penny catechism is th' casket in which is all the knowledge necessary to be known to man; anything outside of it is either silly or dangerous. In it is a full, free, and what-you-fancy explanation of the natural and supernatural worlds, from th' fall of man to the miracle of the five thousand barley loaves and two small fishes, showing us all, including our friend on the fringe of the crowd, that no man can be made good by an Act of Parliament.

—Here, here, said the voice under the plumed hat, that only

stands to reason, an' i t's my opinion, an' I don't care who knows it, that th' Garden of Eden was somewhere among the lakes an' fells of Killarney.

And Sean went away with his secret that he dared to tell to no one there, for he would have been laughed at or brained for telling that he had been in the Garden of Eden; had climbed the wall with much labour and heart-panting; had slid down with a bump on the other side, and had found the place far different from the yarns in newspaper, magazine, and religious manuals which spread the news that through the luscious venery south winds blew so soft that they barely stirred the golden hair of Neve; they filled the spaces with delectable trees languishing lovingly in the silvery mist that went up every morning to water the garden, and so save Adam from having to bend a back. They garlanded every fine tree with delicious fruits, gay in colour and rich in juice, bending so low that Adam on the broad of his back could nibble them without stirring a finger. Gentle animals padded about among the trees, and purred with pleasure, and played tig together, and bent the knees whenever Adam passed by, for he was lord over all that were there. Birds of every hue and cry, fluttering and fluting about everywhere; and neither sign nor sound of death was anywhere near in this sweet garden of rest; perpetual summer, where the nights were naked as the happy couple were, showing all their beauty so that naked night and naked couple mixed and laughed together, peace dropping from the skies, and evening full of the angels' wings.

That's how the mistory went; but Sean found it, when he got there, to be different and disturbed. It was shaking with the roaaoaring, yelelling, squeealing, and growowling of fierce, huge, and unnatural beasts, so that Sean trembled for his life and sought to get back over the wall, but found that it was as hard to get out as it was easy to get in; so the one thing to do now was to keep going on, and dodge the danger. Climbing a little way up a tall horsetail, he looked around and saw that the Paradise was a vast expanse of slime and swamp, with great masses of horsetails, huge calamitic *Mishelaymassmores* towering sky-high, stout-stemmed *Eiraillas* twining round thick clumps of *Sporangia belfusstica*, each striving to destroy the other and reign alone in the Garden of Eden; and everywhere as far as eye could reach or thought could go, there were sprinkled in and out through it all, funguses, brown, grey, black, red, white, and blue, taller than the stately elm, all topped with widely-domed roofs, like great domes of churches, roosting-places for the numerous flocks of the long-baked, snaky-necked, leather-winged ptero-dactyls, who often came between Adam and Eve and a sweet sleep by their rousing way of song, which in sound was something between the trumpeting of a mastodon and the crowing of a mighty fowl, and who were, as we all know, the linnets, larks, and sparrows of that age. All the colours of the land before him were gloomy browns, sad greens, and fading purples, while overhead a leaden, scowling sky kept the heart low and terrified.

Hearing voices ahead, Sean roughly set aside the sharp, tall, green flags thrusting up from the virgin soil and clinging round his legs, and pushed on to the fringe of the rushes. Setting them aside with caution, he looked out over a wind-swept marsh, exactly like the one behind him. Over to the right, near to the mouth of a big, deep, dark dugout, squatted a hairy man and a hairy woman, and Sean knew at once that they must be Adam and Eve, for they had their arms round each other. Before them a thin, short man, sitting on his hunkers, had a flint sheet on his bare knees, and a flint pen was scratching along it, so Sean knew he was busy interviewing them. Beside the man about to take notes, stood a great big fat fellow, with a tremendous grin on his wide-open space, his tangled hair falling into his eyes, his hands keeping a tangle of porifera safely strung around his mighty loins, one of its stems held in the right hand of a little nervous-looking, dull, dumpling-faced manikin with a blue-stone cross hanging on his breast, an umbrella of palm in his left hand, a Roman collar round his neck, all embellished by a look of conceited silliness on his moony face that he and his fat friend took to be thought. Sean crept nearer to hear what they had to say.

—I'm Jeecaysee, the fat man said, the mild knight of the little man, the schnapper-up of God's tremendous trifles; past, present, and to come, grand chief arranger of the greybards at play; awethor of the misuses of divorsety; and this, indicating the little man by his side, is Daabruin, suborned into life to make right what's wrong with the world, and to lead the fiat of heretics to the end of the roaman road; and this gentleman, pointing to the one with the slate tablet and the flinty pen, is a newsman from the city of cod in the land that is over the hills and far away, who has come to get from the first father and mother of men the true facts of how you vaulted into life, and the impressions that struck you when you woke to the beauty and peace of your God-given garden.

—That's it! said the newsman; I want to get at the bottom, and then at the top, of the rumours everywhere about how the first boy met the first girl, see? Everyone has a different slant on the occurrence. F'rinstance, Singasonga of Nota Chagpur says he made the first man and woman out of clay with the help of a spade; the Shillishalliucks of the White Nile say their god, Jokes, made white men from black clay, red men from green clay, black men from white clay, and brown men from blue clay, which sounds a bit far-stretched for me; and the Taaraaraarowa of Tatatiti, chief god of the world, says emphatically that he made the first man from red clay, and when he was asleep, made a female figure from the clay, sawed a rib-bone out of the man, shoved it into the clay figure, and before you could say Eire inverse, the figure lepped up into a lively, dancing woman, tapping a tambourine. But now I'm facing the real McCoy, the pair themselves, ready to get the real goods from boy and girl; and he laid the slate on an algae-covered rock, poised his flint pen, and waited for them to begin.

—Well, said Adam slowly, in the beginning, as you are all aware, there was nothing in existence, for nothing was, for everything was without form, and void, and darkness was on the face of the deep.

—Ah! said the newsman, there was the deep: now let us be clear – what actually was the deep?

—The deep? echoed Adam. The deep was the deep that was there out in the deep, dark days beyond recall – surely that's quite plain to everyone?

—Not to me, said the newsman, shaking his head.

—Maybe, remarked Jeecaysee, the exposition isn't quite clear: we must trust tradition. He turned to Daabruin: Now, vessel of innersense, do your bit!

Daabruin stood stiff, held his temples tight like a man in sudden and violent pain. Stop, stop, stop! he cried; stop talking for a moment, for I see half of what I'm going to say. Will God give me strength? Will my brain give one jump and see all? Heaven help me! I used to be fairly good at thinking. Will my head split – or will it see? I see half, I only see half! He buried his face in his hands, and stood in a sort of rigid torture of thought or prayer. Then a convulsion of revaluation swept over the moony face, and the tense lips opened to mutter, The deep was the deep that was where nothing that was was not.

—Ah! said the newsman; quite; I get you now. It's all quite clear.

—I knew it would be, said Jeecaysee.

—Well, now, about the way the two of you came out of what was once the great deep, eh?

—It was all very simple, said Adam. The Man above just pointed a finger at a tuft of moss and said, Come out of it, Adam! And out I had to come.

—And then? inquired the newsman.

—Then things went like clockwork: the lovely fish in the sea; the lovely birds in the air; the wonderful animals on the land all of which were named and addressed by me; and then, when the Man above saw I was lonely, he put me asleep, took a rib out of my side, and, pointing a thumb at Eve, made herself there.

—Oh, did he now? said Eve, suddenly sarcastic. That's a one-sided story if y'ask me! There wasn't a flash of a second of time lost between the making of us, as everyone knows. We were man and maid together or we weren't made at all; and took precedence over all other living things.

—You were an afterthought, I'm telling you! said Adam sharply. It's there in the Book for anyone to see.

—Ay, said Eve hotly, slipped in with your connivance to give the excuse for making the woman subject to the man. But God spoke before you; and my version, the true version, is there in the Book too, for everyone to see.

—Both of them can't be right, said the newsman conclusively. There's an error somewhere.

—Only so in the unmanageable mind's eye, said Jeecaysee. He turned to Daabruin: Do your bit, my boy!

Again the simplisissimust stiffened, clasped the head between his hands, tossed out bitter murmurs of thought or prayer, and then, casting down his head to gaze on his queer feet, he said, The things told are here to prove the tales. The one here is two, the two one; so what? There is neither first nor second, but two seconds in one first, and two firsts in one second. There is no Adam or Eve, but an Adam plus Eve, and an Eve plus Adam; so though there may be two persons, there is but one indivisible individual, therefore each is *nulla secundus*; therefore though both stories are different, both are identical, for each to the other is an *alter idem*, so all is one, and error is not where error cannot be.

—*Nulla secundus* or *dulla profundis*, Adam's making a wide mistake if he's thinking of getting on top of me, said Eve.

—Now that the question of the two-to-one stories is settled for good and all, said the newsman, let's touch something romantic – Did you fall in love with your good man the minute you clapped eyes on him, or what?

—There wasn't a chance of falling in love with anything else, man. Up to that time he was as good as they make 'em.

—But you were a little shy, weren't you, at first?

—Maybe; but Jeecaysee came along and gave us all the advice we needed. He sang for us *My love is like a red, red nose* and *My love is but a lassie yet*, said that our lives would be divinely arkadian; that in the mystic future we'd grow into two beautiful china figures, a shepherd and his shepherdess, side by side, and close as close together; idols of the happy and healthy peasant and peasantess, giving scope for many sweet songs to Virgil, Ariosto, Dante, and Shakespeare; outliving the pagan gods of stone and brass, innocent boy meets innocent girl today as he did in Eden, so that instead of wonders becoming facts, facts are becoming wonders.

—Glamour! shouted the newsman. Oh, boys, glamour! Here is a story fine and fragrant to be believed in, and enjoyed, by generations yet unborn.

—For ever sweethearts, murmured Jeecaysee; when her hair has turned to silver, he will love her just the same; he will only call her sweetheart, that will always be her name.

—And her hair will never turn to silver, but will for ever be golden, said Daabruin.

—Never afraid of the big bad wolf, said the newsman. For ever busy, for ever tireless, for ever good.

—That's just a little too much to bear, said Eve. A change in one's life is needed now and again. One longs for the luxury of a sigh and a sob sometimes.

—Now don't spoil the story, Eve, pleaded Adam.

—And all this, recited the newsman, writing it furiously down on the slate sheet, in the midst of a loveliness that stretches as far as eye reaches or thought can go. Oh, boys, what a story!

The sudden squealing yell that shook itself through the sodden

air made Sean's hair stand stiff on his head, and he saw the group
tear into the dugout as fast as legs could go. He heard a tumul-
tuous thick splashing out in front in the centre of a rushy morass,
and saw a frightful creature, fifty foot long, with a huge head, a
yawning, yearning mouth, packed with long, fearful, dagger-like
teeth, rending to bits the long, writhing neck of a dinnaseer, while
the two of them squealed like huge whirling steel saws cutting
wildly into flintstone, plunging madly about the slimy, inky
swamp, and sending showers of the mire high into the air. Then
from behind a great clump of carboniferous blacammites there
trotted venomously out, towards the fighting fiends, a horrible
beast, fully a hundred foot long, with an arched back, topped by a
double row of huge triangular bony plates; three long belly-
piercing horns on its ugly head, one over each eye, and one
branching out of its snout; while a long tail, barbed with a row
of fearful spikes two foot long, slashed about at everything within
reach. When he got to the squealing, biting monsters, this
spike-encrusted life lowered his hideous head, thrust it under the
belly of what was rending the squirming neck of the other,
plunged the three deadly horns into it as far as they could go,
and Sean saw the frightful head disappear under a cascade of
blood and tumbling guts, felt himself splashed by the greenish
ooze and the purplish mire scattered into violent horrid showers
by the yelling, squealing beasts rending each other, sinking lower
down into the sucking slime, trying to plunge upward out of the
danger to slide back to a lower depth still, screaming with dim-
felt fright at what lay below them; while the great green-topped
sea of rotting muck crept slowly higher, till the last Sean saw of
the twisting scaly mass was the yawning, yearning mouth with
its fearful daggerite teeth still tearing at the mangled writhing
neck of the dying dinnaseer, hidden at last by a coil of green and
purple muddy bubbles, slowly sinking down into a swaying sea
of thick, unwholesome mire.

After a time, he saw Adam, Eve, and their friends come cautiously out of their cave, to stand at the mouth of it, pale and
shaking. He saw that Jeecaysee kept his back turned to the
bubbling muck, that Daabruin kept looking at his queer feet, and
that the newsman's legs were trembling. Adam glanced nervously
around him, and Eve stared sullenly at the sink and swell of the
blackish-green and purple bubbles, now doing a disturbed dance
of jubilation over swallowing down the horrible.

—Don't let the sobconscious disturb you, said Jeecaysee. We see the beauty only; we are privileged.

—I'm off outa this, said the newsman; thanks for the grand story. And he slunk off, sliding between fern and bracken and rock till he was out of sight.

—Do something, sing something, man, shouted Jeecaysee, catching Daabruin by his shoulder and shaking him; sing to take away the darkness; sing us into sunity, man! And in a querulous and quivering voice, Daabruin sang

> Thou art, O God, the life and light
> Of all this wondrous world we see;
> Its glow by day, its smile by night,
> Are but reflections caught from Thee.

as the two of them crept away, bent double in an effort to camoufledge themselves as animals.

—Old God's rag-and-bone men, said Eve, scornfully, after them. He who is to live for ever is afraid of dying for a day. He has all the saints worn out trying to be jolly on all occasions. He winds his way to Heaven through a maze of beer bottles, wine jars, and pewter pots. He's for ever praying to God to keep the water out of the wine.

—Shush! said Adam, shocked. He's a holy man, and a clever one too. He's a man of infinite jest and more excellent funcy. The angels think the world of him. And a clever one too. Once he said to me, D'ye know, Adam, the farther we go, the nearer we get from where we started. That's the only relatantivity that's true, says he, for it was told to me by a wild knight on a white horse of the Peppers at Notting Hill Gate, his sharp-pointed, towering spire held at the ready so as to pen Pusha Deen Inge firmly to his bethelments. By standing on its head, says he, is the only way the world will learn how to stand on its feet. When a man's the head of the house, says he, you'll find a woman at the bottom of everything. A good man to be near, said Adam, a soft and safe cushion for a parson to lean on.

—We'll go from here! said Eve suddenly. Here we shall never be more than what we are, of the earth earthy, and nurtured in slime; and she girded herself into her robe of lizard skin.

—Go from here! echoed Adam. Are you mad, woman? Go

from the softness and security here to where things may be worse?

—To where things may be better, responded Eve quietly. I've a child coming, and he won't be born here. There will be others too; and in higher ground and purer air they can start to build a Paradise of their own, safer, firmer, and more lovely than anything even a God can give. So on we go, too human to be unafraid, but too human to let fear put an end to us!

And the serpent behind her, the most subtle beast of the field, reared up to his full height, expanded his plumed creast, and said gaily, Evie, allanna, now you're talking.

Immediately the firmament burst asunder and a thunderbolt shot out of it, striking the serpent a frightful blow on the nose, so that his limbs dried up and became useless, forcing him to crawl about on his belly from that day on, which can be verified to this very day by anyone taking the trouble to look at one.

—Let us be going, said Eve, fixing her cloak of skin more closely around her. By another and more dangerous way, we shall come to a finer and a firmer life. Are you afraid? she asked of Adam, seeing him hesitate, and the cold dew of fear beading his forehead; are you afraid?

—Not with you, Eve, he replied, gripping tightly his stout, horn-topped staff; not with you, my love.

And the crowds of lumbering dinnaseer and dipladoci gathered to watch them go, their huge bodies drooping and their scaly eyes dim, and as the mobled mother of man and her mate went by, they raised their heads and called out submissively, Farewell, brave beginners of the human kind, hail and farewell: those who are about to die, salute you!

Under the darkened sky, in the midst of a flash of lightning, Sean saw that the low brow, the timid eye, the shivering step of Adam had changed to the alert walk, the gleaming eye, the lofty brow, and the reddish thrust-out beard of Bernard Shaw. And Sean, bending low under the Golden Bough, followed close behind him.

PROMETHEUS HIBERNICA

IT WAS a bitter day. Winds, cold and nipping, deeply swept up
from the bay, curling crossly round into Beresford Place, trying
to snarl their way through to the heat in the dense crowd packing
with warm life the square that stretched out in front of the King's
elegant Custom House. Here, too, had Parnell stood, defiant,
speaking from the building's wide steps, like a flame-pointed
spear on the people's altar, endurance and patient might in his
beautiful wine-coloured eyes. The rascals, cleric and lay, out-
talked thee, hissed thee, tore at Ireland to get at thee, and God
remembered for many a long year, silencing their voice till He
grew sorry for the work-worn people, and sent another man into
their midst whose name was Larkin.

Through the streets he strode, shouting into every dark and
evil-smelling hallway, The great day of a change has come;
Circe's swine had a better time than you have; come from your
vomit; out into the sun. Larkin is calling you all!

And many were afraid, and hid themselves in corners. Some
ventured as far as the drear and dusky doorway to peer out, and
to say, Mr Larkin, please excuse us, for we have many things to
do and to suffer; we must care for cancerous and tubercular
sick, and we must stay to bury our dead. But he caught them by
the sleeve, by the coat collar, and shouted, Come forth, and fight
with the son of Amos who has come to walk among the men and
women of Ireland. Let the sick look after the sick, and let the
dead bury the dead. Come ye out to fight those who maketh the
ephah small and the shekel great; come out that we may smite the
winter house with the summer house; till the houses of ivory shall
perish, and the great houses shall have an end. And Sean had
joined the Union.

Following afar off for a while, Sean had come at last to hear
Larkin speak, to stand under a red flag rather than the green
banner. On this day the Liffey's ruffled waters were roughly
lapping the granite walls of the quays; the dark-brown tide was
high, and above it, the big white gulls, squealing, went circling
round, tensing their wide wings whenever they went against the
wind that made them turn to cut it sideways. Brown and yellow
leaves, drifting from the little trees along the paths, curled

restlessly along the streets, rustling against the legs of the people
as if eager to find shelter and safety there from the peevish and
vexing wind. A grey, sulky sky overhead was the one banner
flown, but all eyes were on the brave new sign in golden letters on
a green field, running along the length of the building, telling all
that here was the rallying camp of the Irish Transport and General
Workers Union, while over the massive doorway the name Liberty
Hall gave a welcome and twenty to all who came to fight for a
life something higher than the toiling oxen and the bleating
sheep. Here were the sons of the Gael, men of the Pale, brought
up, lugged up, in the mire of Dublin's poverty, their children slung
about at school, while those a little more adventurous than the rest
were carted away to the reformatories of Artane and Glencree.

Aha, here now was the unfolding of the final word from the
evolving words of the ages, the word of the modern, the word
En-Masse, and a mighty cheer gave it welcome. From a window
in the building, leaning well forth, he talked to the workers,
spoke as only Jim Larkin could speak, not for an assignation
with peace, dark obedience, or placid resignation; but trumpet-
tongued of resistance to wrong, discontent with leering poverty,
and defiance of any power strutting out to stand in the way of
their march onward. His was a handsome tense face, the forehead swept by deep black hair, the upper lip of the generous,
mobile mouth hardened into fierceness by a thick moustache, the
voice deep, dark, and husky, carrying to the extreme corners of
the square, and reaching, Sean thought, to the uttermost ends of
the earth. Here was the word En-Masse, not handed down from
Heaven, but handed up from a man. In this voice was the march
of Wat Tyler's men, the yells and grunts of those who took the
Bastille, the sigh of the famine-stricken, the last shout from those,
all bloodied over, who fell in Ninety-eight on the corn slopes of
Royal Meath; here were nursery-rhyme and battle-song, the
silvery pleasing of a lute with the trumpet-call to come out and
carry their ragged banners through the gayer streets of the city,
so that unskilled labour might become the vanguard, the cavaliers
and cannoniers of Labour's thought and purpose.

The voice of mingled gold and bronze went on picturing the
men to themselves – as they were, as they ought to be; showing
them that they hadn't been denied the gift of a holy fire from God;
this man in the drab garments of a drink-sodden nature; that
man whose key of Heaven was a racing record; yonder fellow

fearing to be above a blackleg, refusing to join his comrades out
on strike; and, worse of all, the unsightly scab taking the job of
a comrade out in a fight for better conditions for all. The voice
called for the rejection of the timid one who led them, who hid
in an armchair and let their men be ruled by the strength in a
policeman's baton.

—Who will stand, who will fight, for the right of men to live
and die like men? he called out, the large, strong hand stretched
out of the window gesturing over the head of the crowd.

—We will! came back in a serried shout that echoed along the restless river, making the gliding gulls pause, turn away, and wonder,
as a cloud of chapped and gnarled and grimy hands were lifted
high in the air; strong hands and daring, hands that could drive a
pile, handle a plough, sail a ship, stoke a furnace, or build a city.

—Gifts of the Almighty, went on the voice, labour – a gift, not
a curse – , poetry, dancing, and principles; and Sean could see
that here was a man who would put a flower in a vase on a table
as well as a loaf on a plate. Here, Sean thought, is the beginning
of the broad and busy day, the leisurely evening, the calmer night;
an evening full of poetry, dancing, and the linnet's wings; these
on their way to the music of the accordion, those to that of a
philharmonic orchestra; and after all, to sleep, perchance to
dream; but never to be conscious of a doubt about tomorrow's
bread, certain that, while the earth remaineth, summer and winter
should not cease, seedtime and harvest never fail:

> The bell branch of Ireland may chime again,
> To charm away the merchant from his guile,
> And turn the farmer's memory from his cattle,
> And hush to sleep the roaring ranks of battle,
> And all grow friendly for a little while.

No; for ever. Battles of war changed for battles of peace.
Labour in all its phases the supreme honour of life, broadening
the smile on the world's creased face daily.

The workers of Dublin, Wexford, Cork, Galway, Waterford,
Limerick, and many towns, rallied to Larkin's side. Out of jail
he had come into their arms. Starting in Belfast, Larkin brought
orange and green together as they had never been together before.
On to Derry, city of Columkille and the brave Apprentice Boys.
Down to Cork, then, where the employers marshalled their first

phalanx of bitter opposition. There he was charged with a conspiracy of trying to defraud the workers of their hard-earned money by a witness who had to be sent home because he was drunk; and a Crown and Anchor solicitor who was also the solicitor to the Employers' Federation, harmonizing in himself the glory of God and the honour of Ireland; though one of the two magistrates trying the case, Sir Edward Fitzgerald, had the temerity to declare that every fair-minded man in Cork had the idea in his head that if there was a conspiracy at all, it was a conspiracy of Dublin Castle and the Cork employers to prevent the working men of the city from uniting for their self-defence in the future. But, all the same, for this reason Jim got a sweet little sentence of twelve months with hard labour by the other magistrate on the bench, justifying the righteousness of the lion and the unicorn over the magistrate's head. But the grin came off their faces when the King, after some months had passed, had the common sense and graciousness to grant a free pardon to a fine man who was dragging images of God from a condition worse than that of the beasts in the field of the poorest Irish farmer.

So Jim came out of jail, and in a room of a tenement in Townshend Street, with a candle in a bottle for a torch and a billycan of tea, with a few buns for a banquet, the Church militant here on earth of the Irish workers, called the Irish Transport and General Workers Union, was founded, a tiny speck of flame now, but soon to become a pillar of fire into which a brand was flung by Yeats, the great poet, Orpen, the painter, A. E., who saw gods in every bush and bramble, Corkery the storyteller, James Stephens, the poet and graceful satirical jester, Dudley Fletcher, the Rector of Coolbanagher, and even Patrick Pearse, wandering softly under the Hermitage elms, thinking, maybe, of Robert Emmet, the darlin' of Erin, and his low response to the executioner's *Are you ready, sir?*, of *Not yet, not yet*; even he was to lift a pensive head to the strange new shouting soon to be heard in Dublin streets, loosening the restraining hands of St Patrick and St Laurence O'Toole, holding his girdle, to say *No private right to property is good as against the public right of the people*.

The tramway workers, the worst slaves Ireland ever knew, grew restless, and were trying to key themselves up to make a fight of it. They had no settled job, no settled hours, no settled pay even, for every journey they made was crammed with trivial excuses for a fine that made their wages undergo a weekly shrivel, so that they deprived themselves of what they needed when they gave a penny to Jesus at Mass on Sundays. At midnight, when the last tram had been bedded for the night, to win courage from Larkin's faith they came to Liberty Hall in trains of wagonettes, caravans of toil, playing melodeons, concertinas, mouth-organs, and singing an old Irish ballad, or a music-hall song, as the horses plodded along from the depots of Inchicore, Clontarf, and Ringsend. As the crowded cars pulled up outside Liberty Hall, they were cheered by crowds gathered there, for each arrival was hailed as a reinforcement for an army about to march to battle. The tramwaymen crowded into a hot and stuffy hall, already nearly packed to the doors, the sweat often dripping from the foreheads of the speakers, all of them wiping it convulsively away as they went on speaking; Jim Larkin alone carelessly brushing the bigger drops aside with a sudden impatient movement of his hand, too full of fiery thought to bar the salty moisture from entering into his gleaming eyes.

The employers gathered their forces together too, to harass the workers and stamp their menace out. William Martin Murphy, their leader, who owned the Dublin tramways, Clery's huge stores, and God knows what else besides, determined to get the employers to refuse to give work to any man who was a member of Larkin's Union. Let them submit, or starve. Jacob's the biscuit-makers, Shackleton's the millers, Eason's the newspaper and magazine distributors, along with coal factors, timber merchants, and steamship owners, came along to Martin Murphy and said, We're with you, old boy. What thou doest, we will do; what thou sayest, we will say; thy profits shall be our profits; and thy god, ours too. And so it was. Catholic, Protestant, Quaker, and pagan employer joined hand and foot, flung their money into one bag, and with bishop and priest, viceroy and council, infantryman and cavalry trooper, and bludgeon-belted policeman, formed a square, circle, triangle, and crescent to down the workers.

A foreman came slowly to Sean, a paper stretched out in his right hand, and said, Sign this, you. It was headed by a skull and cross bones, with a tiny cross in a corner, above the motto of *Per ardua add fastra*. The document went on to say:

Under the holy and undivided patronage of St Ellessdee, I, M or N, do solemnly swear, without any reservation whatsoever (cross your heart, and say I hope to die), that from this day forthwith I shall cease to be a member of Larkin's Union, and will forswear his company, give him no aid, in thought, word, or deed, cross to the other side of the street when I see him coming, inasmuch as he has persuaded me to try to bite the hand that doesn't feed me; and I further promise and undertake and expressively swear that I will faithfully serve my employers, assisted by whatsoever Union they may form, or allow me to join; and so I shall incur the beloved and much sought-after brazen benediction of the holy St Ellessdee, and the goodwill of bishop, priest, and deacon, till the act of God, in old age or through an accident, shoves me from the job I'm no longer fit to fill: all this I swear for the third time grinning. Aman. Inscribed with solemn derision on the twelfth day of the eighth month in the year of our Lord, William Martin Murphy. – T. GOMARAWL.

—What's all this mean? asked Sean.

—It means, said the foreman, winking an eye, that Mr Martin Murphy knows what's good for you betther than yourself; so be a good boy an' sign.

—Tell your ignorant lout of a Murphy and his jackal, Bimberton, that I'd see him in hell first!

—Don't be a fool, Jack, said the foreman smoothly, to do in a second what you may regret for a year. Sign, man, an' then go when the pressure gets too sthrong – there's no law again' you signin' the thing, an' breakin' it when you have to.

—Look, Bill, said Sean, a great poet once wrote,

> *A knight there was, and that a worthy man,*
> *That from the time that he first bigan*
> *To ryden out, he loved chivalrye,*
> *Truth and honour, freedom and curteisye;*

and were I to sign this thing, all these things would turn aside and walk no more with me.

—I dunno, said the foreman, and scorn touched his tongue, that e'er a one of those things ever did, or could, walk with any of us. It's only poethry talkin' big. The ten commandments are enough for a working man to go on with – too much, if y'ask me! An' more – you may be a worthy man, but you're hardly a knight.

—Well, I'd be less than a man if I signed, Bill.

—Have it your own way, Jack, but you're no bether than others who will; and raising his voice, he said, If you can't sign, get off th' premises – we want no Larkinism here! And, seeing that Sean hesitated, he added, An' if you try to cut up rough, there's police within call to come an' shuffle you out!

—I'm off, said Sean; but tell your boss, Gomarawl, and let him tell Martin Murphy that I said that they'd auction off the coat of Christ; they'd coin the stars into copper coins; make a till out of the wood of the holy cross; they'd line their hats with the silken sounds of Shakespeare's sonnets; they'd haggle with Helen of Troy about the price of a night in bed with her; and force the sons of the morning, were they hungry, to be satisfied with a penny dinner from St Anthony's Fund: there's nothing they wouldn't do to damn themselves with God, with angels, and with men.

On a bright and sunny day, while all Dublin was harnessing itself into its best for the Horse Show, the trams suddenly stopped. Drivers and conductors left them standing wherever they happened to be at a given time in the day when the strike commenced, to be brought to their sheds by frightened inspectors and the few scabs and blacklegs who saw in Martin Murphy another God incurnate. And the employers kept on locking out all who refused to abandon their Union, mill men, men and women from the factories, from the docks, from the railways, and from the wholesale and retail warehouses of the cities and towns. They came out bravely, marching steadily towards hunger, harm, and hostility, just to give an answer for the hope that was burning in them.

The dust and mire in which the people lived and died were being sprinkled everywhere through the gallant, aristocratic streets; it drifted on to the crimson or blue gold-braided tunics of the officer; on to the sleek morning-coat and glossy top-hat of the merchant and professional man; on to the sober black gown and grey-curled wig of the barrister and judge; on to the rich rochet of immaculate surplice and cocky biretta; on to the burnished silk and lacquer-like satin frocks and delicate petticoats of dame and damsel.

Those who lived where lilacs bloomed in the doorway, where

the dangling beauty of laburnum draped itself over the walls, where many a lovely, youthful rose crinkled into age, and died at last in peace, where three parts of the year was a floral honeymoon – here the dust and the mire came too, and quiet minds knew ease no longer. Magic casements were opened cautiously, and handsome or dominating eyes gazed out on a newer fairyland, a Keltic Twilight growing into smoky tumult, enveloping rough and ugly figures twisting about in a rigadoon of power and resolution.

Standing to arms, the soldiers were confined to barracks; town and country police began to go about in companies; and the horsemen came trotting down this street and up that one. And the clergy, if they weren't denouncing strike organizers, kept fast together in a secret silence. And at the wall of an end house in every tottering street stood groups of mingled black and blue police as if the rotting building had suddenly thrown out a frieze of dark and sinister growth. There they stood, never moving, though every eye turned slow in its socket to follow the figure of every passing man. And every passing man tried to pretend he hadn't seen them; or, if he had, that they were no concern of his, for he was on the Lord's side, out to serve the King, and loyal to William Martin Murphy. Sean, whenever he passed them, shuddered, for in his mind's eye he could see the swiftly rising arm, the snarling face, and feel the broad bone of his skull caving in on his brain, with the darkness of death beside him.

Sean wondered why the clergy didn't stand with the men for their right of choosing their own leader and their own Union. He remembered the Polish poet Mickiewicz's enthusiasm for the haughty, desperate rising of the French Communards, after he had hurried to Rome to form a legion to strike at Austria for the freedom of Italy; how mad he was at the difficulties so civilly thrust in the way of all he wanted to do by crafty, timid, crimson-clothed cardinals. Were he, Sean, able to pick the lock of the massive gate in the grounds of the Primate's palace, or climb in the dead of night over its high, cold, ashlar-moulded walls; creep through shrubbery and gaudy flowerbed, creep through window thoughtlessly left open; pass by secretary and usher, unbeknownst, right into the presence of the right reverend gentleman, reading his breviary, he would catch him by the arm, as the Polish poet caught the arm of the Pope, and say to the Primate what the poet said to the Pope, Good God, man, know that the spirit of God is under the jackets of the Dublin workers!

With six constables sitting on it, six mounted men leading, six following behind, a lorry driven by a scab came slowly down the quays. Suddenly a crowd of dockers were between the leading horsemen and the lorry; another between the lorry and the horsemen following; while a third attacked the foot police, and pulled the scab from the cart, the mounted men trying to shelter their faces and control their frightened horses in the midst of a shower of stone and jagged ends of broken bottles. Before they could recover, the scab was splashing in the river, and then, like lightning, many hands scurried the horse from the cart, dragged the lorry to the river wall, where, with a shout of All together – up! the lorry was raised and sent hurtling down into the river on top of the screaming scab.

The dust and savage creak of this bloody scuffle had no benison of feeling for Sean, so he turned away to go from the place as quick as he dared to move; for, if he met a police patrol, speed would tell them he had been doing something, and a baton might crunch in his skull. So he walked on as carelessly as he could, and oh, Christ! a staggering tatter-clad figure, clasping a jaw with both hands, caught up with him. From a side glance, Sean saw that the figure's jaw had been slashed down by a sabre-cut, and it kept calling out, A handkerchief, a handkerchief, someone! Jasus! is there ne'er a one rich enough among the millions o' Dublin's city to spare a poor bleedin' bugger a handkerchief!

Sean's one handkerchief was safe at home, thank God, and the bit of rag he was using, and always used, except on very special occasions, was too precious to be given away; for there was no way of getting another, for with them rags were as scarce as purple cloth or linen fine; so he kept walking on with the wounded man following. A jarvey driving slowly down the street stopped, umped down, had a look, and said hastily, and with horror, Here, man alive, climb up, an' I'll dhrive yeh to Jervis Street Hospital before half of your dial is missin'; an' you, he added to Sean, jump up, an' hold him on.

Sean hadn't the courage to persist in going on his way; so he climbed on to the side-car, putting an arm round the stricken man to keep him steady, who kept muttering tensely, If I only hadda had a handkerchief, I'd ha' stayed on in the fight. Only let me get a few stitches in it, an' I'm back for the bastard who done it!

Turning into another street, they came on a police patrol, led by a sergeant, who stopped them, asked where they'd been and where they were going.

—Oh, I'm only doin' th' Good Samaritan, said the jarvey jollily; jus' picked him up to bring him to Jervis Street, havin' nothin' betther to do, Sergeant.

—Yous gang o' goughers! snarled the sergeant, I know yous of old. Here you, seizing the wounded man by the arm and pulling him headlong from the car, walkin's good enough for you, instead of plankin' your bum on a car in your Larkinistic idea of proper an' proverbial comfort an' calm. In this war, me bucko, th' wounded'll have to be their own sthretcher-bearers, an' carry themselves to hospital! And he gave him a woeful kick in the backside, shaking him so that he drew his hand from his face, letting the cloven cheek fall like a bloody flap over his chin, giving a howl as his hand caught it again and fingered it back to its proper place; his other hand rubbing his under backbone, as he shambled away moaning.

—And don't be so quick an' ready with your grand charity the next time, you! he said, turning on the jarvey.

—I didn't know, Sergeant, murmured the jarvey. Me an' this good man here helped him, thinkin' he'd met with a purely innocent accident.

—What a pair o' gaums yous are! roared the sergeant sarcastically. Be off with you before I bring you, horse, car, an' all, to the station! An' what are you gawkin' at? he wheeled round on Sean, who was afraid to go or stay. You're another of them that want to change th' world, eh? Well, go an' change it somewhere else, yeh miserable remaindher of some mother's bad dhream! An' here's a hand to help you there; and before Sean knew enough, a heavy hand swung swiftly to his ear, sending him spinning down the street, his vision a blaze of shooting lights, his knees shaking under him as he staggered away, never waiting to give a groan till he was out of sight and sound of the savage group, glad in his heart that it had been a hand, and not a baton, that had clipt him on the head.

The meeting of the locked-out workers, arranged for the following Sunday, had been proclaimed by Dublin Castle. The night the proclamation had come to Liberty Hall, a vast crowd gathered to hear what was to be done. The meeting would be held; Jim Larkin would be there in O'Connell Street. The darkness was falling, a dim quietness was spreading over the troubled city. Even the gulls muted their complaining cries; and the great throng was silent; silent, listening to the dark voice speaking from the window. To Sean, the long arm seemed to move about in the sky, directing the courses of the stars over Dublin; then the moving hand held up the proclamation, the other sturdy hand held a lighted match to it; it suddenly flared up like a minor meteor; in a dead silence it flamed, to fall at last in flakes of dark and film ashes down upon the heads of the workers below, fluttering here and there, uncertainly, by the wind from the mighty cheer of agreed defiance that rose to the sky, and glided away to rattle the windows and shake the brazen nails and knobs on the thick doors of Dublin Castle. Resolute and firm, thought Sean; but they have no arms, they have no arms.

Oh! O'Connell Street was a sight of people on that Sunday morning! From under the clock swinging pedantically outside of the *Irish Times* offices, across the bridge over the river, to well away behind the Pillar, topped by Nelson, the wide street was black with them; all waiting for Jim to appear somewhere when the first tick of the clock tolled the hour of twelve.

In this very street, not so very long ago, the gentle Shelley had stood, handing out to the staring, passing people his Declaration of Rights. From one of the windows of the restaurant, almost facing Sean, he tossed his leaflets of hope and stormy encouragement to the gibing Dublin citizens. Shelley who sang,

> *What is freedom? Ye can tell that which slavery is too well,*
> *For its very name has grown to an echo of your own.*
> *Rise like lions after slumber. . . .*
> *Shake your chains to earth like dew . . . Ye are many – they are few.*

Maybe he is looking down upon this very crowd now, seeing, and applauding, the change that has come to the mind of the Irish workers. Oh! If they only had arms!

—Lo, Jim is there! a voice would say, and the crowd, like a cornfield under a rough wind, would sway towards the bridge; lo, he is here! another voice would say, and the crowd swayed back towards the Pillar.

—There's a funeral to come along, said a voice at Sean's elbow, an' when th' hearse gets to the middle o' th' crowd, Jim'll pop up outa th' coffin an' say his say.

—No, no, another voice replied; as a matther of fact, he's stealin' up th' river in a boat.

—Couldn't be that way, answered still a third, for the quays are crawlin' with polis.

Sean shivered, for he was not a hero, and he felt it was unwise to have come here. He felt in his pocket: yes, the strip of rag and his one handkerchief were safe there. It was well to have something to use for a bandage, for a body never could tell where or how a sudden wound would rise. Although the police were instructed to hit the shoulders of the people, they always struck at the top or the base of the skull. He turned to look back so as to assure himself that he hadn't got too far into the crowd. No; with a quick wheel of his body, and a few swift sweeps of his arms, he'd be out of it, and a few paces only from the side streets opposite the Pillar: so far so good. Maybe the police were out just to fulfil regulations. They had to be wherever there was a crowd; it was customary, and of little significance. If they hadn't wanted the people here, they could have prevented them from gathering by cordoning the street off; and the people around looked quite at ease, and would be very peaceable. They were intent on seeing where Jim would appear, and heads were constantly twisting in every direction. A little way down, on a narrow ledge of a doorway, holding a column to keep steady, Sean saw the figure of a man whose head and face were heavily bound in bandages; and from what he saw of the cap, the coat, and the bit of the face visible, he'd swear it was the man whose cheek hung over his chin but a few days ago. A wicked thing for a man in his condition to come to a place like this, he thought.

—There he is! suddenly shouted a dozen voices near Sean. Goin' to speak from the window of the very hotel owned be Martin Murphy himself! and there right enough, framed in an upper window, was a tall man in clerical garb, and when he swept the beard from his chin, the crowd saw their own beloved leader, Jim Larkin.

A tremendous cheer shook its way through the wide street, and Sean raised his right arm, and opened his mouth to join it, but his mouth was snapped shut by a terrific surge back from the crowd in front, while another section of it, on the outskirts, surged forward to get a better view, though now the cheer had been silenced by a steady scream in the near distance, by the frantic scuffling of many feet, and loud curses from frightened men. Twelve rows or so ahead of him, Sean saw a distended face, with bulging eyes, while a gaping mouth kept shouting, The police – they're chargin'; get back, get back, there! Let me out, let me out; make a way there for a man has a bad heart! They're batonin' everyone to death – make a way out for a poor, sick man, can't yous!

Sean made a desperate try to turn, but the jam became so close that he was penned tight to his struggling neighbour. He felt himself rising, but fought savagely to keep his feet on the ground; and try as he might, he couldn't get his lifted arm down to fend off the pressure on his chest that was choking him. He could neither get his right arm down nor his left arm up to loosen the collar of his shirt, to get more air, a little more air; he could only sway back and forward as the crowd moved. The breathing of the suffocating crowd sounded like the thick, steamy breathing of a herd of frightened cattle in a cattle-boat tossed about in a storm; and over all, as he tried to struggle, he heard the voices of the police shouting, Give it to the bastards! Drive the rats home to their holes! Let them have it, the Larkin bousys!

—Jesus, Mary, an' Joseph be with us now! burst from the voice beside Sean as two sickening sounds told of two skulls crunched not very far away; and Sean closed his eyes, waiting for a blow. The ache in the pit of his belly was agonizing, and the heat of the pressure against him was sending the sweat running in rivulets down his chest and spine.

—We should never ha' listened to Larkin, wailed the voice beside him. Our clergy were always warnin' us, an' we should ha' gone be them! Jesus, Mary, an' Joseph be with us in this hour o' need! If I ever get outa this, I'll light half a dozen candles to St Nocnoc of Duennadurban.

Sean felt he couldn't stick it much longer. Carried along by the ebbing and flowing mass of people, he saw dimly that they had gone beyond Nelson's Pillar; while, topping the crowd, he could see police helmets darting hither and thither, batoning and blustering, batoning, batoning everyone. A minute later his toe struck something soft, and a moment after his feet were trampling a body that never made a move. Now he couldn't get his feet to the ground again, and in a spasmodic effort to do it, he only managed to rise higher so that his head and shoulders looked over the struggling mass of men. He could see no women, though he had heard a woman's screaming several times.

Yes, there was one, a well-dressed lass too, lying along beside the chemist's shop at the corner of Henry Street. The part of the crowd in which he was jammed now took a half-wheel, and he saw they were battling furiously among themselves to be the first to force a way into the narrow lane that led to the Pro-Cathedral. In the pause that came while he waited to be carried to the narrow neck of safety, Sean looked ahead and saw Jim Larkin pulled, pushed, and shoved along by four constables, a crowd of others keeping guard around their comrades, their batons in hand, ready for any head that came within circling range of it. And following some distance away, there, by God! was his friend of the cleft cheek; a sleeve torn from his coat, the bandages hanging wildly round his neck, forced along by three policemen, making things worse by shouting, Up the Dublin workers! Up Jim Larkin! and making Sean shudder at the thought of what they'd make him look like when they got him to the cell and no one was there to see.

Now with an angry surge and a pressure that cracked his ribs, Sean was borne into the narrow way that led unto life; the pressure, pressing in, eased, and his feet touched the ground. A pale paladin of the people, he stood there, his escort fleeing on ahead to crowd into the church and fill themselves with its peace and promise of security. An inward pressure pressing out assailed him now; his breathing could barely keep in time with the frantic flutter of his heart; his head ached ,and the church railings seemed to move this way and that before him. He felt as if he must fall to feel safe. Each time he took a step towards the sidewalk, his foot made a half-circle, and the road seemed to rise and slap the sole of it. Getting there at last, he leaned against the railing, slid down to sit on the pavement and wait for his heart to slow down and his breath to order itself into a quieter commotion. God! it had been a day and a half!

There were the two of them on the top of the building, statuters of St Laurence O'Toole and St Patrick, with their backs to the people, O'Toole, now a commissioner of police, bludgeoning his flock into an improper reverence for law and order. And St Patrick was far too busy to care, with his episcopal nose stuck between the vellum leaves of one of his rarer Keltic books. What one, now, allanna? Book of Kills; the Book of O'Money; the Book of the Ripe and Edifying Thoughts in the Head of Kinsale; the Book of the Old Done Cow; the Book of the Curious Chronicles of Finnegan's Wake (That's over his head); or the

Book of the Revised Version of Cathleen's Thorny Way? More than likely it's Merriman's *Mediae Noctis Consilium* he's poring over now.

God rest you merry, gentlemen, but isn't this a nice book to have burgeoned out of Ireland's bosom! murmured St Patrick to himself. This fellow couldn't have been a true Gael. And I thinking the Gaedhilge was the sure shield of Eire's purity! Well, this book is an eye-opener anyway. Isn't it well that it's in a language that few can read. They'd lap it up if it was in plain English. There isn't half enough police in the country. This is a nice thing to be peeping over the fair hills of holy Ireland. If the English caught me reading it, I'd be ruined! The Irish have always been a worry to me and poor Laurence. He doesn't really know how to deal with Dubliners. You think you have them all nice and handy on their knees, shouting *mea culpa* the way you'd think they were cheering, when, suddenly, one of them'll lep up, roaring, To hell with it all! and, immediately, there's a pack after him, doing the same thing. What a precious, peaceful time the English saints – the few there are – have in comparison! Their sleep hardly ever broken by a row among their boyos below. But I can scarcely sit down to a quiet meal when some excited messenger must come like a whirlwind, sweeping away the little rest one gets nowadays with the wind of his wings, to whisper, You're wanted at once at the bordher, sir; they're at it again! Then to have these simpering, gone-and-forgotten English saints, not a hair astray on one of them, come up to you to admonish and advise: You're not 'arf strict enough with them, Pauddy. You allow them too many indulgences altogether. You really ought to keep them dahn with a stwrong hand. By the Ardaw Chalice, the Cwoss of Cong, and the Tahrahrah Brooch, if I were you, Pauddy, I'd be moh severe. I near lost me temper when that chit of a St Allsup of Shelmexham tapped me on the shoulder to say, Pauddy, the next best thing to do is to change your nationullity and settle dahn into a fine old English gentleman. Only for catching my guardian angel's eye, I'd have put his mitre asthray on his head for him!

It makes it worse that there's some truth in it all. But how, in th' name o' God, could I ever get them to confine their thoughts to dominoes and darts? Sure I know damn well if they did they wouldn't dwell so much on religion or politics. I'll be worn out if this goes on much longer. Then there's that Patricius, insistin' he was the real Patrick, a dangerous fella, goin' round, too, makin' out it was him brought four-thirds of the people into the Church, and all I done was to wangle Armagh into bein' the chief see of th' land; and that poor deluded man, Professor Rahilly, puttin' it down in black an' white, an' sayin' there may have been three Patricks altogether, so that some of the Irish are sayin' there's primae-facie reasons for believin' that St Patrick left Ireland before he came there at all; and that though some Patrick did something somewhere, the real Patrick never existed outside of a stained-glass window, St Patrick's Day parades, the Calendar of the Culdees, picture postcards, and the tune of St Patrick's Day in th' Mornin'! And all this scorn of tradition in spite of what is set down in the Trippertight-tapper-tuttut Life of St Patrick, sworn to as truth in the news by Roddy the Rover with his signature tune added of It could happen here for the glory of God and the honour of Eireann.

Now this Jim Larkin is tumbling my poor flock into turmoil again, snapping away from them their grand lifelong chance of working an exceeding weight of glory from their hunger, wretchedness, and want. It's all getting me down! I was lookin' at myself in a fixed star only yestherday, and I was frightened be the look of sthrain an' weariness starin' out at me. What is Bishop Eblananus of Stopaside doin'?

He seized hold of a passing blink of sun and sent it skimming down to the Bishop's Palace, to tell him to meet him immediately, if not sooner, on the top of Nelson's Pillar to see what they could do to stop the poor from running after things adamnistic and evenescent, instead of cleaving to the things not made with hands, eternal in the heavens. Then he tore a wide strip from the rainbow's end, making a lovely swung seat of it by tying the ends round the necks of two cherubs, Asseguy and Bellboomerang; and sitting himself nicely down in the swing, off the three of them went, dancing through the shining sun, waltzing, gavotering, and schottisching down to the platform of the Pillar, some hundred feet above the tumult in the streets below.

The saint made a perfect landing on the stony square of ground, and as he was passing by for the landing, he had noticed a supercilious look on the battered face of Nelson, and heard a muttered pshaw coming from between his stony lips; but he was too dignified to notice this abortive insult aimed at him by the snobbish and heretical Admiral.

And there, lying flat on his broad back, was the Bishop, Eblananus, feebly fanning himself with his mitre, gasping for breath; the ascent of the hundreds of winding stairs inside the cylindrical Pillar had completely blown him, for he was fairly well stricken in years.

—Pull yourself together, man, said St Patrick, angry at seeing the Bishop in a condition resembling *hors de combat*; this isn't the time for thinking of yourself.

—Take your time, man, till I get me breath; take your time, murmured the good man breathlessly. Curious spot to choose for an episcopal pow-wow.

St Patrick leaned over the balustrade to look at the disorder below, at the little mites of men struggling with the blue-coated mites of policemen striking at the bare hands of the workers raised to shield their heads. He turned towards Eblananus, who had propped himself up against the pedestal on which Nelson stood. Nice position we'd be in, if these Dublin rowdies of yours had been armed, wouldn't we? Will you thry to tell a man what is it they want?

—Everything a man can think of, breathed the Bishop: a pleasanter place be day; warmer shelter be night; more bread for their children; and more time off for themselves.

—Be God! they're not askin' for much! ejaculated Patrick. An' what is this Larkin fella askin' for them?

—All them things too; an' an education that'll allow them, if they so will, to dip into Plato, feel the swing of the Pleiades, to climb the long reaches to the peak of song, to wonder at the rift of the dawn, and to hail with silent happiness the reddening of the rose.

—Oh! Is that all? questioned the saint bitterly. He isn't askin' a lot either. There's nothin' like hitchin' your flagon to a bar! Well, they must be taught that the penny catechism is good enough for them. I wondher what do both of them combined want?

—I can tell you that, said Eblananus, with a tremor in his voice. They want the Old Woman of Beare who once wore a shinin' shift, an' now wears none, to wear a shinin' shift again.

—They didn't use that actual low an' dangerous word, did they?

—They did then, an' all, holy Patrick, apostle of the pure-minded Gael.

—The fact is, Eblananus, said Patrick stormily, you're not doin' your duty be these people. You give them far too many indulgences. You'll have to learn to keep them down with a stwrong hand. If this goes on much longer, I'll change me natio-nullity, an' leave your little Irish colleen in her ould plaid shawl, the playboy of your Western world, the counthry dressmaker, A.E.'s great breath, the eloquent Dempsey, Professor Tim, Mother Machree, and the rest of them, to their own devices. I'll make me home in John Bull's Other Island; I will, as God is me judge, if this goes on! What's preventin' them from patternin' themselves on th' English? Answer me that. No, no answer. Y'never get an answer here when y'ask a decent question. He ran to the railing around the Pillar's platform, leant over as far as he could, cautiously, and again stared down on the street below. Oh! look at them, look at them! Th' shtreet black with them, an' not a one of them with a thought in his head, or a wish in his heart, for me! Well, they're feelin' th' swing of th' Pleiades now! Sorrow mend them! He turned suddenly on Eblananus. Why th' hell, man, don't you come over here an' give them good advice?

—Oh! I've thried, an' thried, an' thried, said the Bishop, petulantly, till I'm tired.

—Well, thry again! shouted the saint. Don't they know the law – that, in its blessed equality, it forbids the rich as well as the poor to resist authority coming from God, to steal bread, to sleep in the open, or to beg in the streets? Have you been teaching them anything at all, man? They must be taught to be trim, correct, and orderly like the English – d'ye hear us talkin', man?

—'Course I hear you – I'd want to be deaf if I didn't.

—Well, roared the saint, losing his temper for the first time in his life, why don't you come here an' shout it down at them?

—Shout it yourself, if you're so eager, an' see what you'll make of it! vehemently replied the patient Bishop, now aroused for the second time in his life.

—Oh! said Patrick in despair, clasping his hand, and turning up his eyes to Heaven. Oh! *Hibernica salubrio, este pesta quaesta essentia terrifica tornadocum!*

—Yah! leered the figure of Nelson, leaning precariously over his pedestal, and shoving his cocked hat farther over his blind eye with his remaining hand, to get a better view; now yous know a little of what we have to contend against to keep yous in the bonds of law 'n order!

—Yah, yourself! shouted Patrick, now beside himself at being jeered at be an intherloper, drummin' the platform with the butt-end of his staff; if all had their rights, me bucko, it's not you'd be stuck up there in a state of honour, but me, or that other dacent man standin' there, Eddy Eblananus, born an' reared only a stone's throw from Lam Doyle's an' th' Three-Rock Mountain. An' who but the foolish Irish lifted you to where y'are?

—Ay, said Eblananus, now on his feet, and standing well out to fix his eyes on Nelson, with a fighting swing of his frock, an' let him be aware he'd be wantin' th' epaulettes on his shouldhers an' th' gold lace on his cocked hat, if it wasn't for the Finucanes, the Finnegans, the Fogarties, and the Flaherties at Trafalgar's Bay, and among the slimy rushes at the open mouth of th' Nile!

—Moreover, me gentleman, went on Patrick, it's not to th' English we'll look for lessons in spiritual or corporal deportment, I can tell you that!

—Let him get down here on th' platform, shouted Eblananus, an', ould an' disabled as I am with a touchy heart, I'll show him a few military manoeuvres that'll stagger him!

—Control yourselves, gentlemen, murmured the stony voice of Nelson; try to control yourselves.

—Control yourself! shouted Patrick up at him. If you could, you wouldn't send your murdherous polis out to maim an' desthroy poor men lookin' for no more than a decent livin', Gah! If me crozier could only reach up to you, I'd knock your other eye out!

Two guardian angels, afraid of a scandal, scooted down from Heaven, seized St Patrick, hoisted him on to his rainbow seat, and hurried him back to where he'd come from; the other, Eblananus', took the Bishop's arm and led him away down the stairs for fear of further mischief.

Along a wide lane of littered bodies, amid the tinkling of busy ambulances picking them up, one by one, pushed, shoved, and kicked by constables, the man with the cleft jaw trudged to jail, the wide stitches in his wounded face showing raw against his livid skin, the torn bandages flapping round his neck; shouting, he trudged on, Up Jim Larkin! Nor baton, bayonet, nor bishop can ever down us now – the Irish workers are loose at last!

DARK KALEIDOSCOPE

SEAN STAGGERED home from a céilidh held in Banba Hall as
the banner of day was breaking out over the squalidness of Bally-
bough, a long, dim, grey cloth tinged with pink, and streaked with
gentle yellow stripes. Force of will kept him on his tottering feet.
Not a soul about to see him, gay-kilted and shawled, blundering
his way homewards. Filled with new wine, they'd say if they
saw him. He was a sick man: he felt it in the core of his brain.
Ill; no one to help; his mother's old-age pension to keep them
both. What it did before, it could do again. From halfway down
his thighs to his ankles his legs were growing numb. He'd felt it
for some time, but just waited for it to go. Rain, rain, go
away. It was getting worse, and now he could barely walk
home.

He had done too much, and hadn't had enough food to restore
the energy lost. Dry bread and tea, with an odd herring when they
happened to be tuppence a dozen. His mother ate less, but she
wasn't suffering for it. Too old to need much; besides, she had
had a better-fed youth than he. Body and mind had done too
much on too little, and he had drained himself of life. This dawn
meant night to him; maybe an everlasting night too.

He got home at last, and sank down on the boards, in kilt,
shawl, and feathered balmoral cap, sleeping curiously there,
with pain as a dream, till his mother wakened him, anxious;
helped him to bed, asking what had happened. He didn't say;
he didn't know. She left a red ticket in North William Street
Dispensary, requesting the attendance of Dr Donnelly, Medical
Man for the District. He came, punched Sean about, looked into
his eyes, murmuring, You're in a bad way, me boy. Head like
to burst, eh? Ay. Legs leaden, eh? Ay. Soles of feet feel as if you
walked on cushions, eh?

—No, said Sean.

—No? Blast it, man, they must! shouted the poor-law doctor.

—Blast you, Doctor, they don't! shouted Sean back at him.

—The Infirmary for this man, he said, turning to Mrs Casside.
It's the only place for him. I'll send the car tomorrow.

—Oh, there's another place, sir, she said.

—Where, me good woman?

—Here. None of us ever went there; none of us ever will, please God.

—Betther than ever you were, ma'am, went there.

—Very likely, sir; they didn't know the difference.

—Well, I've no time to argue; other poor people need my care; and he walked out of the room.

Dr Woods of Gardiner Street came to see him. He was a five-shilling first-visit doctor, half a crown afterwards. He was loved by the poor, so gentle, painstaking; he was a wraithlike figure, said to have but a short time to live, keeping himself going with drugs. He was sent by Seumas Deakin, whom Sean had first known as a member of All Saints Church, Grangegorman, and, afterwards, as a chemist and a member of the Supreme Council of the IRB.

Hanging his coat up on a nail in the door, after a swift glance round the room, sighing languidly, the doctor sat down beside Sean, fingering him with quiet, sympathetic hands, sighing, sighing as he did so.

He sees the world in his own condition, and sighs for it, thought Mrs Casside. What's th' matter with him, Doctor? she asked aloud.

—I don't rightly know, he said, putting his white hands over Sean's eyes, and leaving them there for some seconds, then peering into their depths when he had suddenly whipped them away. I don't rightly know yet. He wrote a prescription. Mr Deakin will make that up for you – a nerve and stomach tonic. Let me know how you feel, say in a fortnight, and if you're not better, Mr Deakin will tell me to come to you; and he sighed again.

He'll come, if Deakin tells him, thought Sean; making sure of his two-and-six. His glance round the room showed him there was no money here. Even kindly, gentle Dr Woods had to think of his wife and children.

—Porridge, Mrs Casside, is the best thing for him; as much as he can eat; and he slid painfully into his topcoat and glided from the room.

Sean was thinking where the porridge would come from, when Deakin came, a few days later, to see him, bringing kingly presents of bundles of the *Review of Reviews*, *John o' London's*, Lane's *Modern Egyptians*, Washington Irving's *Mahomet*, Landor's *Imaginary Conversations*, Butler's *Way of All Flesh*, London's *White Fang*, and George Borrow's *Lavengro* – a rich load of joy, for which Sean thanks him still. When he'd gone, Mrs Casside came to where Sean was lying, the light of Heaven in her eyes, as she held up two small glittering, golden things for Sean to see.

—On the mantelshelf, she said, two of them; sovereigns, gold sovereigns. He knew better than to offer them, so he left them quiet on the mantelshelf so's they wouldn't conflict with our pride. You'll have porridge for a few weeks now.

He looked long at the two shining coins in his hand, for he had never seen such lovely things before. A king's head on one side, St George slaying a dragon on the other; to him they had always been deep down in the cellar of a bank. Love of money root of all evil, said Paul; not this time anyway.

All the movement he made each day was from his bed to this old sofa, his mother's bed by night. For weeks he had lain here, reading, and writing a few things for the *Irish Worker* and for *Irish Freedom*, the latter paper ignoring them; always wondering in his spare time if he would ever walk upright again. The couch was hard; the springs, thick iron, stuck up through the worn-out horsehair, and he marvelled how his mother could sink to sleep on it. Here was a woman enduring torments quietly that would send ecstasy to a saint. The place was poorer than any saint could wish for: he glanced at the bare floor, the old cabinet, veneered mahogany, doing the work of his mother's dresser and his own bookcase; the table, the two old kitchen chairs, the fender, kept together by wire; the butter-box covered with the red cloth; the picture of Nelson, and that much-loved one of Victoria, as bright as ever, with her little crown on her grey head, her purple bodice crossed by a pale-blue sash, and the Victorian Order hanging on her bosom – gaudy guardians of a bleak room. There was the box arrangement too, carrying the musk, the fuchsia, and the geranium, doleful now, and waiting for the spring to come. Someone had given his mother another treasure, a most mysterious plant, for, she said, in winter, sift the soil as you might, you'd find no trace of anything. Yet in the spring it thrust up a rosy tip of life, and in the summer turned into a wealth of variegated leaves, garnished by thick velvety blossoms of a rich red, with a saucy blob of tasselled gold in its centre. She called it the Resurrection Plant; and years after Sean discovered that it was a begonia. It was a lonely time for him, yet his mother had spent the worst of her lifetime here, without a murmur. She and he had hunted the bugs from the rooms, but they never got rid of the fleas, and these tormented him now. How in the name of God did she sleep on such a bed! She must be getting on for eighty now. She who had been buxom, was worn away now to a wiry thinness. She was a brave woman; something of the stoic in her. Seldom he had seen her cry: once, a sudden gushing forth of tears when she saw her dead son Tom; her favourite, Sean thought, though she had never shown it by word or deed; and again, when quiet tears had flowed down her cheeks, the night of his father's funeral, when they sat together by the fireside. Beside Ella's body, she had just whimpered in fright; she had broken down for the first time. Forgot herself for a moment. Her bravery hadn't brought her much. She had certainly served God quietly and faithfully and simply in all the life through which Sean had known her; but God had been stingy in His favours to her. Such a picture as she was deserved a finer frame than this mean, cancerous room. A quiet garden would be a fitter setting, with a few flowers, pansies, mignonette, big-panelled daisies, musk, a peony or two, a clump of gorgeous sunflowers, southernwood that she loved to smell, with big tufts of tansy and michaelmas daisies; oh yes, and maybe one deep-yellow rose with a brown tinge in its rich and silky petals. A tree too – a rowan or a hawthorn, spreading its loveliness over a hard bench where she could sit, and sew, knit, or read, and mark the birds coming into the garden. What bird would suit her best – lark, linnet, thrush, sparrow, or robin? None of these: the lark was too gay; the linnet too delicate; the thrush's speckled breast a little too pompous; the sparrow too humble and commonplace; and the robin too impudent. Which then? The blackbird? Yes, the blackbird; sedate and dignified in his black dress, yet bright in his deep-yellow bill; dignified, yet quick and confident in his walk and flight; a song never boisterous, yet bold and decisive in its deep mellow notes, with a faint touch of sharpness in some of them. The blackbird would suit her best. But her bright sedateness hadn't a green canopy or a blue sky over its head. She would end her days within this dim, drab room. She would get her last look at a patch of sky through the crooked window, over the tops of the musk, the geranium, and the fuchsia – that would be her way to a further life.

Yes, she must be getting on for eighty, he thought, as he watched the gnarled hands stirring the little saucepan of porridge.

Those hands could do many things yet, and she was firm on her legs, and often laughter came purling from her cracking lips. He saw she was stirring mechanically, and that her thoughts were far away. What was she thinking of? Probably of her husband, her Michael; her memory of him seemed to brighten as her body withered, for she really believed they would be together again. Well, he wouldn't hint at anything to frighten the dear delusion. She deserved her dream, coloured with the musk, the fuchsia, and geranium. Her Michael was waiting patiently for her among the asphodels; knee-deep in them now, he couldn't have long more to wait.

Ah, t'hell with it! he thought, he wouldn't stay here to dry up and die! She'd have to stick it, but he wouldn't. Her life was nearly over. She belonged to a different world, the world of submission, patience, resignation; he to that of discontent, resentment, resistance. Whenever she had been ill, he had done for her all he could – cooking, making tea and toast for her, and arrowroot when the funds allowed, lighting the fire, and washing out the damned floor when the end of the week came. But his life was away from her, and he'd have to leave her wandering in her little Garden of Eden among the musk, the fuchsia, and the crimson geranium.

He began to walk stiffly about the room, in great pain, to tip his toes hundreds of times a day, for he wasn't going to lie where he was and wait for God to call him. Though the harness he wore were strings and tatters, he'd die with it on him, resisting to the end.

Asked to be Secretary to a Committee formed to collect funds to provide clothes and boots for women and children of locked-out workers, he borrowed a stick, and hobbled down to be from ten in the morning till twelve at night in and out of Liberty Hall, helping with the Army, and, in his spare time, writing letters appealing for funds to help the women and children of the locked-out workers to cling a little longer on to life, till his heart ached for rest, and he began to set down sad thoughts in bad verses, which was his little space of geranium, fuchsia, and musk.

So here he was in Liberty Hall, seeing all the bright and excited patterns against the dark background of his illness. Always, in the throes of work, the dark grey silhouette of paralysis stared at him behind the moving picture of life. Like the changing designs of red, blue, green, white, and yellow of a kaleidoscope that never shifted from a bed of blackness. Nothing to do but to keep on, crushing out of his thought the gnawing pains in his legs from thigh to ankle; to go as far as his trembling legs would carry him, till he fell down, to wait for the fuller darkness of death.

Strange and vivid things passed in and out, figures in a candle-lighted show. Here was A. E., George Russell, looking like a teddy bear, pouring a cascade of jellied words over Jim Larkin, implying that out of them only a new heaven and earth could be built; shocked by hearing Jim say that bricks to build a new life must be hardened to a fine and fierce quality in the fire of trial.

—Well, what d'ye think of him? asked Jim, when A.E. had gone.

—Can't say, said Sean; no one I know knows him, except the Gaelic Leaguers, and they don't like him. I've read nothing he has written, except some verses in the Christmas Number of the *Irish Homestead*, called *The Celtic Christmas*. He has a great name in a lot of places. He looks to me like a Sanko Panko without his Don, and is a little embarrassed by the loneliness.

—Well, said Jim, most of what he's written isn't for us, except his fine letter defending us in our fight; and we must honour him for that.

A day or so after, in sails the Rev Dudley Fletcher, Rector of Coolbanagher, a strong-looking, stocky man in fully-fledged clericals, bearded like a pard, wearing the Red Hand in the lapel of his coat, full of sympathy with the workers, shaking Jim's hand and mine, wishing us well, and honouring us with a murmured prayer that the workers might win.

He wished he had his paint-box of ten colours handy, all gone, now, but not forgotten, that he might set down in colour the figures that passed him by here. This man, Dudley Fletcher, would appear on a background of grey pain and dark anxiety, in a white robe slashed with a dimmer red cross, upside down, sobriety and sorrow commingled. A. E. would thunder slowly and heavily in under a canopy of multi-coloured fireworks, spluttering and sparkling all around him. Yeats, though he never entered, passed by, and looked up at the windows, in a trailing toga of silver and purple, a mystic rose in his hair, and a lady's golden glove at his girdle. Orpen would hop in, dressed in rusty red and bottle green to sketch the tired and hungry faces surrounding the pale, hardy, handsome face of their leader, Jim. And Countess Markievicz, running around everywhere, would be scintillating in the suit of a harlequin, lozenged with purple, old gold, and virgin green.

In all the time he had pushed a way through a crowd of ragged women, and ragged children, bootless as well as ragged, carrying jugs, saucepans, and even kettles to collect their ration of stew, cooked in the Dagdan cauldron down in the damp and dreary basement, he had never seen the Countess doing anything anyone could call a spot of work. He often had a share of the stew, and sometimes snapped up a chance to bring home some to his mother, who welcomed it when it came, but said nothing when he came home without any; but never once did he see the Countess bearing up in the heat and burden of the day. Whenever a reporter from an English or an Irish journal strayed into the Hall and cocked an eye over the scene, there was the Countess, in spotless bib and tucker, standing in the steam, a gigantic ladle in her hand, busy as a beebeesee, so that a picture of the lady of the ladle might brighten the papers of the morrow; and, significant enough, though many mouths belled the myth of her devotion to the poor, Orpen's sketch of the eskitchen doesn't show sign or light of the good-natured dame anywhere near. The myth, it would seem, appeared in a vision to those who wanted to see it so. Neither did the Countess understand Ireland, even when she was green-costumed in her own selective uniform of the Citizen Army. She differed from Captain White in that while she never understood the workers, and never tried to, he, though never understanding them either, failed, I imagine, by trying too ardently to do so. Gaelic Ireland she never even glimpsed; and the English-speaking Ireland she ran about in was seen as in a wonderful looking-glass, darkly; so different from Alice Milligan, who saw it clear, and was able to fondle it with both her clever hands.

Countess Markievicz lagged far behind Maud Gonne in dignity, character, and grace, and couldn't hold a candle to her as a speaker. Her passionate speeches always appeared to be strained, and rarely had any sense in them; and they always threatened to soar into a still-born scream. Ideas of order she had little, and looked rather contemptuously on any mind that had. She usually whirled into a meeting, and whirled out again, a spluttering Catherine-wheel of irresponsibility. Although he had often seen her handling a gun, he had never seen her fondling a book, and he thought that odd. In her young days she could hardly have been a Cathleen ni Houlihan, and when she grew old she had no resemblance to the Old Woman of Beare. She grew very thin and bony, and in spite of all her irritating and fantastic liveliness, there was, invariably, a querulous look on her face. No part of her melted into the cause of Ireland, nor did she ever set a foot on the threshold of Socialism. She looked at the names over the doors, and then thought she was one of the family. But the movements were no more to her than the hedges over which her horses jumped. She wanted to be in everything and to be everywhere. She rushed into Arthur Griffith's arms, near knocking the man down; she dunced into the Republicanism of the Irish Brotherhood; she stormed into the Gaelic League, but quickly slid out again, for the learning of Irish was too much like work; she bounded into the Volunteers one night, and into the Citizen Army the next. Then she pounced on Connolly, and dazzled his eyes with her flashy enthusiasm. She found it almost impossible to reason out a question, and smothered the reasonable answer of another with a squeal. She seemed never to be able to make any golden or silver thing out of the ore of experience. She tried verses, and failed; she tried painting, and couldn't do any better; and yet she never reached the rank of failure, for she hadn't the constitution to keep long enough at anything in which, at the end, she could see a success or a failure facing her. One thing she had in abundance – physical courage: with that she was clothed as with a garment. She wasn't to be blamed, for she was born that way, and her upbringing in which she received the ready Ay, ay, madame, you're right of the Sligo peasants, stiffened her belief that things just touched were things well done. So she whirled about in her scintillating harlequin suit, lozenged with the colours of purple, old gold, and virgin green, bounding in through windows and dancing out through doors, striking, as she went by, her cardboard lath of thought against things to make them change, verily believing that they did, but never waiting to see whether they did or not. Well, well, may she rest in peace at last.

Recommended in a letter from the friend of a friend, Sean went one day to see another doctor to get a final verdict about his shivering legs. This'll be the third, he thought, and remembering that the number three had often played a curious part in his life, he felt hopeful. The last two were doleful; this one should be favourable. The surgery was filled with the latest gadgets to help a sick man to feel his way about. When he had stripped, he lay down on a swung couch to be thumbed and tapped again. Nerves in knees dead, he was told; and when the doctor had stared into his eyes, he murmured a number of *mmm*'s, adding, I haven't good news for you, young man; it is serious: you have spinal disease, I'm afraid – probably congenital. He gave the dazed Sean a prescription of mingled arsenic and strychnine, to be well shaken before taken, two pleasant kinds of drinks for a warm summer's day. Saint Arsenic and Saint Strychnine between him and all harm! He had got a message as bad as saying that he should live no longer. He felt no interest in wine, woman, or song when he stepped out again into the gay hum of the street. The blue sky was a black one now, and the golden sun but a big brass nail for a coffin. Well, if he was to go, he'd go drinking aromatic tea or wholesome water, and not those other two life-punishing lotions. So he slowly tore up the doctor's kindly incantation and scattered the pieces over the stony street; but when he looked up, the sky over him was as black as ever.

So, though he stumbled, he stood among the crowd in the Custom House square, listening to the English Labour leaders speaking encouragement to the men still fighting the employers: roaring Ben Tillett who cut Dublin into segments with his waving arms; Gosling, comically respectable, spewing out hordes of dead grey words that died dimly before they could reach the minds of the bored men; good-natured George Lansbury, a burning core of fighting faith in his gentle nature; all aglow with words in the midst of squealing gulls, and the boisterous sale among the men of the *Daily Herald*, full of good tidings of great sorrow, its daring pages distended with life and hope, and bearing on its front as a banner a full-paged cartoon by the doughty Will Dyson.

There was Sean, too, among the crowd on that radiant day when the good ship *Jocelyn* sailed in, packed with food, her rigging and lines abloom with flags, her siren shrilling, setting aside the fear of starvation for a month to come, greeted with a cheer that shook her masts when she hove in sight coming up the river. Then there was the busy scene of mooring her to the quay, the opening of the hatches, the first truckload wheeled into the store by Jim Larkin himself, crowned with the aching jubilation of the helping men whose bellies, with those of their wives and their children, would be filled for the first time for weeks. But there wasn't one priestly anointed member of the Christian faith there, from cardinal to sub-deacon, to rejoice with their flock that had been delivered for the time being from the torture of hunger. Here was a miracle of the feeding, not of five, but of fifty thousand souls, and not a stoled follower of Christ there to witness it. There wasn't one of these gentry, from one end of Ireland to the other, who hadn't had that day a good meal, who hadn't had something over and above his daily bread; yet not one of them seemed to sense the silent terror a soul gets from a sagging belly.

As he watched the dockers taking the cargo from the boat, he remembered the day when he was resting his aching legs for an hour at home, watching the sunlight playing with the golden musk and the purple fuchsia, a Mr Henchy, an official – the Secretary, Sean thought – of the Protestant Orphan Society, came suddenly to see him. The youngest son of his dead sister, Ella, had been adopted by the Society, and Sean had been made the guardian of the boy. The Society gave him three shillings a week, payable quarterly, to enable him to fulfil his duty. For some time the boy had shirked the job of going to Sunday school, morning service, and afternoon prayers for the young. Remembering his own experience, Sean did nothing to force him to go, if he found the play of the streets more colourful. So Mr Henchy had come to make a complaint on behalf of the Society.

—You're his guardian, you know, said Mr Henchy, and you are bound to see he is brought up in the nurture and fear of God.

—But don't you see, sir, you're asking me to bring him up, not in the fear of God, but rather in the fear of man? He doesn't want to go: am I to force him?

—It is an obligation, he coughed, and moved uneasy in his chair; an obligation undertaken by you, Mr Casside, in return for what the Society gives the boy.

—That isn't a lot, sir.

—You were very glad to get it! said Mr Henchy sharply.

Sean got up from the sofa, went over to a drawer in the old dresser, took out some receipts, and put them into Mr Henchy's hands. Look at those, he said; they are receipts for clothes and boots bought for the boy, and if you kindly add the amounts up, you'll find that the entire quarter's gratuity, plus two shillings from Mrs Casside, bitterly spared, was spent to get them. Should you have suspicion as to how the money was spent, these receipts will show you.

—I had no suspicions whatever, said Mr Henchy earnestly;

Mr Griffin told me long ago the sort of man you were, and added high praise for your mother. But rules are rules, and the Society must ask you to make the boy attend his religious duties.

—The Society can ask away, said Sean shortly.

—But, my friend, if the Society takes away the grant, the child will suffer.

—Evidently he will suffer either way, sir, and we must try to select the lesser one; for me, I think it better for him to die his own way. If I make him go, he will suffer unnecessarily; if you take away the grant, he will suffer unnecessarily too. I refuse to do it. If you do – well, that is your lookout.

—Your views are odd, said Mr Henchy, with a puzzled and rather shocked look on his face, and hardly show gratitude to those kind people who furnish the wherewithal to satisfy the needs of children in dire circumstances.

—They don't half satisfy the needs – that is my point, said Sean tersely. Look here, sir, and Sean swung his legs from the sofa, and sat so as to face Mr Henchy; would you be content to bring up one of your children on three shillings a week?

Mr Henchy's face flushed, his hands trembled a little, and he rose from his chair. I must be going, he said; I really shouldn't be wasting time arguing. The question is, Are you, as the boy's guardian, or are you not, going to keep the rules of the Society so that the grant may be continued?

—You haven't answered my question, Mr Henchy.

—I don't intend to try, for there is something of an insult in it.

—You are wrong, sir. Come, you are essentially a kind man; and as Mr Griffin has spoken of me to you, so he has spoken of you to me.

—Well, then, he said, mollified, and smiling a little, there's no analogy: you couldn't expect me to wish to bring any child of mine down to the unfortunate level of your little nephew.

—God forbid, sir; but I do wish you to expect me to try to bring my nephew (or anyone's) up to the level of your child.

—But don't you see, said Mr Henchy, that, logically, that would mean the bringing-up of all the children of all the poor to that level too?

—Precisely, said Sean, and to a higher level than that in which your class of children presently stand.

—I confess I don't understand, said Mr Henchy, puzzled.

—Haven't you ever read Bernard Shaw, sir?

—Shaw? Who's he, now? I imagine I've heard the name some-where. He isn't a clergyman by any chance?

—Well, he's a priest of the theatre.

—Oh, I don't take any interest in the theatre.

—Well, sir, you've heard of Goya?

—Goya? No. A foreigner of some sort?

—Well, Raphael, Titian, Constable, Darwin, and the rest.

—Oh, I've a great respect for our National Gallery, and have gone through it, of course; but what has all this got to do with our difficulty?

He hasn't any eye for colour, thought Sean. Here are the golden trumpets of musk sounding at his very ear; a carillon of purple fuchsia bells pealing pensively, and he can hear neither; and there was the rose window of a scarlet geranium behind them, and his eyes were too clouded with worldly things to see it. This man couldn't understand that when Sean's mother reverently touched the blossoms with her gnarled finger, God Himself was admiring the loveliness He had made.

—What I am out to help to do, he said aloud, is to lift our children to the state of enjoying and understanding the visions and ideas of these great men.

—Pshaw! said Mr Henchy impatiently, you're wasting your time. The people you mean prefer the sinful and lowering charms of the public-house. You haven't to deal alone, you know, with decent Protestant children; the great bulk of them are of the Roman Catholic faith – hopelessly ignorant and painfully super-stitious. However, we must think only of our own family of faith, so assuming that you want to give our children a better life – and a gentle, but doubtful, smile spread over his handsome face – isn't our Society trying to do that too?

—According to its lights – very dim ones – yessir; but I would do away with this Protestant charity as I would the Catholic one of St Vincent de Paul: each child has a right to a full life, independent of any charity.

—Oh, that's just anarchy! exclaimed Mr Henchy. It would mean the end of all decent things. Just what that fellow – what's his name? – Larkin tried to do, and look at the state of the poor people now! Hardly any law or order anywhere.

—Mr Henchy, Mr Henchy, where poverty is, there can never be law or order. Sean's arm moved in a sweep to encircle the room. D'ye think law and order could come here, could sit down,

sing, and sleep in a room like this? For such as we, sir, to honour
your law and order would be a blasphemy against God!

—You murmur strange things, said Mr Henchy, strange things
for a Protestant. You mystify me completely. I can't understand
the working of your mind.

—You've said that before, Mr Henchy. That's your trouble –
you can't understand, and you don't try.

—Maybe so. But I must be off now, Mr Casside. Sean could
see he was eager to get away. He placed a white hand on Sean's
shoulder. Be reasonable, man, he said, and listen. I say this, believe
me, in no bullying fashion, but in the kindliest and friendliest
way I can – I am in conscience bound to report to my Committee,
and that Committee is bound to assert the rules, if your charge
doesn't keep them. Now, like a dear man, do try to – not to
force – but to persuade, to persuade the boy to mind his duties.

—I'll tell him, said Sean, that Mr Henchy came to say that if
he didn't go to Sunday school and church, he'd get no more
clothes or boots.

—Oh, not that way; not quite in those terms, said Mr Henchy,
a pained look on his face.

—But that is exactly what you mean, sir. I'll put it this way,
then: If you don't worship God properly, then He'll put it in the
hearts of kind people to give you neither boots nor clothes.

Mr Henchy sighed. Can't you explain to him that as his earthly
father loved him, so does his Heavenly Father love him too, and
likes to see him near?

—The boy's earthly father didn't care a damn about him, said
Sean, so that way won't do. There's no way out of it except by a
big change. Let yous give the lad the whole of his due, and when
he and his young friends come to worship God, let it be by song
and dance and magic story, in gaily-coloured plays, flags, ribbons,
and maypoles; in the music of their own bands, trumpet, cymbal,
triangle, and drum; the louder and fiercer the better. Let them
adore God, not in hypocritical hymn, tiresome prayer, and mind-
torturing catechism, but in the fullness of skipping, a hop, step,
and a lep; the rage of joy in a flying coloured ball, without a care
in the world, bar their own young fears and disappointments.
Then the seriousness of God's face will be broken by a smile, the
very angels will sing and stagger about as if filled with old wine,
and the Church Triumphant will shout and clap her hands,
saying God has come into His own at last!

—I must go, said Mr Henchy; goodbye. By the way, I met the boy as I came in, and I thought he didn't look too well. Maybe he'd better take things quietly for a time. Then he'll go on as usual, eh? Goodbye; and hastily shaking hands, which surprised Sean, he made off without waiting for an answer.

Sean never saw him again, but the money came every quarter from the Society, and no more questions were asked about the boy. Henchy didn't understand. Reared up in a groove, a pleasant groove in many ways, but a dangerous one to us and him. A kind man, made helpless, sometimes even cruel. He never even heard of Henchy again.

A magic shadow-show, played in a box whose candle is the sun, round which we phantom figures come and go. But Ireland was rather more of a kaleidoscope than a shadow-show: always re-shaping itself into a different pattern. Strange pattern here while they talked together: the crosses of Andrew, George, and Patrick twisting uneasy in each other's arms behind a kneeling child in front of a flame from hell, with two dim figures, mouthing methods, were halo'd by whirling crimson gerontium discs, and encompassed about with the blowing of mosque-scented trumpets of gold, and the pealing of purple confuchsian bells.

Religion was ripening in Dublin. God was being worshipped in spirits and in drouth. Well in the background, for fear of a sudden mêlée, he watched the marchers go by, a long, deep, dark, drab mass of men roped together with scapulars, and bespangled with miraculous medals. Friends in England had opened decent homes to receive the starving children of the locked-out workers, and this holy romany ryes were out to prevent their going. Led by their clergy, the marchers, beerded nicely, and supportered by a good conscience, brandyshed sticks and cudgels, bottling their wrath with difficulty; shouting out that everything done against the advice of the clergy was illicit still from a malthuse to a baby powder, the red, blue, brown, black, green, and white scapuleers, scapuliars, drinkaway boys, and slugalowers marched past yodelling and godelling their war-chant,

> *Faith of our fathers, we will love*
> *Both friend and foe in all our strife;*
> *And preach it too, as love knows how,*
> *By kindly words and virtuous life,*

adding sense to it by giving a knock to the head of a father
trying to get his child out of mudesty into life, tearing skin from
the face of a friend helping the father, and the shirts from the
backs of any coming near enough to shout the slogan shame;
four at the front staggering under a banner bearing the inscription of Rear Up the Workers' Chisulers in the Rearum
Novarum Way.

The Scapular Brigade halted, and divided to let a carriage and
pair drive through, and out of it pops a venerable Knight of the
Roman Slumpire, with his portly Dame, he caparisoned with a
wide and flowing beard, yellow and white, the papal colours, she
with the order of Eironical Virtue and Honour aflame on her
bosom, both of them walking as if they had come direct from a
conference in Heaven; harm in harm they went up the steps of
Liberty Hall, down the dim corridors, straight towards the room
where Jim Larkin worked, who, when he heard they were there,
said to show the lady and gentleman in, and up, and in, they came,
to be met with the question of, Well, me good woman and good
man, what can we workers do for you, do for you, do for you,
fair and virtuous lady and noble knight? Have you come for a
share from the urn holding the hashes of Irish art and literature?

—Me an' th' missus, here, said the Knight of the Burning
Apestle, have dropped in on behalf of St Michael an' All Angels,
St Paul, St Pether, and th' other apostles, an' Father O'Flynn,
to place before you their, an' our, undyin' resolutions to prevent
th' hawkin' of our workers' chisulers to decent homes in England,
realizin' that such circumstances would arouse disaffection in their
innocent minds with the holy squalor endured in their own homes,
assured by the remembrance that what is good enough for their
guardian angels must be good enough for them – here he shook
out his white-and-yellow beard like a banner – an' if they only
looked out of the window, they'd see that the might, virtue,
honour, pride, an' holiness of Ireland had gethered itself together to prevent this condamination of our little ones be English
unbelievers, makebelievers, an' fakebelievers, waitin' for th'
chance through gawdiness and comeforth to bounce the child
away from the faith of its fathers.

Asked by Connolly if the Knight and his Dame would take
five children into their own home suite home, the pair were silent;
asked if they would take two, they were still silent; and turning
away to go out, before they could be asked if they would take one,

they were gone, surrounded by clouds of witnesses gay in medi-
evil funcy dross, looking for all the world like pupil halbeer-
dears.

Another twist of the kaleidoscope, and there was the patterned scene, backed by a leaden sky like a sullen face, blotched
with reddish streaks; dark clouds like hair sheltering dull, nickel-
silvered madonna lilies, their pistils out and pointing; a black
cloud, lower down, forming a cavern-mouth from which came
pouring streams of frantic figures wearing on their drab breasts
bright-coloured spots spreading out into the shape of hearts, clubs,
diamonds, and spades; all of them yelling dumb *vivimus vivamus*
into the delicate ears of the figurines of papal knight and papal
dame, all white and gold, standing in front of these squalling
deomens, like chinaware grandees who had somehow climbed
from a scented cabinet and had daringly stepped down on to the
deusty highway. Beyond the veil of these posturing purseline
figurines, and the crowd of roaring, adoring sons of the Guile,
the leaden sky with its clouds and red splotches, looking like the
savage face of an angry yahoovah, English shadows of men and
women were bent and bruised wiring guns, making shells, ham-
mering ships together, burying their dead in their minds by
thousands, and taking their wounded to bloody beds in tens of
thousands; while queues of the very old and very young waited
grouseously for food from morn till midnight, sleeping then that
they might be able to begin again at daybreak; too tired to feel
fear of the faint purr of a Zeppelin sailing by overhead, their ears
stirred soon by the hiss of a falling bomb, to be at once cracked
with the concussion of its explosion, then stuffed with the cut-
short squeal of a housemaid, on her knees washing a doorstep,
as a lump of jagged metal knocked her frillied head to bits;
then came the rumbling, cracking zoom as houses split asunder,
their frightened walls lurching for a moment before they crashed
face downwards, the uproar stabbed by the scream of a woman
yelling out to Heaven, Oh, save my little one who's been buried
under it all!

Sean gave the cap of the kaleidoscope a twist, and there he
was between two comrades who were carrying a round wreath
to one of their Union who had been battered to death by many
police batons. From Tara Street they sallied down one, to emerge
into another street so poor that even the stars in the night sky
seemed to be dimmed by destitution. They penetrated into a

yawning hole that Sean guessed was the doorway, a comrade, the tram conductor, telling him to watch out, for the stairs weren't all there; on to a lobby lit by a dumb religious light, animated by a low murmur of many voices like the sound of many leaves chattering softly on a day of a quiet breeze. First he saw the two tall candles, topped by their flickering wisps of yellow flame; and, between them, higher up on the wall, a crucifix, a little less dim than the shadows around it, seemed to hint, As it is with you, dead man, so it was with me long ago and far away. A crowd of misty men and women, kneeling and standing, hid the dead man, so Sean and his comrades waited till the prayers were said for a chance to lay the wreath where it was to lie. On a small table, covered with vivid blue paper, stood a looking-glass, showing in its depths the candles and the crucifix among the heads of the comforters. The now slumbering fire in the grate, the kettle and saucepans on the hob, with a galvanized bath in a corner, showed Sean that here the family fed, washed, and slept; and a tiny bottle of ink with an old pen stuck in its neck, showed that the correspondence and the children's lessons were done here too. In this one room they are born, they live, they grow old, and then they die. Now he saw the widow, sitting on a chair by the head of the bed, her body bent forward so that her face couldn't be seen. What will this woman do when the shouting dies, the captains and the kings depart?

When the crowd had drawn from the bed, Sean's comrades stepped forward and laid the wreath silently on its foot, crossing themselves, murmuring something meant for a prayer.

—A marthyr – that's what he was, said the conductor; a marthyr to the workers' cause! Look, Sean, he added, turning, look at th' way th' bastards left him!

Sean went forward to have a last look at a comrade who was no more than a dumb message now. There he was, asprawl under a snowy sheet, looking like a mask on a totem-pole. One eye gone, the other askew, the nose cracked at the bridge, and bent sidewise; the forehead and one cheek a royal purple: from a distance it looked well, like a fading iris in a wide patch of driven snow. The mighty baton! Each one an Erin's rod – able at the will of the owner to bud into a purple bloom of death. A warning to Sean. Keep well away from them. That he'd do, for he wanted to live, feeling an urge of some hidden thing in him waiting its chance for an epiphany of creation.

He had had one very narrow escape, when he was dragged from one end of O'Connell Street nearly to the other by two drunken constables. He had been in a fix: had he gone quiet for twelve steps, and then suddenly squirmed out of their grip to make a bolt for freedom, his legs would have let him down in a chase, and he would have given his captors a grand excuse to pummel him to a pulp; had they got him to the station, it would have meant manhandling with fist, foot, and baton, and darkness. He had thought of praying, but his case was too desperate for that; so he clenched his teeth, and was silent while they dragged him along the road from Tom Clarke's shop to Nelson's Pillar, with people stopping on the paths to watch. Then a helmeted inspector had stepped out from a group standing at the Pillar, and had said sharply to the drunken ruffians, Let him go, let him go; and Sean had recognized the voice of Inspector Willoughby who long ago had headed a summons against him for allowing the pipers' band to play past a Protestant church while service was going on – the very church where his father and mother had married, and all of them had been baptized. This was the Inspector's return to Sean for the courteous way he had been received at Sean's home when he came to see him about the summons. The Inspector had saved his life, for Sean had been in no state then to compromise with a beating. When he was released, he had stood staring at the bit of face showing from beneath the peak of the helmet, while the constables stood, grumbling, near. He recovered his surprise, said thank you to the lips smiling under the helmet, bowed, he thought, with grace, and walked slowly away till he got into a side turning; then he had gone hell for leather far to a quiet spot to think it all out.

Still shaken, he stood in O'Connell Street among the crowd watching the funeral of the battered man go past; well hid in the crowd, lest some hearty comrade should pull him, passing, into the procession, for he determined to take no more risks. Here it came, the *Dead March in Saul*, flooding the street, and flowing into the windows of the street's rich buildings, followed by the bannered Labour Unions, the colours sobered by cordons of crêpe, a host of hodden grey following a murdered comrade.

Ay, you, he thought, dotting the upper rich-curtained windows with firmly brushed heads, who have lived far from the life lived by the dead man, or from his own life too. Light-years away from both. Eh, you, up there, lean out a little more, and look a little closer. He can't hurt you now, and his body is quite clean. He has been prepared to meet his God with soap and hot water, for, as you know, cleanliness is next to godliness. He is clad now in clean white linen for the first time in his life; and his battered head lies for the first time on a snowy pillow. Look over, look closer, ladies and gentlemen – there he goes, feet first, stretched out to his fullest; and if the lid was only up, you'd see his face: a big and purple, dead and dreadful blossom, safe now, snug in a calix of lily-white linen.

Twist the cap of the kaleidoscope, and see what it's like: a thick, black sky full of the pale dead faces of workers, life but faintly sketched in each of them, like white, wan moons looking down on a broken purple star falling phut-long out of their own presunctied horrorizon.

UNDER THE PLOUGH AND THE STARS

HARDLY HAD he finished with the Committee to aid the women and children of the workers than, tired and weary, he was called upon to take the Irish Citizen Army in hand, now moving vagely from this place to that, and to put an orderly and adaptable shape on it – a thing he couldn't do to himself; for he was still wondering how long more he'd be able to stir, and in idle moments Despair came to sup with him.

—What's wrong with the Army? he had asked, when called upon to help.

—Oh, man alive, said the conductor, what's right with it would be an easier question to answer – nothing.

—But they looked fine a few weeks ago, said Sean, when I saw them marching in Croydon Park, Connolly leading, and the police trying to look unconcerned.

—That's it – they look fine for an hour; but if they go on in this undisciplined way, the police'll lose that look and we'll be batoned again!

—But what's Connolly, Captain White, the Secretary, and the Committee doing? How can I butt in on their authority?

—There's no Secretary, Committee, rules, or regulations;

Connolly can't give much time to it, so soon there'll be no men.

He got a room, drafted a few sentences, and made out a few rules, short, simple, direct, and wise; sentences that would easily fit into the simplest mind as no sentences in a catechism could; sentences that would sing the workers' song for a fuller life in a few words: *The Land and Air and Sea of Ireland for the People of Ireland – that is the gospel the heavens and earth are proclaiming; and that is the gospel every Irish heart is secretly burning to embrace.* Well, that was John Mitchel praying, and here was O'Casside to say amen. *The first and last principle of the Irish Citizen Army is the avowal that the ownership of Ireland, moral and material, is vested of right in the People of Ireland.* Well, that was Fintan Lalor praying, and here was O'Casside to say amen. The Army stood for the absolute unity of nationhood, and the rights and liberties of the world's democracies. No scab or black-leg could be one of them, and every member, whenever possible, had to be a member of a trade union, recognized by the Trades Union Congress.

These things were heartily agreed to at a general meeting in Liberty Hall, packed with eager men, and the Committee was elected from those present. Strange that out of twenty officials chosen, four were, or had been, of the Protestant way of thinking about Heaven – everybody talkin' 'bout heab'n, an' goin' where? One of those elected, veiled under the name of Richard Brannigan, had been a knight of the Grand Black Chapter of the Orange Order; had served time in a Northern jail for inciting to a breach of the peace in the matter of a Catholic procession; had been presented with a purse packed with sovereigns by the Orange Brethren when he came out; had joined the Gaelic League, as the Roaring O'Kane had done before him; and had now stalked defiantly, in his Belfast way, on to the Citizen Army Committee. A right, good, sensible, energetic man he was, big and burly, with a typical heavy-jowled Belfast face, dour-looking, yet with an exquisitely dry, sly, and spry sense of humour that often sent a twinkle into his serious, questioning grey eyes. Sean often laughed at the dour look of offended agony that swelled his big face when some Army man was blathering without any idea of what he was saying, or when he would stop.

Catching light from the flame of the Irish Citizen Army, the much more respectable sons of Cathleen ni Houlihan, headed by

Eoin Mac Neill, at a packed meeting in the Rotunda, founded the
Irish Volunteers, into which poured many who had fought
Larkin and Connolly, so that it was streaked with employers who
had openly tried to starve the women and children of the workers,
followed meekly by scabs and blacklegs from the lower elements
among the workers themselves, and many of them saw in this
agitation a plumrose path to good jobs, now held in Ireland by
the younger sons of the English well-to-do. Now there were two
Cathleen ni Houlihans running round Dublin: one, like the
traditional, in green dress, shamrocks in her hair, a little Brian
Boru harp under her oxster, chanting her share of song, For the
rights and liberties common to all Irishmen; they who fight for
me shall be rulers in the land; they shall be settled for ever, in
good jobs shall they be, for ever, for ever; the other Cathleen
coarsely dressed, hair a little tousled, caught roughly together
by a pin, barefooted, sometimes with a whiff of whiskey off her
breath; brave and brawny; at ease in the smell of sweat and the
sound of bad language, vital, and asurge with immortality. Those
who had any tinge of gentility in them left the Citizen Army for
the refeenianed Volunteers.

And now began an intensive campaign by both sides for the
in-gathering of arms. The Ulster Volunteers had landed guns in
the North, one day when England's eyes went suddenly blind,
and rich men covered the cost grandly. Mac Neill's army was
much poorer, and the Citizen Army much poorer still. But already
they had got stocks of belts, haversacks, French and Italian
bayonets, long, lithe, dangerous-looking weapons, a number of
revolvers, and about a dozen rifles. Even these had had an effect,
for the grace of civility and bubbling good humour had flooded
the hearts and minds of the police at all meetings. The Citizen
Army began to sing on the march, and Sean began to lose the
fear of a broken head, though he kept wary.

Neither the Army nor the Volunteers was satisfied with
arming: they wanted uniforms. In the weekly paper of the Volunteers, article after article appeared about the uniform worn by
the Volunteers of 1782; and many wanted to be seen going about
the narrow streets of their home homeland, clad in green trousers,
yellow coat, red busby with a blue plume; or black cutaway coat
faced with purple, white pantaloons, top-boots, and brass
helmet with a crimson hackle curving over all. Bravery was to
be twin brother to bravura. The Citizen Army, more wisely,

wanted to be so that they could be a movement, they said, within
the meaning of International Law. In the meantime, till money
was flusher, citizen soldiers were to wear an armlet that was
termed a brassard, of St Patrick's blue, the old Irish colour,
according to Madame Markievicz, and each officer was to wear
a red one. These, it was said, would safely classify them as
belligerents, and so entitle them to the privileges of International
Law when in battle, or as prisoners of war. So argued the chiefs
and lawyers of the Volunteers. The words brassard, the Hague,
belligerent, took wings, flew about everywhere, settling on everyone's shoulder, cooing a soft sense of security into every mind
except Sean's. He argued incessantly and insistently that neither
uniforms nor brassards would be of use to them in securing treatment of belligerents when waging war against the British. You
will simply be, he said, no more to them than decorated rebels.
On the contrary, they will be a greater danger in so far as they
would unmistakably reveal the presence of a foe. They would be
far safer in their ordinary clothes, for, if caught, they could pretend they were there by accident; whereas the uniform or gaudy
brassard would show they were there by intention. He put Shaw's
comparison before them of Ireland's fight with England as a
perambulator up against a Pickford van; and tried to point out
that their military art must be that of strike and dodge; dodge
and strike.

—Shaw's no authority on military affairs, the voice of Captain
White interjected. We can't shape our course from what that
man says; and a loud chorus of hear-hears came from a crowd
the most of whom had heard the name for the first time.

—I say, went on Sean, that the question of belligerency doesn't
exist for us. We will be rebels; worse – we will be traitors, even
terrorists to England, and she will strike without stop or mercy.
It is for us, as far as we can, to force her by dodgery to strike
oftenest at the air. If we flaunt signs about of what we are, and
what we do, we'll get it on the head and round the neck. As for a
uniform – that would be worst of all. We couldn't hope to hide
ourselves anywhere clad in green and gold, or even green without
the gold. Caught in a dangerous corner, there would be a chance
in your workaday clothes. You could slip among the throng,
carelessly, with few the wiser. In uniform, the crowd would
shrink aside to show you, and the enemy will pounce. In your
everyday rags you could, if the worst came, hang your rifle on a

lamp-post and go your way. But you couldn't take your uniform off, for even if you did, a man walking about in his shirt would look as suspicious as one going about in a uniform – that is, if any of you has a shirt.

—We've all got one, said a voice reproachfully; we're decent men.

—It's not a matter of decency, retorted Sean, but of money – I haven't one.

—This is wasting time! said Captain White testily. Without some kind of uniform, the men will look slovenly, and feel it. They'll have no respect for the ideals of the Army, and won't have an incentive to keep together.

Just before this, Jim Larkin had come in, and had listened to what had been said. Now he stood up, and the husky voice agreed with Captain White. Uniforms will give the men a sound sense of *esprit de corps*, and one of homogeneous unity, encourage the practice of discipline, and instil a pride into the men they couldn't possibly feel in their everyday clothing; and a wild chorus of hear-hears from the men showed they agreed with Jim too.

—This discussion, anyhow, is too late, said the Captain, suddenly rising to his feet, a happy smile on his face, for I've already gone guarantor for fifty pounds, the price of fifty uniforms, and Arnott's have already measured the picked men who have been chosen as the first to wear them.

Captain White had fine qualities, and a good many lovable ones, but he had a bad habit of impulsive action without consulting the Committee. This matter of the uniforms had been settled in his own way, after having had a talk about it with Countess Markievicz and Connolly. Here was a commitment of fifty pounds for clothes, and it was left to three or four to get the money somewhere. Three of the Committee, Sean Shelly, an amiable, self-educated fellow, an Aran Islander, Michael Mullen, a prodigious worker, and Sean himself, spent night after night sticking up bills in suitable places announcing an event in Croydon Park, organized to get the money guaranteed by Captain White, dabbing the few clothes they had with paste, and often staggering home at three or four in the morning.

While this work was aswing, the men met to arrange for the yearly demonstration to Bodenstown in honour of Wolfe Tone. It was odd to Sean that Tone was thought of merely as a

Nationalist, out for the rights of Ireland only. All seemed to be unaware that he was also out for the rights of man; that, had he won, Ireland would have stood against control by monarch and prelate; that Paine's *Rights of Man* was more to him than papal bull, encyclical, or decree; that hardships on the clergy wouldn't have made him turn a hair: a democrat away in advance of his time, and well ahead still of the right, left, and step together sons of St Patrick.

But here the Army men were, burnishing button and buckle, and patting out the uniforms into a proper shape to honour the memory of an Internationalist and agnostic, while at a table sat Sean and the ex-knight of the Black Chapter recording the names of those taking tickets, and entering down the money they gave in exchange; when, lo and behold, into the hall came Captain White, quickly, his face flushed and angry, followed by the Countess more slowly, who was followed by Connolly more slowly still. The Captain, standing in front of the table, launched into a violent attack on Sean for not having the money by this time to pay Arnott's, who, he said, were pressing for payment; and but for this slovenly Secretary the Army had, he wouldn't be in the fix of having to pay for the uniforms; all the while, the Countess standing behind him, grinning, Connolly behind her, the old stolid look on his curiously ball-like face. When the Captain's blaze of anger had exhausted itself, Sean stood up to remind everyone that the uniforms had been ordered without the knowledge of the Committee, that he had opposed the getting of them from the very first, as they all knew; but the Captain turned away contemptuously and swept from the room, the Countess trotting after him, while Connolly, more dignified, waddled his slow way out after. Just as the Captain gained the door, the Belfast treasurer roared after him, in his finest northern brogue, Dinna wurry – ye'll get your money bawk! Sean guessed that the Captain had been egged on to this attack by the Countess; for the Captain, unfortunately for himself, didn't think enough about the giving of gifts, and gave to many who deserved kicking instead of ha'pence, even roughly rejecting Sean's advice when he ventured to give it him. But the Festival brought in much more than the cost of the uniforms; and the slovenly Secretary had the joy of seeing the treasurer write out a cheque for what was due to Arnott's, realizing that his hard work made payment possible, though he felt bitter over it all, intensified when he remembered that the Countess and Captain never raised a finger to help them. Give orders, give orders, and let others carry them out.

Then the flag came – the Plough and the Stars. A blanket was spread over a wall, and the flag spread over the blanket so that it couldn't be defiled by the grimy evil of the wall. All pressed back to have a good look at it, and a murmur of reverent approval gave the flag a grave salute – all except the Countess, who returned to the oiling of her automatic with the remark that the flag bears no Republican message to anyone. There it was – the most beautiful flag among the flags of the world's nations: a rich, deep poplin field of blue; across its whole length and breadth stretched the formalized shape of a plough, a golden-brown colour, seamed with a rusty red, while through all glittered the gorgeous group of stars enriching and ennobling the northern skies.

Jim Larkin it was who first said that the Citizen Army should have a banner all on its own, its pattern and sign away from the painted commonplace ones of other national and labour bodies, its symbols showing Labour's near and higher ideals. The one who actually designed it is disputed; some saying A. E., but Sean, later on, asked him, and he denied the honour. A Galway art teacher sketched a realistic pattern, and from this Dun Emer Guild wove the lovely thing now hanging on the soiled wall. It was queer that such a lovely thing should spread itself so proudly in such a lowly place, before a crowd of hardy, rough-handed, dusty-skinned, ignorant men, tempting them to look at it, and seeming to say, Be worthy, men, of following such a banner, for this is your flag of the future. Whatever may happen to me; though I should mingle with the dust, or fall to ashes in a flame, the plough will always remain to furrow the earth, the stars will always be there to unveil the beauty of the night, and a newer people, living a newer life, will sing like the sons of the morning.

But it was hard going. Every possible obstacle was thrust into the way of the Citizen Army. The officers of the Volunteers did all they could to check its growth. They would lend them no hall in which to drill; and no place for an inside meeting could be got from one end of the land to the other. Once they managed by a ruse to get the Town Hall, Kingstown; but this was discovered, and the hall taken away from them, so that the great meeting had to be held outside of it. The Volunteers would give them no help to gather weapons, would give no support to anything the Army did to collect money to pay for what they got. Returning good for evil, the Union and the Army did all they could to help any Irish-Ireland activity; but great bitterness tinged the distant relations between the two of them. The Wolfe Tone Committee were hesitant about letting the Army travel down to Bodenstown, and when Sean went to their meeting to get the tickets, there was a discussion as to whether it would be wise to give them.

—They don't like us Volunteers, said Con Colbert, and they're a tough lot, aren't they?

—I'm afraid they are, said Bulmer Hobson.

—They are a tough lot, said Sean, and that is part of their glory, for in that they resemble the Boys of Ormond Market whom Wolfe Tone sighed to have beside him when he went into battle for Ireland. But, on a vote, only one hand was raised to invite them to come.

Then Tom Clarke came in, and took the chair. His bright eyes gleamed when he was told all that had happened. Of course they'll come, he said, and welcome. They are Irishmen, and damned good ones too. Special carriages would be there for them, and he and O'Casside would make them as comfortable as possible. And he proposed that as the Irish Citizen Army were the first body in Nationalist Ireland to become armed, they should receive the honour of marching at the head of the procession. But Clarke's intervention didn't hide from Sean that the workers wouldn't get much from this crowd if ever they came into power. These aren't Internationalists; they aren't even Republicans. They aren't able to see over the head of England out to the world beyond. They would be lost among Desmoulins, Danton, Couthon, St Just, and Robespierre, and Marat would frighten the life out of them. Their eyes can see no further soil than their feet can cover. A frail few would stand at ease under the workers' banner. They would be the heralds of the new power, having time but to sound the reveille, and then sink suddenly down into sleep themselves.

Never mind: to plough is to pray, to plant is to prophesy. Again, as in an age gone by, the plough will with a wreath be crowned, and wise men will twine the garland; and the stars will last, and those who have loved them fondly will never be fearful of the night.

IN THIS TENT, THE REBUBBLICANS

SEAN CASSIDE had left the IRB long ago, though he still
swung forward to help them in anything that came his way. His
criticisms had given offence, and he had been summoned to
visit one of the Supreme Council to be warned; summoned to
meet the man who had been so kind to him in his illness, and who
now told him that he had been selected to tell Sean in all friendliness that they were very displeased with him; that his criticisms
did no good to the Movement; and that they must cease: and
Sean knew now that he would have to cease troubling Deakin
for a renewal of his prescription.

—Who has done more for the IRB in relation to his condition
and chances than I? he asked. Isn't it because the criticisms are
justified that they want them stopped? he asked again. Quite a
few have got jobs through its influence: have I? Bar ill-health,
pain, and poverty, I have got nothing. Nor do I want anything;
but I am determined to hold on to what is mine own; my way of
thinking, and freedom to give it utterance. Otherwise the little
life I have would cease to be life at all. Here's a question: do you,
or do you not, think Bulmer Hobson the best editor we can get
for *Irish Freedom*? But Deakin mumbled that he hadn't been
empowered to argue about the literary gifts of Bulmer Hobson.

—We can't argue on what doesn't exist, said Sean. What I want
to know is if you think his editorials inspire our members?

—That isn't the point, said Deakin. What I want to know is if
you are prepared to obey us, and stop your criticism?

—No, I'm not, said Sean. I've criticized their inner policy only
in the Circles; their public policy and tactics set out in the Press,
I'll criticize whenever I think they need it.

—Is that your final answer? he asked sharply. Am I to say you
refuse to obey orders?

—You can put it that way if you like; and as far as ceasing to
say what I think is concerned, you can tell them all to go to hell
for me!

—There's no more to be said, said Deakin; goodnight; and he
turned to propounding a prescription. Sean took the hint, rose
up, left the shop, and neither saw nor heard of Deakin for years.
He knew, of course, if he asked, or even if he left the bottle, he'd

get his prescription renewed readily; but he knew he would never neither ask nor go. Anyway, he thought to soothe himself, the feast of porridge was long ago over, and what good would the potion be without the porridge?

They were a queer lot, as queer as himself, and Sean was sorry to leave them; but the one precious thing he had, he'd hold. It seemed to him though, that, for democrats, they were damned intolerant. Yet most of them were, if not actual, at least potential agnostics, and all of them anti-clericals. He knew few of them who could be called practising Catholics, though he had had one experience how the faith lay crystallized in the inner corner of their minds. He got the monthly *Irish Protestant* from a friend, and in one issue was astounded to see the leading article praised the Men of Ninety-eight, and with the article went the verses telling of *The Wake of William Orr*, one of the leaders executed as a rebel. The article had been written by Lindsay Crawford, who, in some way or another, had been attracted by the New Irish Movement. Sean hurried down to Tom Clarke's shop with the journal.

—Look, he said, shaking Tom out of a doze which he was enjoying in a corner behind the counter, look and read – you'll find something to stir you there!

As soon as Clarke's brilliant eyes saw the title of the paper, he flung it back at Sean, saying excitedly, and with no little venom, Take it away – I don't read such slanderous rubbish! Take away that anti-Catholic rag!

—I don't want to make a Protestant of you, man! Sean said, savagely, surprised to see that the fear of a bigot lingered even in the bold heart of Tom Clarke. Here was a most intelligent man, ready to face a firing squad, afraid to face a Protestant paper, and a rather stupid one at that. If anything, I'd but try to make an atheist of a Catholic, said Sean, and then only in an argument of the Catholic's own making, prepared, as a man, to give an answer for the hopelessness that is in me. This issue of the paper praises the Irish who died for Ireland, and says that the Protestants should be the vanguard in Ireland's fight for freedom.

Tom Clarke seized the paper, skimmed it with his gleaming eyes, turned, and said with rapture, Here Sean, quick, get three dozen of them; go where you think they are, and get them – this is the best I've read for years!

Every aspect of this man showed weariness and age. His

fifteen years of distorted life in jail, added to fifteen years of
silent defensive fighting for mind and body, had fretted away
the outward semblance of strength and virility. The full and
happier growth of his life had been sucked away into uselessness
and pain. Almost all his loyalties to the colours and enjoyments
of life had been burned away, leaving but a slender, intense flame
of hatred to what he knew to be England. Free himself, now, he
plucked impatiently at those who wanted to let bad enough
alone. Watch him locking up his tiny shop, slipping the key in
his pocket, then giving a swift turn to where a Committee
waited for him; a warm, rough, tweed overcoat belted firmly at
his slender waist, a broad-brimmed hat set firm on his greying
head, the frail figure went straight on, taking short, rapid steps
with a tiny spice of jauntiness in them; straight on, looking neither
right nor left, to where a drooping Committee sprang to interested
alertness when he came among them, and bent low over the task
of moulding the bullets that would tear rough and roguish gaps
open in some of their own breasts.

The prominent ones of Dublin never, on the whole, tuned
themselves in to the hum of a prayer-book. The rifle brown and
sabre bright were what they stretched romantic hands to, rather
than to the more romantic cross; the shout of a battle rather than
to the chanting of a hymn. The cowl, the Roman collar, the
swing-high-swing-low of the church bells and bulls didn't bother
them much; and the *pro bonem* clericallous but brought to their
minds the purrannual squeal of the bishops in their Easter pos-
turels against whoring, gambling, stock-raising without a marriage
licence, and the threat of a hot welcome to hell for anyone who
became a Fenian.

Pity, though, few of them cared a thraneen about art, literature,
or science. In this respect, even, they weren't International. A few
of them, one of the Plunkets, MacDonagh, and McEntee,
paddled in the summertime in the dull waters of poor verse;
but gave hardly any sign that they had ever plunged into the
waters that kept the world green. No mention of art, science, or
music appeared in *Sinn Fein* or *Irish Freedom*. To them, no book
existed save ones like *The Resurrection of Hungary* or the *Sinn
Fein Year Book*. None of them ever seemed to go to a play, bar
one that made them crow in pain and anger. A great many of
them were ignorant of the finer things of the mind, as the on-
slaught on Synge showed. Even Mangan was beyond them. All

of them knew his Dark Rosaleen by heart; sang it so often that one got tired of her sighing and weeping, longing to hear her roar out vulgar words with the vigour of a Pegeen Mike. But Mangan's splendid Ode to The Maguire was known to hardly any of them, or, if known, never mentioned. In all the years of his sojourn in Irish Ireland, he never once heard it mentioned. Thomas Davis was their pattern and their pride. He sang for them every hour of the day, and, if he happened to tire, his poor imitator, William Rooney, Griffith's great butty, sang instead. In a literary sense, they could have chosen a king in Mitchel; instead they put a heavy gilded crown on the pauper Davis. Almost all of them feared the singing of Yeats, and many were openly hostile to him; though few of them could quote a line from a poem of his. All they treasured of him was the dream which fashioned the little play about Cathleen ni Houlihan, a tiny bubble, iridescent with a green tinge. Their plays in Irish and English were frightening. Sean saw a play called *Seabhac na Ceithre Caoile – the Hawk of the Slender Quarters –* produced in the Rotunda as a prime piece of imagination; and he sorrowed for a month afterwards for the hard-earned shilling he had given to it. Apart from Pearse, Seumas Deakin, and Tom Clarke, few of the others showed any liking for book, play, poem, or picture.

Patrick Pearse, while filled with the vision of a romantic Ireland, was also fairly full of an Ireland sensitive, knowledgeable, and graceful; a doer of things noble, and a lover of things beautiful; and through his remarkable school of St Enda, showed he was eager to coax others to come out of the dim thicket of convention into a clearer light, and the finer conception beginning to creep into the more modern Irish thought. The word, said he, for education in Irish is the same as that for fosterage; the teacher was a fosterer, the pupil a foster-child. To foster was not, primarily, to lead up, to conduct through a course of studies, and still less to indoctrinate, to inform, to prepare for exams; but primarily to foster the elements of character already there. Pearse told of a famous Irish king (so we see Irish kings thought of things besides war) who gathered about him numbers of boys, children of friends and kinsmen, giving them a constitution, and allowing them to make their own laws and elect their own leaders. The king provided the most skilled to teach them art, the bravest to teach them chivalry, and the wisest to teach them philosophy. He devoted one-third of the time he saved from state affairs to

teaching them, or watching them at play. And if any stranger
came to the Dun at that time, even though he were a king's en-
voy, demanding audience, there was but one answer for him:
the king is with his foster-children.

We should rise up against the system, went on Pearse, that
tolerates as teachers the rejected of all other professions, rather
than demanding for so priestlike an office the highest souls and
the highest intellects of the race. I think the little child-republics
I have described, with their own laws, and their own leaders,
their life face to face with nature, their care for the body as well
as the mind, their fostering of individualities, yet never at the
expense of the commonwealth, ought to be taken as models for
our own modern schools.

This was the man whom Sean selected as the head and front
of them all, and, in his limited circumstances, he did all he could
to help him. When Pearse organized a pageant round the story of
The Cattle Raid of Cooley, to raise money for his school, the
funds allowed by a hundred handbills to be printed to tell the
world of the venture. Sean ran to Jim Larkin, who got his own
printer, West of Stafford Street, to do five thousand more, and
these Sean handed out, day after day, in the busiest streets, ignoring his hunger, his aches, his grey-minded anxiety about his
legs; in heavy rain he stood, without an overcoat, and with his
boots starred with holes. This wasn't due to deliberate bravery,
but to a dreamy and unrealistic ignorance of what would happen
when he could walk no more. He was too much afraid to think
about it long. Jim Larkin supplied the turf, and the paraffin in
which to soak it, to make the camp-fires round which the Men of
Eireann sat on their way up to attack the north.

The pageant was held in Jones's Road Park, and the opening
night was one of torrential rain, so that all who came crowded
into the large hall of the grandstand, to crouch there, saturated,
gloomy, and low in heart as man could be. Pearse sat, the nadir
of dejection, his grieving figure telling us that once more the
damned weather had betrayed the Gael; while Douglas Hyde,
who came to open it, roared out eulogy and boomed out windy
joy, all the time the wind shook the sodden wooden walls, and
the rain slashed down on the roof above them.

Wind and water, thought Sean; we want only the fire now.

That came on the last day of the great event. The Boy Scouts
had been careless with the oil, and had let a lot of it swim about

the floor; then some hasty hand had flung a glow-match into a
pool of oil, and in a moment the grandstand and the dressing-
rooms were crackling. Such a scene! All the performers dressed
for the pageant thought of their everyday clothes, and the money
and watches hidden in the pockets, and ran from their places to
save their goods. Pearse, still brooding on Cuchullain, was
knocked over, and a great cry went up from the crowd to put the
fire out, someone! From the balcony above the Boy Scouts flung
down the clothes in heaps; and there was a terrible din of sorting,
while red-shirted, brass-helmeted firemen shoved them aside and
sent jets of water on to the flames. After a while, poor Pearse, with
a few gaily-clad performers, wandered over to a smoke-stained,
sweating fireman standing halfway up the blazing stairs, plying
water on the flames, his hardy, sooty hands shaking with the
quivering of the jerking hose.

—Do you think, Mr Fireman, murmured Pearse, mounting a
few of the steps, carefully to one side, to prevent his polished
boots from being stained by a stream of blackened water flowing
down the other one, Do you think you'll quench the fire soon
enough to let us go on with the pageant?

—I'm not thinkin' whether we will or no, said the fireman
gruffly; that's your pigeon.

—Quite, said Pearse; but you should know, and we'd be
grateful for a guess.

—The pageant's all about the great Cuchullain, you know,
said a Gael from a bottom step up to the fireman.

—That so? he asked sarcastically. Begod, we must do our best
for that fella! Aw, get outa me way! he said suddenly, thrusting
Pearse aside, an' give a man room to spit!

—Poor Ireland! murmured the Gael on the bottom step; the
rough language of him; poor old Ireland!

But the fire was quelled, the firemen went away, the pageant
went on, and Sean saw again the Boy Corps of Emain Macha
playing hurley, to be stopped by a messenger telling them that
Connacht was marching on Ulster, and that Ulster's chumpians
were in the punishment of a trance-stupor for great unkindness to
a pregnant woman, that Cuchullain, having fought Maeve's
army for many days, was now in a deep sleep, and that they
would have to take his place, which they did, all dying in defence
of the black north. And in the whirl Sean thought he saw the
Men of Eireann, clad in all the colours of the rainbow, marching,

their Chiefs dashing about in chariots of brass, bronze, and buck-
skin, shaking spears that entangled the clouds, and waving swords
long as a summer's day, silver-handled, with knobs on; Sean
saw the fight on the Ford, all fair and even between Cuchullain
and Ferdiah who wore the same old-school tie, and were sworn
friends, so that Cuchullain didn't like to polish his friend off,
but had to, though he knew poor Ferdiah was sure he'd kill
him, and lie on top of the beautiful daughter of Queen Maeve for
half a naked night as a gift of honour to him for killing a comrade; and hard it might have gone with Cuchullain but for the
staggering pain his wounds gave him, and for the mocking of his
charioteer standing by who told him he was getting soft; so
Cuchullain took his hero's hurroo-leap upwards, and, coming
down, shot the gae bolg, or magic spear, right through Ferdiah's
buddy, who fled into eternal darkness murmuring

Oh! the bitterness of leaving all that richly went before;
Finding in the older darkness nothing new, and nothing more.

And deep Sean sighed with him at the loss of a night's unrest
with the fair Findobhair, for Sean had felt that way several times
here. In a corner of the grounds a Fancy Fair had set itself down,
the rent it paid covering some of the pageant's cost, and while
the Gaels strutted where Ferdiah and Cuchullain were fated to
fight it out, the gulls flocked to where gay red, green, yellow, blue,
and black pennons showed the way to the roundabout, the wheel
of fortune, the aunt sallies, the crown, anchor, and club convey-
ance promising a three-to-one reward, but rarely giving it, and
to the other jollities, regardless of the fact that their country's
harp slumbered, and lay in oblivion near Tara's old hall, with ne'er
a kind hand to enliven its numbers, and strike a rude dirge to
the sons of Fingal. Divil a much better he was himself, for when
he could snatch a few minutes of idle time before the performance,
he'd hurry to the roundabout to watch the girls swinging round on
the horses; for often, when in full career, the swift breeze would
get entangled in their skirts, twirling them away from where they
ought to be, giving his excited eyes a flash of a coloured garter
embracing a rounded leg. Once he saw a fair one's dress roughly
caressed by the wind; her skirt went wide, showing a trim leg
with a taste of white thigh over the rim of her stocking; and as
she whirled round, he saw that she saw what the wind showed him,

and she smiled, lifting one leg over the other so that the skirt hid less, and she became fairer than the evening air clad in the beauty of a thousand stars; but the grey, cloudy curtain of his wretched condition came slowly down between, and shut her out of his sight.

It was funny to see the agony on the faces of the Gaels when the roundabout organ blared out loud, grinding out Tara-ra-boom-de-ay with brazen impudence, aided by the mechanical roll from a grim drum, forcing those in the pageant to raise their voices, and those of the audience, nearer the Fair, to cup their hands to their ears to catch the sound of what was said. Pearse, dreamy and colourful in his pageant raiment, with a comrade Gael strode to the booth where the proprietor of the Fair sat, watching wares and workers; and 'he Gael requested, rather pompously, that the steam-organ should be silenced while the pageant ran its course.

—'Deed an' I won't, she said indignantly, and it's cool customers yez are t'ask it! Th' music gives a thrill to th' gallop of th' horses, an' it's part o' what th' people pay for. I paid a good rent to get in here, an' it'll take more encouragement than I'm gettin' to see me safe outa th' hasty bargain. Stop your own show, an' let th' poor people, lettin' on they like it, come here to join in a heartier amusement. Yez can go back, gentlemen, for me organ's not goin' to be lullabyed be any other opposite money-makin' manoeuvre.

—Listen, my good woman, said the Gael persuasively, we request its silence only while the pageant is in progress. You know the pageant deals with the life and deeds of the great Cuchullain during the Tawn Bo Cooley; the deeds of him who was the comeliest among the Men of Eireann. Surely you'll do that much for Ireland's greatest hero who had the ninety-and-nine gifts, who was famous for the lightness of his lep, the weight of his wisdom, the melody of his voice, and the fine form of his face? You'll surely silence the organ to let us do honour and show due reverence to this great man, Cuchullain?

—He musta been th' divil an' all from what yez say; but I've never seen or heard tell of him in any circus or show I met, an' I'm gettin' on for sixty years now. Where'd he live? Was he one o' th' boys who stood be th' great O'Connell for Emancipation?

—Oh, no, no, ma'am! said the Gael testily, glancing with pity at Pearse, who stood with head bent, listening; Cuchullain had nothing whatever to do with O'Connell. Cuchullain lived his short and glorious life thousands of years ago – long before St Patrick thought of coming near us.

—Oh! That musta been in old God's time, mister. Anyway, here's a lady doesn't want to be versed in the doin's of them who haunted Ireland before th' time o' blessed St Patrick, an' I'd advise yez to think similar. What Cookullin was or wasn't doesn't throuble me. An', anyway, even if I hadda heard of him, no Cockullin 'ud make me give over doin' what was me due to do; so like good an' decent men, Coocoolin yourselves outa th' way, an' leave a body in peace to knock out a livin'!

—Poor old Ireland! said the Gael, shaking his head sadly as he and Pearse returned to do the best they could through the boisterous blare of the steam-organ.

And there it was on the green sward before him – *The Cattle Raid of Cooley*, with its mimic figures, coloured gaily in the flood-light, growing mighty through the mind's misty thought of what happened far away and long ago. The Boy Corps of Armagh playing hurley, veiled in blues, greens, reds, browns, and purple; the stopping of the game by the Messenger, Pearse himself, to tell them that Cuchullain, weary with the battles of many days, was asleep, and the Boy Corps would have to defend Ulster from the Men of Eireann till Cuchullain could stand to fight again, for the rest of the Ulster champions were in a trance-stupor as a punishment for great unkindness shown to a pregnant woman. And the boys stood and fought Maeve's great army till they died, but held on till Cuchullain grew strong again to fill the gap. And here were the Men of Eireann in battle array, all because of a quarrel between Oillol of Cruachan and Queen Maeve, his wife, over which of them possessed the greatest wealth in raiment, jewel, and cattle on the hills; measuring and valuing all they had, but finding that each was equal to the other, day by day, for in that day, nor bishop nor archbishop nor cardinal was there to have more than either. But Maeve knew that the White Bull of Cruachan would lick anything among her own kine, so she gathered her powers together to seize the Brown Bull of Cooley, reported on all sides, and vouched for by Roddy the Drover to be the *capax imperii* among jovine bulls, so that she'd be one up on poor old Oilleololo. And here was the bould Cuchullain challenging Maeve to send her champions out, with a Come on the whole of you, one by one, to meet your doom, and when

I'm done with you, a lot of you'll be like little green leaves in a Bible; and won't your Maeve be glad when she's at home with her feet on the fender, while the old kitchen kettle keeps singing a song, and Oillol, if he can get away, to smoke another pipeful in the shade of the old apple tree.

The last came Ferdiah to fight with the hero, and Cuchullain's heart near failed him, for Ferdiah wore the same old school gorget that he wore himself; but there was no way out, so they fought by day, and rested by night for a lunar month, till Cuchullain, full of wounds and mad with anger, could stick it no longer and killed Ferdiah without any hindrance; then came the caoining skirl of the pipes, and the sad rolling of the drum, mingling with the hues of red, brown, green, and purple kilts and shawls, ending a scene of a song that in colour, form, dignity of movement, and vigour of speech made the loveliest thing that had ever patterned the green sward of the playing-field of Jones's Road, or any other field the world over; fairer than anything the bowler-hatted Gael could think of now, much more do.

A pity death pulled Pearse away from his school, for he was a pioneer in what has now become the common sense of education. He hated the system that kept colour and life far from the child, content to stuff a delicate mind with a mass of fact and information. Ay, indeed, said Pearse, I knew one boy who passed through several schools a dunce and a laughing-stock. The National Board and Intermediate Board of Education damned him as a fool before men and angels. Yet it was discovered that he had a wondrous sympathy for nature. He loved and understood the ways of plants, and he had a strange subtlety of observation – in short he was a boy who was likely to become an accomplished botanist. A father of another boy said to me: He's no good at books, no good at work; he's good for nothing but playing a tin whistle. What am I to do with him? And the distressed father was shocked by Pearse saying: Buy a tin whistle for him.

No timid cloak of a papal count hung from this man's shoulders; no Order of Knight Commendatore of St Gregory or St Silvester sparkled on his breast: the scarlet or white cloak of Cuchullain was good enough for him, and, in his soldier's cap, a jaunty sprig from the holy oak of Derry Columcille whispering in his ear the words of the saint himself: *If I die, it shall be from the excessive love I bear the Gael.* Not for Pearse the glory that was Greece nor the grandeur that was Rome; nor even the sacred grove, olive grove, or mountain of Judea: he fixed his thoughts on the vivid and pathetic greatness of Ardee, Emain Macha, Derry, Beann Edair, Tailltin, Cruachan, Tara, and Usneach, grander than Greece or Rome; and holier to him the lonely grave of Bodenstown, where Wolfe Tone's valour has changed to dust, than the place where St Patrick is said to be pinned down to an everlasting slumber. Pearse was the one prominent Gael among the leaders of the militant movement who fought the battle of Ireland from the midst of the faith, well in the stream, not of Gonzaga or De Sales or Loyola, but of Columcille, Aidan, Finbarr, Enda, Kevin, Columbanus, and Brigid. Such as he couldn't be near the swashbuckling canakin-clink Catholicity of Chesterton, who put up a tavern sign on the gate of Heaven and made it into a Jolly Abode.

Ah! Patrick Pearse, you were a man, a poet, with a mind simple as a daisy, brilliant as a daffodil; and like these, you came before the swallow dared, and took the Irish minds of March with beauty. A Catholic with whom the roughest unbeliever could be safely silent, not from shame, but out of respect for your gallant and urging soul; a Catholic who almost made one see that Ireland's blue sky was Brigid's poplin shawl; that the moon and stars were under Mary's feet, the Virgin-born on her breast, stretching out little leal hands that were to guide to a Father's home the long-banished children of Eve. Beside Pearse, men might listen to the jangling bells, and think them musical; might watch men bend sleek, slick knees, and think they honoured humility; might see men fast, and still think it sensible; might drink insipid water, and taste the wine; for your austerity was ever bright, your snowy mantle of rigid conduct was ever girdled by a coloured scarf, and golden buttons closed it over you; nay, on the very head of grinning Death itself you stuck a smiling star.

Ah! Patrick Pearse, when over the hard, cold flags of a barrack square you took your last stroll and wandered to where the rifles pointed to your breast, you never even paused, for that was what you guessed you'd come to; you came close to them; the stupid bullets tore a way through your quiet breast, and your fall forward to death was but a bow to your enemies. Peace be with you, and with your comrades too.

All the colour and song of Pearse was shadowed by the level dullness of the Sinn Fein campaign, led by Marthur Gruffith, who was busy scraping all the leisure time he could from his pullitical work to damn poor Synge and slight Yeats, damning him for his good verses. Perhaps his nerves were aching after the hysterical tornado of activity to give birth to a *Daily Sinn Fein*, when the short neck of Gruffith stretched out as far as it could go, demanding help from every loyal Gael to bring forth this new thing that would establish unity in Ireland for ever; down the British Empire; and carry Ireland up to the top of delectable mountains. At last it was born with the loudest cry Ireland had heard so far, a sullen face on it, dull and futile, no more a living daily than an out-of-date Salvation Army *War Cry*. It gasped out a kind of a curious life for a short while, then went to its bony, mean, and silent death, forming itself into a cold monument to Gruffith's consequential conceit at having been able to bring it out at all. During its spare days of wailing life, the paper gave one rowdy, gaudy, ranting gesture when some poor fool, uniformed and daring, came to some fancy-dress gathering wearing a long golden-haired wig, and dressed in a long white robe having a brilliant red heart in the centre of its breast, entering among the dancers with a boisterously-dressed girl hanging on each arm. Gruffith at once saw his chance of getting into touch with the people, not through his politics, but through his piety, so an article denouncing the foolishness as blasphemy and sacrilege splashed the paper from side to side; though some of his Sinn Fein friends, a few years before, had sent greeting to Viviani, who had told the world that that very evening he was going to put out the lights of Heaven; but, afterwards, found that he wasn't quite tall enough. The howls for the expulsion of the blasphemer from job, house, and home, helped by *Sinn Fein*, deafened Dublin, and soon the Confraternities added their hyena yelling, till the city was a howl from one end to the other, driving the thoughtless fool from his job, then his home, till finally, by night, a cargo-boat took him to where God wasn't so well known; but the griffithian St George, though he slew his dragon, didn't get any further with the people; and the valiant paper, after its great fight for the good character of God, soon took to its bed and died there, another instance of the high rate of infant immortality in Ireland. But like a Boy Scout, Griffith had done his good deed for the day, for God, and Cathleen Mavourneen.

Under the sulky green tent that Dublin called the sky, these odd figures moved about and about, the huge, sable, wide-winged

Morrigu, Ireland's bottle-crow. watching from the tent-pole top.
There goes Bulmer Hobson with a gigantic volume of Mazzini's
sermons strapped between his shoulders like a nobsack; and
Yeats, trying through a loose seam in the tent's roof to catch a
glimpse of the round green eyes and the long wavering bodies of
the dark leopards of the moon, as he murmured longingly, *I will
arise,* and go to Inisfree; and George Russell rushing round,
booming, *Come, acushla, with me to the mountains old, There the
bright ones call us waving to and fro – Come, my children, with me
to the ancient go.* There stood the full-bearded Plunket, in his
papal count's cuniform, patting the head of a young man, De
Valuera, who was putting a poser to the old gentleman about the
equality of *abc* to *xyz*; and there by the door of the tent was
Griffith neglecting his practice of a Hungarian funtasia on a
fuddle to prevent Jim Connolly from attaching a red tassel to
the flap of the tent. And there was the Old Lady in black, Gregory
by name, planked up against Nelson's Pillar, watching, and
deciding that no Rebubblican name was wordy to cut away any
of de bark on her topper beech; though those of Pearse and
Clarke would have done well enough. And there, in his go-cart,
threading through one street into another, goes the toy Catholic
Viceroy, chanting the Irish ballad of *Is truagh gan mise i Sasana*;
the go-cart having to stop here to let the Volunteers come down
this street, having to stop there to let the Irish Citizen Army go
up that one; while from the window of a snug, Tim Healy, having
a slow one, looks out on the world, to murmur as the Viceroy
passes, *The time's not far distant when them that are up will be
down, and them that are down will be up, and your grand Viceregal
Lodge will be no more than an Uncle Tim's cabin.* There goes
Padruig Pearse hurrying through the centre of the city, saying
swift to any who tries to check his stride, *Stay me not: I have a
rendezvous with Death*; and Erskine Childers following hot-foot
after him, calling out to him to wait a minute, and he'd be there
too; and after Childers, Mellows and Rory O'Connor, with a
string of vague forms following behind, hurrying, hurrying to
make the isle a nation, free and grand; while the great crowd
of the plain people jostled and pushed them, regardless of their
dustiny; for, concerned with finer things, each of the plain people
clutched a key-of-heaven prayer-book in one hand and a buff
British ring-paper in the other – preservers of the Irish soul and
body; and all the time, unknown to most, in the core of the

tumult, the timber-merchant labourer, Mutt Talbot, iron hoops and steel chain tight round his body, boring into his belly and wearing a way into his spine, a gonner on God, at the crack of dawn, squirmed about atop the steps of the Pro-Cathedral, waiting for the door to open, creeping in towards the altar when it did, hiding and chiding himself in a cloud of *mea na meala culpas*. A hero of Irish holiness! Proved, too, by the fact that when, one day, Mutt Talbot suddenly fell dead, as soon as his clothes were removed it was found, rumour definitely stated, that the iron and steel round the poor body had blossomed into hardy laurel leaves and scented honeysuckle. Over all, atop of the tent-pole, the huge sable Morrigu clapped her wide wings in glee, croaking joyously, *Thou art not conquered yet, dear land; thou art not conquered yet*; and Sean sat on a pediment of a column keeping up the façade of the Post Office, reading, reading the new catechism of the *Communist Manifesto* with its great commandment of Workers of all lands, unite! And in all the shouting and the tumult and the misery around, he heard the roll of new drums, the blowing of new bugles, and the sound of millions of men marching.

ST VINCENT PROVIDES A BED

ANOTHER IRRITATING trouble began to further bruise Sean's confidence and hope: a tubercular swelling began to rise up on the right side of his neck. He had had them when he was young, and he remembered (he was always remembering these things, possibly because he had so few blessings to count. Count your blessings one by one – well, he wouldn't have to work overtime) hours of swirling pain from one of them, when his mother, acting on neighbourly advice, had painted it three times a day for weeks with iodine. He thought he had got rid of them for ever, and it was maddening to feel one of them thrusting itself out again. Jesu! what is the pleasure of life, asked an Elizabethan, but the good hours of an ague! Jim Larkin, noticing it one day, sent him up, with Councillor Partridge – one of Labour's finest souls – to the Charles Street Tubercular Clinic; and there he

was rudely handled by a rough-shouting doctor, who apolo-
gized, after Partridge had whispered something in his ear. The
doctor muttered that he was tired after a long day, and Sean,
standing up to walk out, said he was tired too, and had more
cause to feel uneasy. Partridge, amiable and holy, smoothed
Sean's anger, and the doctor gave him the only aid he could –
a note saying he had examined the patient, and hereby certified
that he needed surgical attention.

Larkin said he must go to Vincent's where the Union had
several beds; but Sean decided to try the Protestant Adelaide
first. So off he tramped, where the house-surgeon took the note,
and listened patiently to Sean. Then he said, tersely, there was
no bed, and there wouldn't be one for a year. Just as Sean was
fixing on his hat to go, a senior surgeon, Dr Thompson, came out
and stopped a minute to listen, and looked at Sean's swelling.
Some little time before, he had lost an only son in the war, and
in a burst of pity said to his comrade doctor, Oh, make out a bed
for him, and give the poor devil a chance! When he'd gone, the
house-surgeon, indignant, turned to Sean, saying, He knows
damn all about it! If I do as he says, I'll have to pitch some other
poor devil out to let you in, and what good would that do? Why
the hell didn't he go in and make a bed for you himself?

So, armed with a request from the Union, he became No 23
in the St Laurence O'Toole ward of St Vincent's under a sister
named Gonzaga, a delightful woman, most popular with the
patients; never lax, always lenient; always cheerful, with a gay
greeting for everyone. Afterwards, he discovered that some of
the other nuns seemed to be jealous of her popularity. But now,
he innocently passed in by the heavy, wide, double-folding door,
glancing at the great bronze gong in the vestibule – looking like
the languishing shield of Oscar, now dedicated to God – giving
different numbers of strokes for the different sisters, with a long,
solemn one for the Reverend Mother. He turned left down the
long tiled corridor, with high french windows along its way, on
one side, giving on to a lawn on which, in brief moments of
leisure, sisters paraded determinedly up and down, decidedly
reading some pious manual, so that not a moment should be
allotted to the unthinking world. He passed by the gaudy image
of St Michael shoving a tough spear throughout the twisting
body of a spitting dragon; perhaps a white-coated surgeon
flitted by, giving importance to a quick walk or a decorous trot,

on his way to, or coming from, doing damage to some poor body. Silent nuns, on duty, soft-slippered, glided to and fro, went in, came out, eyes half closed, lips faintly forming the soft names of Jesus, Mary, and Joseph. Any words ventured there were modulated into the sad smile of silence, as if speech itself was bandaged; then up a few steps at the corridor's end, if he remembered right, to St Laurence's ward, the saint himself, frocked, cowled, and tonsured, at the entrance, standing deep in stony meditation, as if he had vaulted into upper thoughts so as to muffle his hearing from the half-repressed sighs of anxiety and fear that dignified the rough bosoms of those who lay stretched out on the beds within. The ward was a big one, long and lofty, with rows of beds on each side. At the far end was a huge fire-place with a bright fire blazing, for though it was a warm day, the hot-water system had gone agley, and big black kettles simmered on the hob ready with healing or cleansing heat, should a patient need it. Over the fireplace, filling the breast of the chimney with sorrowful significance, stretched a great black cross on which hung the yellowish-white figure of Him who is, and was, and is to come, silently manifesting forth the curious, majestic mystery of pain. Sean glanced at it very often, and wondered that the patients seemed in no way disturbed by it. Indeed, they seemed not to notice it, and when he had been a few days there himself, it ceased to trouble him with more than a casual thought. The patients passed by as indifferently as those who did the same on the first day of the first crucifixion. The symbol was never men-tioned – yes it was, once: when a bright young man, convalescent and about to leave, cast a longing eye on a pretty maid who was sweeping the floor, and murmured longing, lustful words about her fine and charming figure. One of some who were listening moved away, saying afterwards to Sean, Did you hear him? Right under our Lord on the cross, too! I was mortally ashamed. Yes, at times it came before them, and this genuine man was shocked again when Sean said, I'm afraid your Lord on the cross is getting used to far worse things than those hot words from the heart of a young man eager to endorse life in the arms of a maid.

Because of the defect in the water system, Sean was given a bed-bath by three nurses; and, for two of them were pretty, his mind rambled into some unholy thoughts, to be silenced by a nun dropping on her knees in the middle of the ward to honour the Angelus, the nurses flopping down too, so that when the hot water cooled, Sean's damp body got cold, and he shivered. One of the nurses, feeling the tremor, said, You'll get your death, and tried to sling a blanket over him with a sudden movement, but it covered his feet only, and Sean coughed to prevent a laugh at his ridiculous outlook in the middle of the Hail Mary, fearful they'd imagine he was laughing at the invocation, though he felt that the Blessed Virgin Herself, if She did exist, would have laughed along with him. He didn't catch his death, for they put hot-water bottles in with him, and a soothing glow soon overspread his body, and gave him an open mind for thought to enter.

The war was singeing England badly, he thought, as he stretched gloriously into the heat of the bed, and the English stood now with their backs to the wall. The black, white, and red banner of the Germans was cocking a snoot even at the naval forces of her foe, and Gott Mit Uns looked forward to being the enforced motto of the world. England's ancient bustians of Eton and Harrow were filing her reputation. The well-mortared manners, the sleek minds, and tidy thoughts, born of Eton and Harrow, and reared into meanhood by Balliol, Brasenose, Corpus Christi, Patterhouse and Emmanuel, Trinity and Magdalen, were of little effect in a rough world, even when they were helped by the Abdominal Council. They were old-fashioned, stiff-jointed, and still swooned delusively among drawbridge and barbican. England had been warned to put her house in disorder some time before, during the inilligant row in the Commons over the curtalement of the power moneyfisted in the *viva veto vita* of the House of Lords. Yet England never despaired, and still took her ministers out of silk-lined bandboxes, sedately-coated, neatly-trousered, delicately-gloved, and technically top-hatted, repeating everything their forefellows had already said so well and so often, stepping out, and passing on, like a solemn file of geese and gander – Salisbury, Balfour, Bonar Law, Bannerman, and now Asquith, ponderous with a pile of classical knullidge, who calmly went on convulsing England's life into elegant argument; and scotching Ireland's life into a vellumized declaration of Home Rule curled up on a purple cushion, ready for the Irish to rede and hang up in the front parlour as a period piece between the picture of Robert Emmet in an Ireland surrounded by silence and gloom, and that of St Patrick in an Ireland full of the light that never was on sea or land.

But when the Lords were attacked, all the decency and debonair in manners became frayed into a gorgeous orgy of vulgarity, stupidity, and ruffianism (English authority quoted); for when the *rara avis*, Asquith, got up to move the motion emending the power of miniver and muskwaw, he was jowled over with the curses, blasphemies, squeals, jeers and shouts of the Opposition, so indecorous that the marble saints in Westminster Abbey opposite had to clap their hands over their ears and chant Hallelujah, I'm a bomb! in unison, to keep their minds free from cant.

Afar off, sitting on the very end of the Thames Embankment, her eyes fixed on the revolving light of Eddystone, focusing memories of Drake and Frobisher into her mind, Britannia heard the whooproar, and jumping down from her stony seat, she flung her shield over her back, tucked up her skirts, and flew to where her sons were sitting. Bursting in on the bawling men, she hurried to the Speaker's chair, she hammered her trydent on her shield to gain silence, but AM went on bawling to keep PM from speaking.

—Eh, eh, she yelled, yez lot of Babbylon baboons, are yez not goin' to show any regard whatever for the mother who bore yez? What'll th' world say to all this hollerin', I ask yez? – and seeing Asquith blush for her common speech, she at once showed her learning by shouting, This lingua longia Horridens blasphemodicum, setting a parlous example to the Irish over the sayway; college-bred chaps yez are too, all, from the banks of the cher, boys, cher, and the cam of the good companions!

Encouraged by this, the Speaker spoke; thumping the dusk in front of him, he cupped his hands over his mouth, stretched as far as his forwardness could go, and shouted, Eh, there, eh! D'yez not hear the lady talkin' to yez? That's enough, boys! Have yez forgotten all about Ghengist an' Hoarsa, an' holy Edward, called the Confusser? Steady, boys, steady! We'll fight an' we'll canker again! Looka, the Welsh are laughin'. Criccieth, boys, play criccieth! An' the Irish are enjoyin' it all, too. Erin'll remember these days of scold again' us. For th' honour of th' auld Hoose, boys! What th' hell's th' Silver Rod doin'?

And all the time, calm, pale, silent, dignified, Asquith stood, quoting quietly, How can men die better than facing fearful cods for the cashes of his fathers and the temples of his goods! High up in the Speaker's Gullery, frilled ladies from Mayfair,

Grosvenor Square, Mile End, and Canning Town, shouted and
squealed, standing up on their cheers (English authority quoted),
and the PM's lady was horridly scribbling a nota-bene to the
bony-faced Grey, appealing to him to be a little more bellicose,
and chime in with help for the poor PM against the great I
AMs, which he did with some fine strokes that rung the hearts of
many there.

But nothing could stop the clangour, though the Silver Rod
ran here and there like a man who was bats in the belfry, beseeching them to remember their better natures, all in fine vain;
and once, passing by the front bench, Britannia, mistaking him
for a disturber, gave him a vicious prod in the behind with her
trydent, causing the man great pain, and forcing him to turn to
say, more in sorrow than in anger, that no genuine lady would
do that to a gentleman, upsetting her so much that she fell into
a comma, bringing the row to a full stop while an usher of the
House made a dash to help her, getting her carried off to Guy's
Hospital before any more damage was done. The Speaker,
realizing it wasn't possible to restore the campus mentis, took his
chance to postpone proceedings, ordering the Silver Rod to shut
the windows, lock the doors, and put out the lights on all that
happened there that day.

Strange how placid it seemed to be in an hospital! Stones,
bricks, and a few sheets of glass, helped by pain and suffering,
hid the busy world away. All was dimmer and quieter now that
the night had fallen, with but one nurse left in the ward to guard
against the needs of the quieter hours. There she was, all but her
head hidden in a deep armchair by a blazing fire, her head resting
on its back, her hands folded over an abandoned book, her senses
sinking into a vigilant sleep; while the fire made more vivid
parts of the lamentable crucifix overhead, throwing other parts
into an uneasy purple shadow.

Hail Mary, the Lord is with Thee – there it goes, the night-
mustering mutter of the Rosary, the words, only half formed,
falling rapidly from the mouths of those whose heads Sean could
dimly see by the humble light given by two small, crimson-
coloured bulbs, one at each end of the ward. Haimary th' Loris-
withee blessearthouamonwomn, it circled the ward lazily, rose
to the ceiling, and died away in the sad sleep of the patients;
and Sean recognized the voice of the leader as that of Den Daffy,
in for urethral stricture, due for an operation soon, and dreading

it: a big, burly, bald-headed docker, own brother to Sylvester Daffy who had been tried for the alleged killing of a scab by cleaving his head open with a navvy's shovel, during the big lock-out; but he had been released without a stain on his character when it was discovered that the blood on his shirt came, not from a human body, but from the bodies of fleas, crushed when he found leisure to kill them; own brother, too, to Cock Daffy, one of the best football backs Dublin had ever known.

—Jesus! came a sharp scream from a centre bed. I can stick it no longer, I'm tellin' yous! And the scream from the man with cancer in the tongue went skirling about the ward, bringing to a keener wakefulness the drowsy murmur of Holmarmotherogo prayfrusmisrablesinnrs nowana thourofhoudeath. The head of the night nurse left its haven, and stiffened to listen, and turned to where the cry came from; then turned back, and sank slow to rest again when the murmur of prayer and moaning of pain mingled amicably together.

Again the animal-like yelp of pain circled the ward, and again the head of the nurse left its soft nest, to turn quick, and face towards the stricken patient.

—You'll have to stick it, Eighteen, she said, sharply; you've had your morphia, and you'll get no more; so sink your head into the pillow, and don't keep the other patients awake! And Sean heard the yelping die down into a muffled moaning. Heavy breathing showed that the patients had woven their anxiety away into sleep; the nurse's head again lay on the back of her chair, and nothing was left with Sean's thoughts but the two soft red lights, and the dreary madrigal of moaning from the centre bed.

If one only knew, he thought, there's a helluva lot of moaning in the world today; and it would grow; grow till the common people came to themselves. Humanity's music would be as sad as ever, but it wouldn't remain silent much longer. New thoughts were being born, not only in a cry, but in smoke, flame, and cannon-fire. Half the Christian world had just discovered that the other half no longer deserved to live. The slime, the bloodied mud, the crater, and the shell-hole had become God's kingdom here on earth. Deep trenches led to the delectable mountains; and a never-ending line of duckboards led to where they could see Him even as they themselves were seen. Our Father which art in Heaven, Thy kingdom of Communism come! In every ravine,

on every hill, through every golden cornfield tens of thousands of
Irish wriggled and twisted to death, their dimming eyes dazzled
by the flame from a scarlet poppy, their dulling ears shocked by
the lilting notes from a rising lark. The ghosts of them who fell
at Dettingen, Fontenoy, and Waterloo were clasping their colder
arms around the newer dead.

The whole city was sadly coloured now with the blue of the
wounded soldier. They were flowing into St Vincent's as room
could be made for them. Mr Tobin, the head surgeon, had lost
an only son in Flanders, and it seemed he couldn't see enough of
forms similar to what his son last looked like. Every free moment
he plunged into the middle of those well enough to talk, and
would stand there silent, for he was almost stone-deaf, and could
hear only a shout given into a circular disc with a delicate connexion to a rod stuck into his ear. Where did you get your blighty,
son? he'd say to a wounded man, sticking the rod into an ear,
and inclining the disc towards the soldier's mouth. When he
heard the faint echo of the place's name, he'd murmur, Ah! my
son spent his last moment a long way off; but yours was near
enough, son; near enough. He seemed to think when he was
close to them, he was closer to his son. When on the roof of
the operating-theatre, a group of them sang Tipperary, Tobin was
in the middle of them, trumpet in ear, his old, slender wavery
hand trying to keep time: trying to conjure up the ghost of his
son from the songs and stories of the wounded men. You wouldn't
get a mother doing it, thought Sean. She'd feel it too deep. She'd
conjure up her boy's ghost out of the coloured shadows he left
behind him. Neither in noise of song nor murmur of story would
she bring back the sad, sunny dust of his shape again, but in the
deep and bitter loneliness of remembrance.

Sean found out that the nuns didn't seem to love each other as
sisters should. The Order was celebrating a Jubilee, and great
agitation and stir blossomed out in the building. Evergreens
were strewed in the wards, and special meals given to all patients
who could eat them. One ward, empty for renovation, was to be
a theatre in which doctors and nurses were to give a home-made
show. Sean was busy helping, and when Sister Gonzaga – who
was the life and soul of the activity – said, Chairs, more chairs for
our theatre, Sean rushed into his ward and began to whip up the
chairs, one of which stood by the end of every bed. Going out, he
ran into Sister Paul.

—Where are you going with those? she asked sharply.

—Sister Gonzaga asked for them, he said busily; she wants all she can get.

—Leave them back where you got them! Sister Paul said angrily; at once, please!

—But Sister Gonzaga wants them, said Sean, surprised, and sure that Sister Paul hadn't heard what he had said.

—Does she, indeed? sarcastically. Sister Gonzaga has no authority here; and Sister Paul now tells you to leave them where you got them. And for the future, never touch a thing in this ward without my permission; and Sean had gone back ashamed, for many had heard the rebuke, and he was furious that he should be humiliated for trying to help. He went down to the grounds, and took no further part in the celebration.

It was a little embarrassing now, for, since the battle of the chairs, Sister Paul passed him without a nod or a smile. But she was scrupulously fair, and there wasn't the slightest difference shown between him and the other patients. Indeed, she was more polite to him now than to the others. To one she would say, Sixteen, give nurse a hand with the lockers. To Sean it would be, Twenty-three, would you please give nurse a hand with the beds; but the polite request was always cold, and his short bow of obedience was colder still. Several times he meant to go, but he lingered, and clung to the hope that he had furnished himself with the skill to heal his ailment. So he waited for the operation guaranteed to remove whatever danger lurked in the lump on his neck.

Sister Paul was still cold, but she was kind on the morning of the operation. Under the warm blankets on the operating-table she had stroked his arm, and smiled down reassuringly. Sean had determined to give as little trouble as possible, and when the ether was offered, he breathed the stuff in without a murmur or movement. Once when the stuff came out in a fuller flow, he had half turned his head away, and had felt the grasp of sister and nurse tighten on his arms; but he had murmured that the move-ment was involuntary; the scent of the ether isn't that of the honeysuckle; but that he'd move no more. One thing troubled him – that under the power of the drug he'd loose all his rich knowledge of profanity on those who were trying to help him. But when he was coming out of his sleep, he sang Alliliu na Gamhna and the Palatine's Daughter at the top of his good baritone voice, the nurses in the ward standing round to listen to him, and when the songs had ended, the theatre nurse bent over him to whisper coaxingly, Sing us another, Twenty-three, another in Irish, please do! And through the haze of the drug that still dimmed his eyes, he swung into Mary of Ballyhaunis. When he had got a little hoarse, Sister Paul came over to warn him to rest, saying, There – that's enough. Have a rest now; and stroking his forehead, added, You were a great soldier, and gave us no trouble whatever.

So he lay, thinking, his neck feeling as if he had had his head sawn off with rough and blunt-edged tools; but he went on thinking, feeling no ill-effects from the ether. He heard a patient telling another that one more ward had been given over to the wounded English. The sky over Dublin now was covered with a red cross. And on the top of Ireland's lowest mountain, on its purple cushion, reposed the Home Rule Bill. Strange how Asquith thought to cajole the Irish into love of everything but their own. The poor devil must know nothing about us. What was Connemara to him? Or the Decies? Knights of Dingle, or Earls of Desmond? Did he know anything outside the bounds of Downing Street? To Sean his job seemed to be an easy one. The England he governed was a big, gilded, angel-protected clock, and the Prime Minister was the little figure that popped out to blow a bugle and tell the hours. His lady seemed to show that her lord didn't know all he needed to know. He woefully, wilfully disregarded the wise words of his lady, a woman of great intelligence and wide perspicacity, who said, I have never understood how anyone could be proud of having either Jewish or Keltic blood in their veins. I have often been painfully reminded of the saying – A Jew is around your neck, or at your feet, but never by your side. Keltic blood is usually accompanied by excited brains and a reckless temperament, and is always an excuse for exaggeration. When not whining or wheedling, the Kelt is usually in a state of bluff, or funk, and can always wind himself up to the kind of rhetoric no housemaid can resist.

Eh! there, Sister, hold on a minute! Didn't you write to Johnny Redmond, a day before, or a day after, telling him that he had the opportunity of his life in setting an unforgettable example to the Carsonites if he would go to the House of Commons, and on Monday, and in a great speech, offer all his soldiers to the Government? Did she say that now? A grand idea. Shows brains. It showed, too, that the Kelts, however excited their brains might be; however they might bluff and funk things; however they might wheedle or whine, were good enough to go forth and die so that Margot Asquith might live her old life without any hindrance. And quite a lot of Jews, too, ceasing from hanging around necks or flopping at the feet of others, went forth to die for Britain and Big Ben.

Be fair. Mrs Ah says she has devoted friends among the Jews; one of them, Rufus Isaacs, Earl of Reading, – one of the best fellows that ever lived. But then Rufus, though by race a Jew, was – British to the core. Encore! Markoni him well. And – He has the laugh of an English schoolboy. Oh! boy. Nice little chap, must be. But listen, thought Sean, addressing an imaginary audience in the ward, listen: She likes Rufus, not because he is a Jew, but because he is British to the encore. The less a Jew, the more she likes him. I daresay if a Kelt could be English to the core, she'd like him too; or an Indian. If only these could manage to be English to the core, even to the *esprit de corps*, how much happier the world would be! Sitting on top of it, rolling along, singing a song! But can't you see the vainglory and silly impudence of such an opinion? It's right, it's proper; but it wouldn't work.

Sean was thinking how long he could manage to stay here.

The doctor had said the wound was healing remarkably well, and the beds were in great demand. St Vincent was being pestered with petitions for help. A few days more, at the most, and he'd have to quit this clean, airy place, the pleasant bed, the fine food, and the peace and quietude surrounding the sick. He was still measuring the time of possible respite when Sister Paul sent to say she wanted to speak to him quietly in her office. It was a cell-like little place, with a narrow austere desk of polished pine, and a spare, simple, round-topped seat before it as its sole furniture. She was standing in front of the desk, scorning the seat – mortifying herself, thought Sean – in her cream-coloured working-habit, her cap, white as snow, almost hiding her passive face, a dark stream of heavy rosary beads hanging by her skirt, and a large brass crucifix agleam on her bosom. He stood silent there, beside her, while she fiddled with some papers, waiting for her to begin speaking.

Sent to tell me I've got to go, he thought; the good hours of the ague are over.

—Well, Twenty-three, she said calmly, your wound's healing splendidly, and there is little more that we can do for you here. What you want now are good food and plenty of fresh air and sun. I've just got word that you are to go for a fortnight to our Convalescent Home; but it will be two weeks or so before there's a vacancy, so you'll have to remain with us here till they're ready for you.

A month altogether given him to get into some shape to face the harder future: that was good. It was damned kind of them. He felt like cheering. Thank you, Sister Paul, he said earnestly; you have all been very kind to me.

—Now, we must think of the future, she said, as if she hadn't heard what he had murmured – after you leave the Convalescent, have you a job to go to?

—A job? No; I'm afraid not, Sister.

—Oh! That's not so good! Where did you work before you came here for treatment?

—Nowhere, he said. A few odd weeks of work, here and there, are all I managed for the past year or more.

—A few weeks only! You must be a lazy fellow, she said tartly.

He was shocked into some silent moments by this remark. It was unexpected. He felt a surge of resentment sweeping through him. His rosy hope was growing grey. Oh! well, St Vincent's wasn't an abiding city, and he'd just have to move on.

—Not lazy, Sister, he said; no, no; not lazy. For many years I have worked, never missing a single quarter while a job lasted. I have worked myself into a knowledge few labourers possess. I have made the night joint labourer with the day, working for the Irish Movement, and for my own class – no, not lazy.

He was staring into her face, now turned to him fairly for the first time, and he saw her as she appeared to eyes that were good. She was of medium height, and inclined to become buxom. She had a round, rather heavy, rosy face of pleasant plainness, with rather cold blue-grey eyes like chilly corners in a warm room. She had the appearance of dignified bustling about her work, as if she was half forcing herself towards perpetual abnegation; so set on activity that she seemed nervous her thoughts might stray for a moment from what she was obliged to do: an uneasy Martha among some Marys in the house of healing.

—But why couldn't you get steady work? she went on, turning

her head away to gaze down again at the ledge of the narrow austere desk. It seems curious to me.

He wondered how she'd look if he sang Hallelujah, I'm a Bum!

> *Why don't you men work as other men do?*
> *How th' hell can we work when there's no work to do!*

Instead, he murmured quietly, Oh, I don't know exactly. Perhaps I was a little too prominently in the lock-out, and made too much of a rendezvous of Liberty Hall.

—Ah! now we're getting nearer to it! she said acidly. Liberty Hall! Poor deluded men! You were on the side of those fellows, Larkin and Connolly, who did so much harm to our poor people, is that it?

—Yes, that's it, Sister, he said gently.

—In spite of the fact, I suppose, that they were ready to hand over our dear, Dublin, Catholic children to those who would set about upsetting their faith?

—You do them something of an injustice, he said firmly; I am intimate enough with those two fellows – as you scornfully call them – to know that neither would stand for such a thing.

—Well, maybe they wouldn't, she said slowly, and a little grudgingly; but they were willing, you must admit, to thrust our dear children into grave danger. You should know that the people who wanted the children would be all too ready to try to pervert the faith of our little ones.

—I don't believe it for a moment, he said vehemently; the workers' movement isn't out to thry that sort of thing! We are wholly indifferent to the faith held by man, woman, or child, Sister.

—There you are! she said quickly. You shouldn't be indifferent to what faith is held by your members. It is a question of our eternal salvation, and what we have to bear in this life is as nothing to what we may receive, through the goodness and mercy of God, in the next. Have you actual knowledge that these English friends of yours wouldn't want to interfere with the faith of children left in their charge?

—As far as actual knowledge goes, Sister, I am as uncertain they wouldn't as you are certain that they would.

—Well, she said, flushing, at least you should be able to see what this dangerous and unchristian tumult has done for you!

That's a homer, thought Sean. I take things patiently, Sister, he said; there are wounded soldiers after every war.

—And you don't hesitate to come for help, and healing for your wounds, to those who don't in any way agree with your activities, do you?

Another homer! thought Sean. This was a sharp and a bitter thrust, tempting him to reply in a kindred bitterness; but he kept silent for a few moments, for bitterness wouldn't be a meet return for the care she had given him, or the food supplied for the past three weeks.

—I daresay I shouldn't have come, he said; that was a sad mistake. And he stood, silent, waiting for her to dismiss him.

—You're talking nonsense now, she said; you know you did well to come here. I hope your stay at the Convalescent will do you good – I am sure it will. You can go, now, Twenty-three.

He went back to the ward, his breast tight with rage so that he could breathe but rapidly. Had he any right to be angry? Maybe Sister Paul felt aggrieved that he was where a member of her own household of faith ought to be. That was only natural. There were many waiting to be given a bed; many more now that the Tommies had taken up so much room. When the Adelaide had refused, they had taken him in, and had helped him as much as they could. Had he a right to that help? He held he had – as much as another. But maybe Sister Paul had a different opinion, and she was right according to her belief. She would be but following the direction of him after whom she was called: Let us do good unto all men, especially unto them who are of the household of faith. Especially – there was the order. He was there on sufferance, and sufferance wasn't the badge of his tribe. She might have said her say more softly; he was poor and, in a way, helpless. Not helpless – he could go.

He wrapped his razor, soap, brush, and face flannel in an old ragged handkerchief, and thrust the little bundle into a pocket; and went over to Nurse Kelly making bandages in the centre of the ward.

—I'm going, he said; you can give my bed to someone else; and he went from the ward, barely glancing at the tonsured head of the stony St Laurence, deeper in thought than ever; down the corridor, past the armoured Michael still thrusting a spear through a twisting dragon; past the great gong just as the porter was giving it three strokes, out by the broad doorway, into the Green opposite, and over the bridge by the pond, under the trees, he took his first few steps homewards.

PREPARE, EVERYONE WITH WEAPONS

IT WAS a warm and lovely day. Sean, having eaten his breakfast, had taken his stick to go out, for his legs were feeling more numb than ever, and quivered threateningly at times. He slid over the stone wall bordering the railway, and wandered to a grassy bank where demure dog-daisies were jostled by flaunting poppies, scarlet and gay, looking like gaudy whores invading the home of Quaker girls. Clearing a space, he sat down with a sigh of relief, for a cup of tea and a slice of dry bread didn't fill a body with any desire for dancing. He would forget Irish republics, dark rosaleens, and red flags for the moment, and try to be at peace, for peace comes dropping slow, dropping from the veils of the morning. No, no, Yeats; there can be no peace where poverty is, and your own cry to go to Inisfree shows there is little of it in your own heart.

He leaned back against the dry trunk of a dead thorn tree, looking like what he himself would be when this damned paralysis got a proper grip on him. But doctors weren't always right: no one could be always right. He gathered into his hand a spray that was circling round the dry trunk, and admired its tiny blossoms, purple and yellow. Quaint flower, pliable stem, handsome leaves – an interesting plant, and poisonous! Children called it *the deadly nightshade*, warning younger ones against its beautiful red berries, and tearing it down whenever it crept too near to their homes. Eat them, they'd say, an' you'll die in terrible pain. Well, thousands had died in terrible pain who had never eaten of these beautiful berries. He had read that this plant was close to the tomato plant whose fruit, it was said, was very good to eat. He had often seen them, red and luscious, lying in shallow wooden boxes, fringed with purple-and-yellow tissue paper, among green cabbages in the greengrocer's shop. He wondered if he'd like

them, for up to now he had never tasted one. Come to that, he
had never tasted a lot of things. What now? Well, peaches,
pineapple, figs, apricots, or those funny-looking things called
bananas. It was some years now since he had tasted an apple, a
plum, or a strawberry, or any fruit, be God, now that he thought
of it! If he were a knight-errant, with an escutcheon, he'd bear as
a motto, Poverty Must Go – *Declenda est pauperium*, or whatever
the hell the Latin was.

Ay, indeed, and there's the spud too, related to this poisonous
plant. Same flower almost, though bigger, and possibly like that
of the tomato too, though he'd never seen it growing. Well,
everything had something to say for itself, and even this dangerous
plant, at least, jewelled the hedges in autumn.

Il Poverino – that was St Francis who had beatified poverty,
a *mariage de convenance* between Heaven and Hell. It was indeed
easy for some who had inherited wealth to achieve a rapturous
poverty; not so easy for those who had inherited poverty to show
it with a fine form and bright colours. There was nothing in either
dire poverty or great wealth: both were undignified, both were
vulgar. Of course, the personality of St Francis made what he
touched rich, and gave to everywhere he went a veil of grandeur.
But what about the poor devil whose personality had neither
grandeur nor richness, and in whom poverty itself destroyed the
flickering personality a simple, certain life might have saved?
No, St Francis, excuse me, poverty must go.

Apricots! Must be good to eat. My oath! Go, bind up yon
dangling apricots, was a warning to Richard's poor queen that
all wasn't well with her man; and wasn't it apricots that seemed
to have made the Duchess of Malfi feel sick when she was with
child by Antonio? They came to us, too, wrapped in coloured
tissue; and peaches, sheltered in greater richness, silver tissue
mostly, each in a little nest of its own. A feast of vision! Well,
such as he had but little to do with the kindly fruits of the earth.
How often had he prayed to God that He might give and preserve
to his use the kindly fruits of the earth, so as in due time he might
enjoy them! The time wasn't due yet – that must be it.

He turned his head away from the blossoms beside him to
glance at the wretched back yards of the poor houses jutting out
into the railway wasteland. All muddy, drab, and crumbling; not
a single flower abloom in one of them. In almost every yard the
week's washing fluttered from knotted lines – a red cotton dress,

white rags of sheets, blue blouses and drawers. Three cheers for the red, white, and blue! The banners of the poor leading the battle for cleanliness.

Well, there was peace here, at least. He had no ties at the moment. He had left the Council of the Citizen Army over a difference with Madame Markievicz, moving a motion that she should either give up her connexion with the Army or the Irish Volunteers. The vote had gone against him in a curious way. She had voted for herself; a strange thing, but typical, thought Sean, for her to do. Tommy Foran, President of the Union, who had never attended one meeting of the Committee, put in an appearance at this, and, of course, gave his vote of confidence in Madame. Even with Tommy's vote and her own, she had but a majority of one; and had she refrained from voting for herself, as Sean did, like a fool, the vote would have been an even one. But Madame on this result built up a demand for an apology, and Sean obliged by resigning, and leaving the Army for good. He could relax now in a kind of a way. He looked down at his boots. God help him when the winter came again. When summer's here, winter isn't far behind. He smiled grimly as he remembered Father Jimmy Breen stopping to advise him one day, and he stumbling along Seville Place: *Keep your feet warm an' dry – that's th' chief thing*, he had said in his shrill, nasal voice. One splash of rain, and his feet would be wet and cold. Oh, to hell with this sighing when the sun shone, the birds sang, and the flowers bloomed!

Some young voice shouting his name made him turn his restless head, and he saw a boy, who lived a few doors down, running across the waste, breathless and capless.

—Mr Casside, Mr Casside, he said, puffing, great news! Millions of Volunteers have gone marching – down to Howth, they say – an' thousands of police an' Scottish Bordherers have folleyed them, packed in thrams!

—What for? Why? Didya hear anything else?

—Somethin' 'bout guns comin' in at Howth. Everyone's talkin'!

Up he jumped, caught his stick, crossed the waste ground, slid over the wall, and hurried up Seville Place to go to Croydon Park, on the road to Howth, where he guessed some of the Citizen Army would be drilling. As he turned right from Seville Place, on to the main road, a body of Scottish Borderers were marching by, followed by a jeering crowd, throwing tin cans, stones, or any suitable thing they could lay hands on, some of them thumping hard into the backs of the men, a few hopping off the backs of their heads. Sean saw one young soldier, almost a boy, pale as death, limping along, his frightened young face screwed tight to keep the tears back, supported by the protecting arm of an old non-com, who turned while Sean looked, to glance savagely back at the crowd.

Suddenly, without a word of warning, several rear ranks wheeled right about, brought their bayoneted rifles to the charge, and, scattering over the street, came at a swift run towards the crowd, which broke, turned, and fled away in all directions. Sean found himself in danger again. He would be spitted like a fowl if he didn't run. In an instant he conjured the speed of his old hurling days into his shrivelling legs, and flew, flew faster than Master McGrath flew after the hare, into McGlade's newsagent and tobacconist shop, just before McGlade himself banged the shop door shut as the butts of several rifles hammered on it, and the gleaming point of a bayonet shot through one of the panels. He sat down on the floor to modify the beats of his heart, and wonder how speed came to animate his legs. Silence of intense listening filled the shop, while McGlade gawked cautiously from an upper window to watch till the coast was clear.

Paralysis me arse! thought Sean; no potent or potential paralysis could furnish me with the speed I got into me legs today. Fire of life is in them still. I wonder, now, is it that I'm not getting enough to eat? That may be it, coupled with the fact that I've long been trying to do too much.

McGlade came down to say the soldiers had gone on, and the coast was clear, so Sean lumbered to his feet, went out, and ran into Sean Connolly, the one who'd worked with him in Jason's, now a member of the Citizen Army. He was full of the gun-running, and was on his way, too, to Croydon Park to pick up more news of what was happening. As they went on down the Strand, along came two young men, haversack and belt showing they were Volunteers, casually, as it were, supporting a third between them who, though walking wearily, was half reclining in their arms, his head resting sideways on his left shoulder, while the look on the faces of his comrades was that of ignoring all, but seeing everyone.

—What's happened to him? asked Connolly, anxiously, turning to walk back with them, as did Sean too, not wishing to delay aid to a hurt man.

—Gun-running, said a Volunteer laconically; bayonet thrust; Howth.

—Get a cab; I'll get a cab, said Connolly excitedly; he shouldn't be walking!

—No, it's awright, said the Volunteer consoledly; doesn't want a cab; 'tisn't that ugly, an' walkin's a better advertisement.

They were now just in front of an advertisement hoarding on which was a huge poster of a vast hairy bull slanting down a tremendous shaggy head to stare at a small balloon-bellied bottle of Bovril; and there the two of them stood to look after the two Volunteers bearing home their poor hurt comrade.

—Alas! my poor brother! said Sean mockingly; and, as Connolly looked sad and embarrassed, he added, Don't look so solemn, man; the three of them are thoroughly enjoying themselves.

Just as they had begun to move on again, they were startled to another stop by a distant volley of rapid rifle-fire.

—What's that? what's what? exclaimed Connolly; listen!

—The Scottish Borderers letting bang at the crowd, murmured Sean.

—Murderers, said Sean Connolly, his face pale and tense, merciless murderers! But Sean saw again the look of tired resentment on the soldiers' faces, the dust on their khaki coats, the stones hopping off their heads and backs, the young boy twisting his face to keep back tears of pain, and the grim face of the veteran with a steady arm around him, helping him along.

When they got to Croydon Park, they found about thirty of the Army in a state of dubious excitement, all of them talking, and none of them listening. When they saw Sean Connolly and Sean coming up the drive, they ran over, several saying rapidly, The Volunteers are scatherin' everywhere, an' flingin' everything away!

—An' why th' hell don't some of you go an' get some of the scattered things? asked Sean. This is a chance you may never get again. Wait a minute! he added, as all of them started off; look, go different ways, say five or six in each group, and let each group decide who is to be non-com to lead the way. And mind, boys, no rowing with any Volunteer; if one needs help, give him all you can; only disregard those who fling anything away. Pick up guns, or anything else you can find, and bring them here – see?

—If we see a fellow timid-like, said one of the men, couldn't we whisper there was soldiers in some bushes farther along so's he'd slide his gun away from him?

—A fine idea, said Sean. A number of you had better stay here to mind whatever may be brought back.

Later on they came back, jubilant, with a number of guns, belts, haversacks, and even a few bayonets, and a quantity of ammunition. The guns were heavy and clumsy-looking – Mausers, some said; and they were fed with ugly, thick-bodied bullets. They were stored away in the house, the men keeping whatever else they had found as their personal property.

Later in the evening, a motor-car swept up the drive, and a cocky cuchullain Gael sprang out before it stopped, followed by a tired looking man with a greyish moustache, cut brusquely in a military way. He wore a bowler hat, and polished brown leggings were tightly fixed on to his legs. Long afterwards, Sean heard that he was Colonel Moore.

—Hello! said the cocky Gael cheerily; we've just slipped down here, Sean, to collect the guns you've got.

—Guns? echoed Sean. What guns? We've no guns – this is a place of peace.

—We know the kind of a peaceful place it is, said the military gent.

—If you know that, then, why waste time coming here to look for guns?

—We have heard your men have taken a number of guns, mislaid by Volunteers in the excitement of a collision with the British Authorities; and we have come to claim them.

—Have you now? said Sean; that's kind of you. Let's get this thing down sensibly, for you seem to be excited yourselves: who told you we had guns?

—We didn't come here to argue with ignorant men! said the military gent testily. These weapons are the property of the Volunteers, and it is a dishonourable thing to try to keep them.

—We aren't altogether ignorant men, said Sean, and we don't wish to be impertinent; but you are turning the question now into an ethical one. You first alleged you were told that guns were here; that these guns are Volunteer property, without proving that a gun, because it is a gun, must necessarily be a Volunteer gun; and that the keeping of a gun, unproved to be a Volunteer gun, is a reprehensible thing to do. Who the hell are you, anyhow?

—All that is necessary for you to know is that we have the

authority of Volunteer Headquarters to demand the surrender of whatever guns you have.

—Look here, my friend, said Sean smoothly, laying a gentle but remonstrating hand on the military gent's sleeve; but the hand was shaken roughly away, and the military gent stepped back to be farther away from Sean; Oh, well, if that's the way the wind blows, went on Sean, it's just as well to let you know that the writ of Volunteer Headquarters doesn't run here. This is part of a Union premises, and the men, not you, sir, are in control here. Look, he said, turning to the cocky Gael, the two of you had better go.

—This isn't a brotherly way for the Citizen Army to treat the Volunteers, said the cocky Gael.

—Oh, if you want to be brotherly, said Sean, then divide the guns equally between us – they'll be in good hands. How many did you get altogether?

—That's a question concerning the Volunteers alone, said the military gent tersely.

—Aw, take your chum away, said Sean to the cocky Gael; he shouldn't be let loose. He gestured towards the car; pack him back into his cushions, and bring him home – the figure is getting a little too stiff.

—If they aren't surrendered decently, said the military gent, there'll probably be more about it.

—How more about it? questioned Sean.

—The Volunteer Authorities aren't likely to allow their property to be pilfered in this unseemly and unmanly way.

—Aw, said Sean, you've got property on the brain. Do you good to read what Wolfe Tone thought about the rights of property. And, if I were you, my man, I shouldn't be drumming threats into our tough ears, for we are apt to resent them.

—Ay, are we, growled a big Citizen Army man. We've faced an' fought authorities bigger'n Volunteer ones, so it's safer for certain people to keep from chivvyin' them as wear the Red Hand in th' sides of their hats!

The cocky Gael and military gent got into their car, and off they went down the drive, without even getting a smell of a cartridge.

When Jim Larkin came back from England, a huge bank of clay, buttressed by thick planks, was built; targets were fixed on the planks, and soon the Dublin people began to hear the roaring report of the Howth guns as Citizen Army man and Volunteer shot to improve their aim by practice. Nelson from his high post stretched his neck when he heard them, and wished for the other eye so that he could see better. St Patrick on the top of Tara shook with anxiety and foreboding, for what he heard didn't sound like bells. No one could foresee, no one knew that these ugly signals were the songs heralding the coming of Easter morn.

THE BOLD FENIAN MEN

LARKIN WAS gone, and Connolly was going, to the great joy of some of the Labour leaders whose harts panteth after a cushy job as a deer's panteth after the water brooks. They were never at heart's ease while either of these leaders was near; but now, like wise and sensible men, they could, thank God, set about knocking fighting Unions into safe, prudential enterprises. Larkin had gone to America, and Connolly had left his Union to give all he had to the Citizen Army. He began to write patriotic verse that shivered with wretchedness. His fine eyes saw red no longer, but stared into the sky for a green dawn. A play of his called *Under Which Flag?* blundered a sentimental way over a stage in the Hall in a green limelight, shot with tinsel stars. All the old-age punchioners of commonplace outcries were poured into the pages of *The Workers' Republic* week by week; legions of words, each the same in stature and appearance, mob-capped and mock-cussined, dumbly plodded over the paper, unled by a single officer-word in sword and sash to justify the long, swing-song, dull purrade.

The World War was waxing over Europe, and Ireland was enjoying the hardships suffered by her enemy. The advanced Nationalists carried the name of Von Kluck about on the tips of their tongues. *Dark Rosaleen, The Men of the West*, and *Clare's Dragoons* were near forgotten by most Gaelic Leaguers, Sinn Feiners, and all IRB men, whose favourite songs now were *Die Wacht am Rhein, Deutschland über Alles, Was ist des Deutschen Vaterland*, and the sky grew greener. But all the time, the stoutest men from hill, valley, and town were pressing into the British

Army, and long columns of armed Irishmen, singing Ireland's latest love-song, *It's a long way to Tipperary*, went swinging by Liberty Hall down to the quays to the ships waiting to bring them to a poppy-mobbed grave in Flanders. The IRB worked hard sticking up fly-by-night posters calling on Irishmen to keep out of the British Army, while the journals *Sinn Fein* and *Irish Freedom* warned them that the coming fight must be, not for Catholic Belgium, but for Catholic Ireland; but the swinging columns went on marching down to the quays to the ships that go down to the sea. H. H. Asquith, Prime Minister, stood side by side with John Redmond at a recruiting meeting in the house of Dublin's Lord Mayor, but the forest of British guns and bayonets round the building kept his voice from travelling; and Dublin roared out her contempt for the pair of political brokers, but still the swinging columns of Kellys, Burkes, and Sheas tramped to the quays, and, singing, went forth to battle for England, little nations, and homes unfit for humans to live in; for while the sky was green for some, for many more it turned to the solid and salutary buff colour of a ring-paper.

Connolly determined to try to damn the stream of men flowing out of Ireland, and was seized with the idea that he could turn the sky green for all to see by hoisting a flag of the same colour over Liberty Hall. He had banished the Committee, and now ruled alone; so, after being thoroughly rehearsed, the Citizen Army, numbering about one hundred and seventy men, paraded outside, and Connolly, followed a pace behind by Madame Markievicz, inspected them. Connolly wore his new dark-green uniform for the first time, and didn't look too well in it, for he had a rather awkward carriage; and bow-legs, partly ensnared in rich, red-brown, leather leggings, added to the waddle in his walk. He carried an automatic gun in his left hand, the barrel resting in the crook of his arm. Madame having dressed herself in man's attire to fight for liberty, was in full green uniform too, and carried a big automatic pistol on her thin hip.

There was a dire sparkle of vanity lighting this little group of armed men: it sparkled from Connolly's waddle, from the uniformed men stiff to attention, and from the bunch of cock-feathers fluttering in the cap of the Countess. But it was a vanity that none could challenge, for it came from a group that was willing to sprinkle itself into oblivion that a change might be born in the long-settled thought of the people. There they stood – a tiny speck of green among a wide surge of muddily-garbed watchers, still and silent too, as if from their listlessness they were draining out their last drop of energy and hope into this tiny goblet-group of men so that they might go forth and make a last short fight for them. Here was the purple heart of Ireland.

Now the escort marched with the flag, carried by a young girl, and not a murmur broke from the big crowd watching, Sean, a little loose on his legs, and nursing a septic neck-wound, among those in the front rank. Not a cheer went up when Connolly declared to his men that as soon as the old green flag flew from the roof, the Irish soldiers passing by would swing left, assemble before the Hall, and vow that they served neither Kaiser nor King, but Ireland. The flag was borne to the roof, fixed to the traces, and as it broke out on the breeze, the men of the Army presented arms, and the great crowd cheered as if the breaking of the flag meant the ending of time for England.

Not an Irish soldier passing by to the quay, led by bands playing *Garryowen* or *Let Erin Remember*, turned aside; not one of them turned a head to glance at the lonely banner flying from the roof-top, lonelier now that the crowd had gone, pathetically flapping a call no one heard; loneliest at night waving, seemingly, among the stars, tired and drooping, but still fluttering a faint message to those tough men of Dublin City who now slept, waiting for the dawn to come to go in full marching kit down to the ships, and set their sails for Flanders. It was a childish thought for Connolly to harbour: it was a fiery-tale, a die-dream showing a false dawn that no soul saw.

But Sean knew that Connolly's men would fight, and the Irish Volunteers would stand by them; but he knew in his soul that they were going the wrong way about it. Their methods were those of the days of the redcoats, busby, and plume; salute your superior officers, fix bayonets, and charge, boys. These uniformed batches of men attacking, holding, and defending particular positions couldn't hope to measure themselves against the heavy forces that would be sent out to down them. Once they were cut off, they were as good as gone. The arrangements were too open, and the idea that the British wouldn't use cannon, vouched for by Connolly, Pearse, and others, maddened Sean. Capitalists of England won't destroy capitalist property here, said Connolly, and so said Pearse, and so say all of us. I tell you they will, shouted Sean; And I tell you they won't, shouted back those who heard him. They used artillery in the streets during the Franco-Prussian War, said Sean, and at the siege of Paris the French soldiers battered their way over the Communard barricades with cannon-fire, careless of what property the bursting shells destroyed.

He sent an article on the question to *The Volunteer*, but it was never published; he wrote to Connolly and Pearse suggesting a debate, but heard no word of reply from either. He argued that the fight would have to be mainly an underground one; that to risk a thousand men, or even half that number, in one concentric fight was foolishness. He pointed out that the Boers, a much more formidable army than any Ireland could put into the field, had to adopt the method of surprise attack, the quick arrival, the ambush, the quicker get-away. When the Boers tried to pit a big force against a far bigger, and better-armed one, in a stand-up fight, they failed badly, as Cronje did, and Prinsloo after him. It was the fighting of De Wet, Delarey, and Botha that gave them the time to win terms from the victorious British that were the beginning of a great Afrikander nation. Take off your uniforms, he advised, and keep them for the wedding, the wake, the pattern, and the fair. Put on your old duds that make you undistinguishable from your neighbours; send out detachments of fifty so that when you've got to run for it, you may lose no more than five or ten, while with an embattled thousand you'd lose the lot.

Once or twice, with the help he gave at St Enda's Fête at Jones's Road in his mind, deluded with the thought that it was in Pearse's mind too, he tried to catch a hold of him; but he was always shunted off by staff officers with vivid yellow tabs on their buzz-fuzz buzzoms, centres, right-hand and left-hand men, and picko-thninnies of the Irish Movement. Afterwards he ceased to rage at the thought of this treatment, for a ragamuffin like him, with his oozing neck, near-sighted eyes, trembling legs, tattered clothes, and broken boots must have been a shuddering sight for Gaelic gods to see. Besides, when he was excited, he had a habit of taking God's name in vain to punctuate his points; so they turned aside, giving him a look of horrified contempt as they went their way. A swearcrow he must have looked to the lot of them, defiling Ireland with his cawing of Irish into their tenderly-turned ears.

Sean was to see more nonsense still: Wally Carpenter, son of a Wicklow Englishman, caught him by the arm one day and hustled him into Liberty Hall. Wally was hardly five foot high, with tiny hands, feet, and head; sentimental to a tearful degree, but with a hard core of grit in his tinyness.

—Wait till I show you, Sean, he panted, pulling him along one of the narrow passages; you'll soon see something you'll like – make you near jump for joy! He opened a dim door that had a red cross in paper pasted on a panel, and shoved Sean into a little, dirty, dismal room. Look, he said, there's a bit of wot you fawncy!

When Sean's eyes got used to the dimness, the grimy walls, the cobwebbed windows frightening away the beggarly light that lurked in the lane outside, he saw, stretched on the dusty floor, four flimsy camp-beds, each of them covered with a glaring white sheet looking like shrouds, their whiteness over the soiled floor showing them up like lilies afloat on the top of a murky pool.

—For th' wounded in the fight, said Wally proudly; lovely, aren't they? When Connolly showed them to me, I felt as I'd like to kiss him!

—Why th' hell didn't you? asked Sean. More childishness. Good God, man! he said, turning on poor Wally, can't you see this is naked foolishness? A child's patthern of war! Look! he added, gripping the thin little arm, if anyone near you gets a bullet in him, tell him to yell for an hospital where the facts of wounds are known; where a splint's a splint and a probe's a probe, and where there are surgeons who know how to handle them!

·Connolly began his madnight route marches, sometimes ending with a furiosius attack on Dublin Castle. He seemed to see the beautiful Cathleen ni Houlihan immured within, pining away, chained hand and foot with ring-papers. The capture of the Castle would mean nothing, for shortly afterwards the fighters would find that in taking the Castle they had but been taken themselves. Behind this romantic façade Connolly was shoving the Volunteers forward, quicker than they wanted to go. His men were kibing their heels. Quicker, quicker, and Volunteers crossed and recrossed Citizen Army men, route-marching, drilling, raising the wind of war. In between this criss-cross of armed Irishmen wove the sparkling, half-galloping equipage of the Viceroy, drawn by four silky-skinned animals ridden by outriders in velvet coats, white breeches, and long-peaked jockey caps; followed by red-breasted lancers, brass-helmeted dragoons, or plumed hussars trying to weave an elegant binding embroidery through the more rough-and-ready pattern with which Ireland was busy, determined to cover up for ever every sign and thread in it of coloured conquest.

The Easter vigil was nearly over. Thousands were crumbling tobacco in the palms of their hands, preparing for the first smoke in seven long Lenten weeks of abstinence; the time had passed for forcing oneself (if you were lucky) to swallow sharply-tasting potted herrings, leathery strips of salted ling, and tea without milk. Steak and onions, bacon and cabbage, with pig's cheek as a variation, would again glorify the white-scrubbed kitchen tables of the Dublin workers. Dancing for the young; the rollicking call into Eden would again swing into life to the tune of *Hoosh the Cat from under the Table* or *Lift the Roof Higher*; older ones, thinking of their children, would be getting ready for a trip to Portmarnock's Velvet Strand, or Malahide's silver one; and those who weren't would be poring over the names of horses booked to run at Fairyhouse on Easter Monday. The danger aglow in an All-Ireland Parade of the Volunteers had passed. It had been whispered, only whispered, mind you, that it had been planned by a few of remember-for-ever boys to suddenly change the parade from a quiet walk into an armed revolt. A near thing. Only for God's gillie, Eoin Mac Neill, Chief of Stuff, and Bulmer Hobson, God's gillie's gillie, the Volunteer Sacredary, neither of whom had been told about the plan, but who caught the wisp of a whisper, the deadly dreama would have been on top of the people. But these two sent out couriers in trains, on horseback, on bicycles, in donkey-carts, and on roller-skates, running, galloping, and puffing all over the country, to countermind the whole thing, and so muted the silver trumpets that had lifted themselves up to call to the great race that was to come. So the country stretched itself before the fire, examined the form of the horses, filled its pipe, and watched the pig's cheek simmering on the fire for the morrow's dinner, thanking God that the long threatening hadn't come at last.

And on Easter Monday, off they went to the races, to their velvet strands, or got out their pretty frocks for the night dancing, all in a state of grace after the Easter devotions, full up of the blessed *joie deo feevre*; part of the country coming to the city to see the Museum, the Four Courts, the Custom House, and the Pro-Cathedral; while up one street Roger Casement, surrounded by armed detectives, was being taken to a boat chartered to land him at the nearest point to Tyburn; and down another street Bulmer Hobson, in the midst of armed IRB men, was being taken where he could do no good. All was quiet as a none breathless in madoration. Then down the centre of O'Connell Street, silent but for the tramp of their feet, came hundreds of armed Volunteers and Irish Citizen Army, led by Pearse, Connolly, and Tom Clarke, to halt, wheel, and face the General Post Office.

—There go the go-boys! muttered an old man, half to himself and half to an elderly, thin lady beside him who had stopped to help him stare at the Volunteers. Well, Mac Neill put a stop to their gallop! What th' hell are th' up to now? They seem to be bent on disturbin' th' whoremony of the sacred day. Goin' in, eh? Wha' for, I wondher? Can't be wantin' postage stamps. Can't be to get th' right time, for there's a clock in th' window. What'r they doin', ma'am? I dunno. Somethin' brewin'? Ma'am, there's always somethin' brewin'. I'm seventy, an' I've never known an hour that I didn't hear tell of somethin' brewin'. Be God, they're takin' th' clock outa th' window! That's odd, now. Looka, they're smashin' out th' windows with their rifles! There's a shower o' glass – right over th' passers-by! That's goin' beyond th' beyond. Tha's, tha's just hooliganism. We betther be gettin' outa here – th' police'll be here any minute! Didn't I tell you before, ma'am, I dunno! They're shovin' out the Post Office workers; pointin' their guns at them. We betther be gettin' outa here while we're safe. Houl' on a second – here's someone out to read a paper. What's he sayin'? I dunno. How th' hell can you expect a fella to hear from here? Oh! pushin' th' people off th' streets, now. Eh? G'on home, is it? An' who are you t'ordher me about? Takin' over th' city? D'ye tell me that? Well, you're not goin' to take over me! I'm a peaceful man out on a peaceful sthroll on a peaceful day, an' I stand be me constitutional rights. Gun-fire here soon? Arrah, from where? From where, ma'am? I dunno, I'm tellin' you! He says he's speakin' in th' name of th' Irish Republic, so now you're as wise as I am meself. Th' police'll soon explain matthers. Don't be talkin', looka what's comin' up O'Connell Street! A company o' throttin' lancers – full regalia with carbines, lances, an' all! Comin' to clear th' Post Office. Don't be pushin' me ribs in, ma'am! Hear th' jingle of them! This looks like business. Here we see, ma'am, the Irish Republic endin' quicker'n it began. Jasus, Mary, an' Joseph! th' fools are firin' on them! Here, get outa th' way, ma'am, an' let a man move! Near knocked you down? Why th' hell are you clingin' on me tail for, then? Didn' I tell you hours ago that it was dangerous dawdlin' here? D'ye hear that volley! Looka th' police runnin' for their lives! Here, let's get outa this; we've dilly-dallied too long where we've no real business to be!

—Oh, looka them breakin' into the shops! Isn't that provokin', ma'am? After all, th' boys are out for somethin' higher. Looka this fella comin' along with a gramophone. Eh, sonny boy, where'd you get that? Didja hear that answer? Go an' find out! Uncivilized lot. Looka these comin' with a piano, no less! Didja hear that? Give them a shove! Cheek, wha'? Look, they're bringin' out hand-carts an' prams. A sad day for Dublin's fair name. What's that fella in beard an' knickerbockers doin'? Pastin' up bills. Willya read that – callin' on the citizens to do nothin' to dishonour the boys. Why doesn't he mind his own business? Sheehy-Skeffington? Never heard of him. One o' Ireland's noblest sons? Is it on for coddin' me y'are? If he was less noble an' less unselfish, I'd ha' heard a lot of him? Maybe; but he's not goin' to be let dictate to me. It's none o' his business if I want to rifle, rob, an' plundher. Looka! There he goes, now, with two others, in a web o' soldiers! That doesn't look like he was noble. What was that, now, went whizzin' by me? A bullet? You're jokin'! I can tell them, if they harm me, there'll be more about it!

The tinkle of breaking glass wandered down the whole street, and people were pushing and pulling each other, till through broken windows all the treasures of India, Arabia, and Samarkand were open before them. Sean watched them as they pulled boxes down on top of themselves, flung clothing all over the place; tried to pull new garments over their old ones; while one woman, stripped naked, was trying on camisole after camisole, ending with calm touches that smoothed out the light-blue one that satisfied her at last. All who were underdressed before, were overdressed now, and for the first time in their frosty lives the heat of good warm things encircled them.

He heard the humming zipzz of bullets flying a little way overhead, and guessed someone was firing to frighten the looters; so he dodged into the doorway of a shop to put a protection between him and them. A solidly-built man came trotting along carrying a large jar by the handle against his right thigh, while from his left hung a pair of vividly yellow boots. A sharp ping sounded, and the jar separated into halves, letting a golden stream of liquor honour the road. The man stopped, and gazed at the jagged neck of the jar left in his hand.

—Jasus! he said, not a dhrop of it left – the wasteful bastards!

Sean squirmed round an angle of the doorway to get a look into the shop. Through the great jagged hole in the window he saw the inside was a litter of tossed clothing, caps, shoes, collars, and ties on which people were trampling, and over which they were jostling each other; ignoring the value of what lay on the floor or what was spread over the counter, for the hidden value of what lay neatly folded in the still-unopened boxes. One man, alone, was rooting among a heap of caps on the floor, feverishly planting one after the other on his head, and flinging to the far end of the shop those which didn't seem to fit. Another, trying by main force to pull a delicate-looking pair of tweed trousers over a pair of big thick boots, was cursing loudly when he discovered they wouldn't go, and cursing louder still when he found he couldn't get them off again. A third was holding his old coat tightly between his legs while he excitedly thrust raggedly-shirted arms through the sleeves of a brand-new one; while yet another was calling out that if anyone came across a seven-size in socks, they might let him know. And there, too, was the old man, leaning on the counter directing with his stick a younger man on a ladder, busy searching among the boxes on the higher shelves.

—What's in that one to your left? he shouted to the man on the ladder; to your left, man! Shirts? What kinda shirts? Ordinary cotton ones? Aw, don't waste time clawin' them things! They can be picked up anywhere. That box to your right – to your right! Good God, man! D'ye not know your right from your left? De Luxe written on them? Throw them down, throw them down! Where'r you pushin', ma'am? This isn't a spring sale. You'll have to keep ordher if you want to do business here. Wha'? How th' hell do I know where to direct you to the ladies' department! One, two, three, four, five, six, an' one for Sunday – they'll be about enough for the time bein'. Have a look for a box marked pyjamas – I always had a notion of wantin' to feel how they felt on a fella. Wha's that? What do they want th' ambulance for? A woman's been shot? Wha', just outside? Who done it? A sniper, or somebody? God Almighty, where's our boasted law an' ordher!

Sean watched their wonderful activity, and couldn't desecrate their disorder with dishonour. All these are they who go to Mass every Sunday and holy day of obligation; whose noses are ground down by the clergy on the grindstone of eternal destiny; who go in mortal fear of the threat of a priest, he thought; but now he was glad to see they hadn't lost their taste for things material. In spite of the clergy's fifing and drumming about venial and mortal sin, they were stretching out their hands for food, for raiment, for colour, and for life. If the lilies of the field, that neither toiled nor spun, could be lovely, how much more that these whose lives were a ceaseless labour should be lovely too? The time would come when they would no longer need to take their kingdom of heaven by violence, for they would build it themselves, and warmth, adornment, and satisfaction in the midst of fair sounds and bright colours would be their own.

When the shooting seemed to have got less, Sean slid cautiously out of his shelter and, keeping close to the walls of shop and house, made his way home. Darkness had fallen, and his near-sighted eyes could see but a few feet in front of them. Coming to the bridge across the canal at Spencer Dock, his semi-consciousness heard a calm, tired voice say somewhere, Halt! Who goes there? A few steps farther, and the voice, tired no longer, terse and threatening, said again, Who goes there! In the hesitating shock of seeing nothing, he managed to say, Friend, and a moment after, passed by the dim form of a soldier with the rifle at the ready, who passed him by with the advice of, Answer quicker, next time, friend. A narrow squeak, that! A few seconds more of hesitation and he'd have been high among the stars. Watch your steps, Sean. A little farther on, his breast almost touched a bayonet as another voice said, Who goes there? Murmuring, Friend, the bayonet was lowered, and a soldier's voice said, Pass on, friend. They were dotted along the road up to the corner of the street that held his home. Pouring in by the North Wall, and no one here to stop them. Poor ould Ireland!

He halted at the doorway thrust through with the knowledge that it was dangerous for him to be abroad at night. His eyes were blank in the darkness. He thought of the things that had happened, and wondered how it would all end. It was a deserted city now, but for those who fought each other. The pubs had emptied, the trams had jingled back to their sheds, the shops were shut. Lansdowne Road, Rathmines, and Rathgar gathered up their fine clothes and ran home; the janitors of the Bank of Ireland came rushing out to slam-to the great iron gates with a clang, turning the thick lips of the lock with hurried hands, and the sentries rushed into the guardroom; those coming home from Fairyhouse had been stopped by British barricades, and choruses of How th' hell am I goin' to get home ascended to God and His blessed saints. And Sean, standing in the doorway of his house, gazed back towards the centre of the city and saw a great plume of flame rising high into the sky: the first passion flower had blossomed.

The next day, early, not allowed to cross the canal, Sean took a longer back way over the railways, and got to the nearer fringe of the city where talk was furious, and wild guesses were made of what was happening.

—Th' attack on the Castle's failed, and Sean Connolly, the modest and noble, had died, murmuring that he died for Ireland. And you can't even climb through O'Connell Street, the dead are piled that high in it. An' th' Sinn Feiners have taken th' Bank of Ireland!

—What!

—Occupied it; overpowered the senthries, shot them before, shot them behind, and flung their riddled bodies at the foot of King Billy's statue.

—No? God, what'r we comin' to! With th' Bank of Ireland gone, we'll all be ruined. How'r we goin' to get our old-age pensions; an' ring-papers won't be worth a damn!

—An' – listen, man alive – an', an' th' figures of Liberty, Fortitude, an' Justice that stood on th' top of the ayste side of the Bank is sthrewn over th' wide world. Smithereens they are now; rubble; dust.

—No! An' th' others, Hibernia, Fidelity, an' somethin' – what's happened to them?

—Them? Aw, them was took down an' brought in for safety till betther times came. Just in time.

—But wait till I tell yous: a fella standin' on the Park Magazine Hill says he could see plain an army of Germans marchin' forward dead on th' horizon. No I don't mean frontier – I said horizon. Which horizon? Dtch dtch! There's only one horizon, man, an' it's th' place where th' sky an' earth meet together. You hope it's thrue? Well, I don't; it's bad enough now between our own and the English; but what would it be between the three of them? Only the lark in the clear air 'ud be safe then, an' he'd have to fly higher than usual.

Sean was behind his mother when she gawked out of the window in the back room, seeking to see something of what was happening.

—There's some soldiers in th' church tower, she said, the last word blending with a crackling roar, while the two of them staggered about the room, choked and blinded from a cloud of powdered mortar thick as a white thundercloud.

—I'm shot, Jack, she whimpered; but feeling her all over, he found she wasn't; and he hurried her into the other room where she lay down, panting, on the old horsehair sofa. He gave her a drink of water, then coaxed her down to a neighbour below who set about making a cup of tea for her. As he was going back to see what had happened, a number of soldiers, in charge of an officer and sergeant, came in and went upstairs with him, leaving two men to guard the outside door. The officer stood beside Sean, a revolver in his hand, while the sergeant searched the back room. After some time, the sergeant came out and whispered to the officer.

—Come downstairs with me, said the officer to Sean.

They placed him stiff against the wall of the house, outside, while the sergeant searched him, taking off his old boots to have a look inside, a soldier kneeling on one knee before him, butt of rifle to the knee, the bayonet but a foot away from Sean's chest. They were searching for an automatic, they told him, and he wondered how one could fit into either of his boots. A violent explosion in the wasteland beyond the wall bordering the railway sent a storm of stones, tufts of grass, and bunches of poppies sky-high, showers of them falling around Sean and his searchers. Another, and then, a second later, a vicious ping on the wall beside him, sent Sean word that some sniper was having a shot at the soldiers around him. The officer slid down the street into a shop, and the soldiers, bending low, followed him, leaving Sean stretched out against the wall, alone, watched by neighbours who were peeping from their doorways in the houses lower down the street. He took his outstretched arms from the wall, turned in, and mounted the stairs to his home. While by the wall, he had felt that his end was near, and had had a stiff time trying to hold on to his pride and dignity. Now he was shaking, and tense with fright. Either the badly-aimed shells fired from the gunboat *Helga* or the sniper's bullet may have saved his life. For a long time he had tried to keep out of danger, and as often had found himself

in the thick of it. Three times, at work, he had had narrow escapes:
once when a bucket had been whipped from a swinging hand by
a train passing by at fifty miles an hour; once when a scaffold
had collapsed, and he had come down with it, escaping with a
bad shock and many sore bruises; and once on a high roof,
cleaning glass, a fellow worker, in a hurry to show the foreman
how alert he was, stepped on a plank, leading over the glass,
before him; the plank had snapped, the glass had given way, and
the poor devil had fallen forty or fifty feet, to be smashed to
pieces on a concrete floor below. And today, he and his mother
had had a stream of machine-gun bullets sweeping between their
two heads, making a hash of the wall behind them. How often
during the riots of drunken policemen had he escaped a batoning?
More often than he wished to remember. He didn't like this sort
of thing at all. As he grew in grace and wisdom, he was growing
less and less of a hero. Like the fine and upright Alderman Tom
Kelly, he wanted to die in bed surrounded by medicine bottles.

Good God! looka th' mess the back room was in! The one old
palliasse they had had been ripped open with a bayonet, and the
dirty feathers had been scattered about. Their one mattress, too,
had been torn the same way, and the straw, mixed with the
feathers, littered the floor. And all this on top of his aching,
trembling legs, and oozing neck. Had he been made of less sterner
stuff, he'd have sat on the edge of the ruined bed to weep. But he
must sway his thought away from an inclination to tears to hard
resistance, and an icy acceptance of what was beyond his power
to avoid.

He lighted some sticks, put some water into a small saucepan,
and made himself a cup of tea. In the old dresser he found a small
lump of a loaf, and cut himself a slice; no more, for the neighbours
might send back his mother any minute and she'd need her share.
But he ate all the bread there, for he wanted all he could get to
modify with new strength the energy lost through his oozing neck,
his aching legs, and troubled mind. He was sipping the tea, when
in came a sergeant and two Tommies, and his heart sank again.

—'Ere, you, said the sergeant, motioning towards the Tommies,
go with 'em; the church; 'urry! Why? never mind the why. They
'as their orders – that's enough for you.

—Whose orders – the Lord Lieutenant's?

—Naw! Company officer's. 'Urry!

Sean sighed, and slipped a volume of Keats into a pocket, put on his cap, and went with them to the church. In the porch a young officer sat by a small table, a notebook before him, pencil in hand. Name? Address? Age? Occupation? Sean saw the officer bend a searching look at him when he said, Unemployed. Another search. What's this, eh? Oh, a book! Poetry – harmless enough. Why don't you join the Army? No interest in armies – not even the Salvation Army. Civil answers, my man, will serve you better. Into the church with him.

Soldiers were asleep, asprawl, in the baptistery; others snored lying on the tiles of the chancel; and an armed sentry stood at the east end and west end of the church. Piles of haversacks, belts, boots, and rifles were heaped on, and around, the Communion Table. But two other prisoners were there, each widely separated from the other. It was strange to be this way in a church where he had so often sat as a worshipper, in which he found his first genuine, educated friend – the Rector. How angry he would be if he knew the soldiers were making themselves at home in the House of God! Do This in Remembrance Of Me were words forming a semicircle above the Holy Table.

That whole evening, and throughout the night, he sat wearily on the hard bench, finding out that things even of beauty weren't joys for ever. He could but give now the faint smile like a star shining through autumn mists. It was a wry smile, but it wasn't a tear. Even here, even now, even so, perhaps he was one with those

> Who love their fellows even to the death,
> Who feel the giant agony of the world,
> And more, like slaves to poor humanity,
> Labour for mortal good.

The deadly whiteness of the lilies was here upon him; but not the deadly whiteness of the snow: not yet, though sunken from the healthy breath of morn, and far from the fiery noon and eve's one star.

He had to put every thought of anxiety about his mother away from him. Sit here; say nothing – that was all he could do. What use would he be at home, anyway? We were all helled by the enemy. The neighbours would keep her on her feet till he came back, and they took counsel together. In spite of his pride, his bowels yearned for a share of the Maconochie stew some of the soldiers were eating.

The next evening, all the lusty men of the locality were marshalled, about a hundred of them, Sean joining in, and were marched
under guard (anyone trying to bolt was to be shot dead) down a
desolate road to a great granary. Into the dreary building they
filed, one by one; up a long flight of dark stone steps, to a narrow
doorway, where each, as he came forward, was told to jump
through into the darkness and take a chance of what was at the
bottom. Sean dropped through, finding that he landed many
feet below on a great heap of maize that sent up a cloud of fine
dust, near choking him. When his eyes got accustomed to it, he
saw a narrow beam of light trickling in through some badly-
shuttered windows, and realized he was in a huge grain store, the
maize never less than five feet deep so that it was a burden to
walk from one spot to another, for each leg sank down to the
thigh, and had to be dragged up before another step could be
taken. It took him a long time to get to a window, and crouch
there, watching the sky over the city through a crack in the
shutters. A burning molten glow shone in the sky beyond, and it
looked as if the whole city was blazing. One ear caught the talk
of a group of men nearby who were playing cards. He couldn't
read Keats here, for the light was too bad for his eyes. More
light, were the last words of Goethe, and it looked as if they
would be his last words too.

—I dunno how it'll end, said one of the card-players; the Ger-
man submarines are sweepin' up th' Liffey like salmon, an' when
they let loose it's goodbye England. My thrick, there, eh!

—I heard, said another player, that th' Dublin Mountains is
black with them – coal-scuttle helmets an' all – your deal, Ned.

—Th' Sinn Feiners has taken to an unknown destination that
fella who ordhered the Volunteers in th' counthry to stay incog-
nito wherever they were – what's his name? Oh, I've said it a
hundhred times. What's this it is?

—Is it Father O'Flynn? asked a mocking voice in a corner.

—No mockery, Skinner Doyle; this isn't a time for jokin'. Eh,
houl' on there – see th' ace o' hearts!

Then they heard them, and all the heads turned to where Sean
was crouching at the window; for in the fussy brattle of ceaseless
musketry fire, all now listened to the slow, dignified, deadly boom
of the big guns.

—Christ help them now! said Skinner Doyle.

Next day, he heard his name called from the hole at the end of

the store where the sentry stood. Wading through the corn, he
was told to leap up, and leaping, was caught by a corporal who
helped him to scramble to the floor above. He was to go home for
a meal, accompanied by a soldier, for while the rest were permitted
to disperse home for an hour, they were suspicious of him because
his room was the one that received the fire from those searching
out a sniper. He was covered with the dust of the corn, and though
he had pulled up the collar of his coat to protect the wound in
his neck, he felt the dust of the grain tearing against its rawness
and felt anxious about it. But he had to be patient, so he trudged
home, silent, by the side of the soldier. When he sat down, and,
in reply to the soldier's question, said there was nothing in
the house with which to make a meal,

—Wot, nothink? asked the soldier, shocked. Isn't there some-
wheres as you can get some grub?

—Yes, said Sean; a huckster's round the corner, but I've no
money to pay for it.

—'E'll give it, 'e'll 'ave to; you come with me, said the Tommy;
Gawd blimey, a man 'as to eat!

So round to Murphy's went the Saxon and the Gael, for food.
Murphy was a man who, by paying a hundred pounds for a
dispensation, had married his dead wife's sister, so that the
property might be kept in the family; and Sean thought how much
comfort and security for a long time such a sum would bring to
his mother and to him. The soldier's sharp request to give this
prisoner feller some grub got Sean a loaf, tea and sugar, milk in
a bottle, rashers, and a pound of bully beef. On the way back,
Sean got his mother, and they had a royal meal, the soldier joining
them in a cup of scald.

In the sky the flames were soaring higher, till the heavens
looked like a great ruby hanging from God's ear. It was tingeing
the buildings with a scarlet glow, while the saints stretched their
ears to catch the tenour of the Irish prayers going up, for each
paternoster and ave maria mingled with the biting snarl from the
Howth guns, and the answering roar from Saxon rifle, machine
gun, and cannon, that were weaving a closer cordon of fire round
the Sinn Feiners, the fire creeping towards the group of innocents
blessed with arms in their hands for the first time. Now it was
above them, licking away the roof from over their heads, and they
were too weary to go on trying to put it out. Their haggard faces
were chipped into bleeding jaggedness by splinters flying from

shattered stones and brick; the wounded were in a corner making their moan to themselves, while a few men and women were risking their lives to get the seriously hurt away to some hospital, wending through falling walls, fire and brimstone, and gauntlets of burning buildings. The grey-green Volunteer uniforms now no longer looked neat; they were ragged, and powdered thick with the pulverised mortar clouding from the walls. The fighters now looked like automatons moving unsteadily about, encased tightly in a fog of dust and acrid ashes. They were silent, unshaven, maybe muttering an act of contrition for things done before they went to war; wan-eyed, they persuaded their drooping lids to lift again, for drowsiness might mean a sudden and silent death to them. Those handiest with a rifle kept firing into the flames coming closer; a few, hoarse and parched, still tried to control the flame with tiny buckets of water, their leaders, before a wall of flame, standing dignified among them, already garlanded for death; gay outwardly, and satisfied, their inner wakefulness wondering how they'd fare when the world faded. They had helped God to rouse up Ireland: let the whole people answer for them now! For them, now, tired and worn, there was but a long, long sleep; a thin ribbon of flame from a line of levelled muskets, and then a long sleep. For evermore, Ireland's Easter lilies would have a crimson streak through them.

The thyme had turned to rue. And through the ring of fire and smoke, passing by the flying bullets, went the brown-robed Capuchins, bending over the wounded, unable to do much, but standing by their people and the danger. Father Aloysius, with a white apron on a broomstick, hurries to the British barricade to ask for a surgeon, but an elegant Colonel Taylor turns his back on him and leaves him there alone with the Tommies and with God; and later on an equally elegant captain does all a man can do to help the minister with humane thoughts and a courteous address. And Cathleen ni Houlihan, in her bare feet, is singing, for her pride that had almost gone is come back again. In tattered gown, and hair uncombed, she sings, shaking the ashes from her hair, and smoothing out the bigger creases in her dress; she is

> Singing of men that in battle array,
> Ready in heart and ready in hand,
> March with banner and bugle and fife
> To the death, for their native land.

A rare time for death in Ireland; and in the battle's prologue many a common man, woman, and child had said goodbye to work and love and play; and many more in an hour or so would receive a terse message that life no longer needed them. There they are, lying so quiet – a child surprised in the doorway; an old man stretched in the street; a young man near a lamp-post which he had clutched when the bullet struck him, and down which he had slid when he died, his curiously white face containing wide eyes staring upwards, as if asking the sky why this had happened, a stiff arm still half encircling the lamp standard; a young lassie in holiday attire, lying on her face, maybe hurrying home when she heard the uproar, but going too slow, for on the brilliant white blouse a purple patch of death was spreading over the middle of the back; an old woman on the floor of her tenement room, alone, her blood seeping through the ceiling below: all of the goodly company of the dead who died for Ireland. Jesu, have pity! Quiet, comrades, quiet. It was necessary that you should die for Ireland too. You didn't want to die. I know, I know. You signed no proclamation; you invaded no building; you pulled no trigger; I know, I know. But Ireland needed you all the same. Many will die like that before Ireland can go free. They must put up with it. You will be unknown for ever; you died without a word of praise; you will be buried without even a shadowy ceremony; no bugle will call your name; no gunshot will let loose brave echoes over your grave; you will not be numbered among the accepted slain. But listen, comrades, listen: Whitman will be there to meet you; he will marshal you into the march-past with the greater dead; on the cornet he will give you a shrill salute. Listen – there it goes! Forward! March!

Here comes Paudrig Pearse down the silent street, two elegant British officers waiting for him. He comes steadily, in no hurry; unafraid, to where two elegant British officers are waiting to meet him. His men have been beaten; the cordon of flame has burnt out their last fading hope. *The struggle is over; our boys are defeated; and Ireland's surrounded with silence and gloom:* the old ballad is singing in his ears. He wears a topcoat, for the Easter sun has gone west, and a nipping breeze blows. It is the wind of death blowing keenly on this brave man's pure face. His eyes droop, for he hasn't slept for days. He has lain down, but not to sleep. Soon he will sleep long and well. He feels this is no defeat; that to stand up in an armed fight against subjection is a victory for Ireland. So he stands silently, and listens to the elegant British officer demanding unconditional surrender. The fools, the fools! So he agrees, and hands over his sword; bows, and returns to marshal his men for a general surrender. Soon Whitman will be shaking his hand, and reciting,

> *Vivas to those who have failed!*
> *And to all generals who lost engagements, and all overcome heroes!*
> *And the numberless unknown heroes equal to the greatest heroes known!*

The sky had gone black and the rain was falling; cold rain, with the sting of vanishing winter in it. Along the silent, empty street small groups of men come marching. They are tired, tattered, and sleepy, hungry shadows of the neat, trim, and steady Volunteers who had marched the opposite way a week ago. Crowds behind the soldiers cheered when they saw the proud but woebegone men come marching through the blackened lanes of smouldering buildings. They marched silent; no whistle or lilt came from any parched lip or dry throat: the time was past for song. The hot, bitter vapour from charred wood, leather, and cloth seared their nostrils; and cinders, smoking red in the centre, strewing the street, crunched under their passing feet. Down they came, covered with hundreds of rifles, with machine guns trained on them, thousands of soldiers staring at them piling their poor arms in a heap; the Tommies wondering and bewildered that such a pitiable pile of metal should try to overthrow the might and power of England's armed forces.

—Larfable, I say. Th' wild Irish. Drink gores to their 'eads! Cawn't savvy 'em. Never knows w'en you 'as 'em. Don't arst me, mite. Blinkin' lot of' em oughter be in a 'ome! Wot was bitin' 'em? Barmy, th' lot of 'em. Wot did they do it for?

A dream! To make again the white sails crowd in on Ireland, so that her harbours, the finest in the world, could hardly hold her ships; to set up the sale again of our potteries and textiles; Huguenot poplins woven since Jacquard de Lion first sang *The Palatine's Daughter*; crowded bales of supreme cloth, red, green, green russet, and yellow to Cologne, Naples, Catalonia, Ypres, and the Rhine. To send out fine marbles, green, red, jet, and dove grey, fine and smooth, as Spenser vouches for in his *Faerie Queen*, to Bologna, Brabant, making palaces for princes of Lithuania; to give to the civilized world again beef, lard, tallow, bacon, butter, wax, wool, tanned leather, well embroidered; hawks and horses, gold from Wicklow, and silver from Tipperary, coined and uncoined; to send the whitest linen to the Netherlands, Italy, and the city of Chester. To make the land a centre of prime books, well tooled and illuminated, like them of old, the book of Fenagh, of Monasterboice, the psalter of Cashel, and the Red Book of the Earls of Kildare.

So that St Furze might again become the patron saint of the fierce O'Flaherties, and the Feast of Brendan on May the tenth could be safely kept again in Galway by the ancient dwellers on the quay street; that the Dublin men might be free to again become members of the Corpus Christi Guild of Coventry, and make a new path round that fair city; and to be able to send clean white boards for the church of Salisbury, and oak and elm beams to England to be made into galleys and shapely vessels of a fine length.

—Whhoorish! shouted a sergeant; is it treadin' on th' tile of me coat yez want to be now? Oirish, an' prawd of it, wot?

—Ay, and so as to again excel in carving rich and diversified designs on all churches, within and without the walls; to build round towers higher than the high ones already here; to have multitudes of great bells and lesser bells aloft in bunches in all suitable and desirable places; and to have piles of rare images, altars, gems, and hundreds of square miles of painted glass for all our church windows.

—And mike Iahland a plice fit for 'eroes to live in, Paddy, eh wot?

Ay, and our famous fairs will no longer cower away in old, unhonoured corners, but step into the open again, like the Fair of Telltown, known to all the lords and ladies of the well-mapped world; the Fair of Garmain, the Fair of Clapping of Hands, the Fair of Opening Eyes, the Fair in the Valley of Squinting Windows, the Fair of the Foggy Dew, the Fair of the Valley Lay Smiling Before Me.

—Never 'eard of 'em, Paddy; musta been in old Gord's time.

And the Fair of Fairs of the Blessed Saints, twelve in number -- Cing Bully of the Boyne of Contention, Carzen of the Papes, Mishe Lemass More, a Talbot a Talbot, Lily Bullero, Shantee

Ohkay, Roody the Shrover with his Pendraggin Piety, the Irish
Sweep who Beat Miraculous Melody from a Drum, Elfie Byrne
of Ballyblandus, Guffer Gaffney, Prayboy of the Festerin' World,
Billora et Labora O'Brien, and Gee Kiaora Jesterton the Laughing Diwine.

And where are these precious things now? Buried in the black
ruins, hidden in heaps of rubble, scarred with the venom of fire.
All our dear dreams gone: tread light, soldier, for you tread on
our dreams. These Sinn Fein madmen have tossed them into insig-
nificance; their blow at England has fallen on the head of
Ireland, and all is lost as well as honour.

—I wouldn't tike it too much to heart, daddy; no use of gettin'
riled wif us – we didn't start the shindy.

—Make no sport of me, soldier, for there's no Fergus of the
kindly tongue now to cool a man's anger! To hell with yous,
spawn of Cromwell! May none of your race survive; may God
destroy yous all; each curse of the holy Book of the Psalms and
the prophets upon yous fall!

—Easy, easy, there, daddy; have a heart!

Oh! Every cedar in the land is down; every Irish oak has fallen!
There's not that much wood left would make the lintel of a door.
The starry head of the Old Woman is lit now but by the death-
light in the eyes of them about to die. Listen! Listen all! And a
dead silence swept the land, and all the people listened. There
they go – clear on the air of a misty dawn: a volley; another, and
another. What Irish heart is thrilled now by the eagle's whistle?
What Irish ear bothers about the notes of the cuckoo calling
summer closer? What foot will move to the sound of a violin
making merry with sound? What hand will light a bonfire to
welcome a joy?

The listening people hear the quick, short, sharp steps of Tom
Clarke over the stony square of Kilmainham. There is the squad
waiting, khaki-clad, motionless, not knowing the argument.
Here, in front, halt! A brown-robed friar stands aside, hurrying
prayers over his rosary beads. There is no bravery here save in
the thin figure with its arms bound tight; a cloth over the gleaming
eyes. The guns suddenly give forth a jet of flame, the figure jerks
rhythmically, slides awkwardly to the ground, twitches for a
second, then lies for ever still. Ireland has scored another victory
over England, for the people begin to ponder over what this man
has done, and search for everything he has said, that what was

spoken by the prophets might be fulfilled – he will be remembered for ever.

Then another came forth to die, with head, usually bent, now held high, for Pearse has bidden farewell to the world, though he still holds Ireland by her rough and graceful hand, loth to let it go: farewell to St Enda's, its toil, its joy, its golden brood of boys; farewell to Emmet's Fort, to the Hermitage, the lake in the woods, the scented hayfield; farewell to the azure sky, the brown bog, the purple heather of Connemara; farewell the pageants that wheeled broad palaces into simple places and turned greyness into magic colour; farewell the jewelled quaintness in the thoughts and play of children. – Oh, farewell! The moments have grown bigger than the years.

The face of Ireland twitches when the guns again sing, but she stands steady, waiting to fasten around her white neck this jewelled string of death, for these are they who shall speak to her people for ever; the spirit that had gone from her bosom returns to it again to breathe out hope once more, and soon to sing.

Ere the tiny curl from the gun-muzzles has hid in the upper air, the flames lash out again, and Connolly, last of the lost leaders, loses his place in life, and becomes a marbled memory.

Black prison vans, packed with prisoners, cavalry with naked swords before and behind them, move swift through the streets. Crowds, silent and sullen, watch them go by at the street corners, and stare at white faces pressed against the tiny grating at the back of the van, striving for a last glimpse of Erin ere they walk the decks of the ship that will carry them to the prisons of England. And the Castle is alert and confident; files all correct, and dossiers signed and sealed for the last time. Now the Irish may be quiet, and quit their moan, for nothing is whole that could be broken. And the glasses are full of wine, and cigar-smoke incenses the satisfaction.

But Cathleen, the daughter of Houlihan, walks firm now, a flush on her haughty cheek. She hears the murmur in the people's hearts. Her lovers are gathering around her, for things are changed, changed utterly:

A terrible beauty is born.

Poor, dear, dead men; poor W. B. Yeats.

Sean O'Casey
Frank O'Connor

SEAN O'CASEY wrote his first evocative and richly entertaining autobiography in six volumes over more than two decades, re-creating in Vol. I the days of his Dublin childhood. The second volume tells of his coming to manhood and includes episodes later used in his play RED ROSES FOR ME. Each volume is essential reading for a proper appreciation of this major Irish dramatist.

FRANK O'CONNOR 'A Master' – The Listener 'Perfect' – The Spectator

Also in PAN is the enthralling and entrancing story of O'Connor's life from schoolboy to revolutionary to librarian and his association with the Abbey Theatre.

These and other PAN Books are obtainable from all booksellers and newsagents. If you have any difficulty please send purchase price plus 7p postage to PO Box 11, Falmouth, Cornwall. While every effort is made to keep prices low, it is sometimes necessary to increase prices at short notice. PAN Books reserve the right to show new retail prices on covers which may differ from those previously advertised in the text or elsewhere.